EMILE OLLIVIER AND THE LIBERAL EMPIRE OF NAPOLEON III

EMILE OLLIVIER

EMILE OLLIVIER
AND THE LIBERAL EMPIRE
OF NAPOLEON III

by

THEODORE ZELDIN

*Fellow of St. Antony's College
and Lecturer of Christ Church, Oxford*

CLARENDON PRESS · OXFORD
1963

Oxford University Press, Amen House, London E.C. 4

GLASGOW NEW YORK TORONTO MELBOURNE WELLINGTON
BOMBAY CALCUTTA MADRAS KARACHI LAHORE DACCA
CAPE TOWN SALISBURY NAIROBI IBADAN ACCRA
KUALA LUMPUR HONG KONG

Printed in Great Britain by
The Camelot Press Ltd., London and Southampton

PREFACE

THIS book is not a biography of Emile Ollivier but a study of his conduct as a politician and of his work as chief minister of Napoleon III's liberal empire. It could not have been written but for the kindness of Madame Geneviève Troisier, who very generously allowed me unrestricted access to her father's papers. I should like to express my gratitude to her and also to Madame Anne Troisier de Diaz. I wish to thank in addition Mr. Raymond Carr, Mr. James Joll, and Mr. Steven Watson whose advice and constructive criticism have been extremely helpful; Dr. W. C. Costin, M. Louis Girard, M. Pierre Guiral, and Professor and Mrs. Kenneth Kirkwood for suggestions and comments from which I have derived great benefit; Mrs. J. Dean for her invaluable secretarial assistance; and not least the archivists and librarians who guided me through their collections and obtained obscure works for me.

I dedicate the book to my old tutors at Christ Church and to the Warden and Fellows of St. Antony's College, in deep gratitude.

CONTENTS

ABBREVIATIONS

O.P. Ollivier's private papers.

D. Ollivier's manuscript diary.

J. Extracts from this diary, published as *Journal 1846–1869*, edited by Theodore Zeldin and Anne Troisier de Diaz (1961).

A.N. Archives Nationales, Paris.

A.D. Archives Départementales.

B.N. Bibliothèque Nationale, Paris.

E.L. *L'Empire libéral*, by E. Ollivier (1895–1918).

CHAPTER 1
THE NATURE OF OLLIVIER'S EARLY REPUBLICANISM

EMILE OLLIVIER has a unique place in the history of the second empire, and an important one, for he exercised a crucial influence both on its domestic evolution and on its foreign policy. After having been a leader of the opposition to Napoleon III, he deserted the republican party to become the emperor's chief minister in 1870. For a time his success in transforming his new master from a despot into a constitutional monarch seemed to justify his conduct and perhaps even his claim that he was destined to be one of the great politicians of the nineteenth century. The youthful Gambetta had said that Ollivier combined 'the passion of Fox with the political genius of Pitt' and a visitor to Paris wrote that 'all speak with great great respect of Ollivier'.[1] However, after only seven months in office, his 'liberal empire', which he had vaunted as a régime of peace, plunged France unprepared into the disastrous war with Prussia and lost her Alsace and Lorraine. His reputation at once sank as low as it had only shortly before stood high. Ever since, he has been remembered essentially as first a turncoat and then a bungler. That such a man, it was now said, 'should have been built up into a statesman, in good faith, is incomprehensible. That he should have been entrusted with the destinies of France was a crime.'[2]

Has posterity treated him unjustly? Was his conversion to the cause of Napoleon III inspired simply by ambition for office, or by muddled thinking? Is it right to regard his liberal empire as a hollow sham inevitably doomed to failure, in that it was an attempt to effect an impossible reconciliation between

---

[1] I. Tchnernoff, *Le Parti républicain au coup d'état et sous le second empire* (1906), 274; Lady Amberley, 14 March 1870, *The Amberley Papers*, ed. B. and P. Russell (1937), ii. 323.

[2] M. Du Camp, *Souvenirs d'un demi-siècle* (1949), i. 240.

an essentially authoritarian empire and liberal principles? Was it no more in fact than a feeble parody of the Hundred Days and Additional Act of Napoleon I, with Ollivier playing the role of Benjamin Constant, whom he openly admitted to be his hero? Did he cause so many of his countrymen to take him seriously simply by his bewitchingly melodious, silver-toned rhetoric?

The purpose of this book is to examine Ollivier's career afresh, to try to understand his aims, his motives and his work. By investigating his origins and early life, it will seek to ascertain the precise nature of his republican opinions, to see how they compared with Bonapartism and so to discover in what way he betrayed them when he went over to Napoleon III. By studying his rise to power and the detailed achievement of his ministry, it will try to assess how far the liberal empire was inaugurated with a serious purpose, whether it can be written off as a mere epilogue to Napoleon III's reign, or whether it has in fact a significant place in French political development. Finally, by penetrating into the generally neglected period of his life after 1870, it will attempt to explain why he was never restored to favour, and why he remains condemned to an ambiguous and mediocre notoriety, despite the spark of genius Zola saw in him, despite the 'brilliant qualities' Bergson declared he possessed, and despite his seventeen volumes of self-justifying memoirs, which Toynbee has said make him—as a historian of his own times—almost the equal of Thucydides.[1]

Emile Ollivier, on his paternal side, came of fiery radical stock.[2]

---

[1] E. Zola, Œuvres complètes ed. M. Le Blond (1927–9), xix. 426; Discours de réception de M. Henri Bergson, Séance de l'Académie française, 24 January 1918, 7 ; A. J. Toynbee, A Study of History (1951 ed.), iii. 287–321.

[2] For his family see M. T. Ollivier, Emile Ollivier, sa jeunesse (1919); Z. Marcas, Emile Ollivier (1865); notes in O.P.; and references in P. Masson, Les Bouches du Rhône, encyclopédie départementale (1924–35), xi. 374; G. Perreux, La Propagande républicaine au début de la monarchie de juillet (1930), 261 n.; E. E. Y. Hales, Mazzini and the Secret Societies (1956), 73, 90–91, 171; G. Weill, Histoire du parti républicain en France (1928), 12 n.; P. Dubosc, Quatre mois de république à Marseille (1848); E. Castre, Le Conseil général des Bouches du Rhône (1912); A. G. Garrone, Il Figlio di Mazzini, off-print from Il Ponte (Florence, May–June 1951); P. Guiral, Marseille et l'Algérie, 1830–41 (1957), 159.

His grandfather had fled from his home in Vannes to join the army of the revolution, rather than become a priest as his parents wished, and in old age, settling down as a village schoolmaster in the more congenial south, near Toulon, he had nurtured himself on the republican heroes of antiquity. His father (who was accordingly named Demosthenes) was a conspirator in the democratic cause, devoting his life, as he put it, to 'increasing the number of defenders of the masses'. He was a Carbonaro under the restoration; he was imprisoned at least once for his share in their plots; he was on the side of the revolution both in 1830 and in 1848—sufficiently prominent to be Mazzini's host when the latter visited Marseilles and sufficiently dangerous to be exiled when Napoleon III destroyed the republic. Demosthenes' brother (Aristides) was a merchant who used his profits to subsidize Italian revolutionaries.[1] It has always been assumed therefore that Emile Ollivier was essentially a republican by birth and that it was thus all the more inexcusable for him to have gone over to serve his father's persecutor.

Closer examination, however, reveals that his background was not as simple as it appeared to be. He derived his ideas not only from his father but from a dozen different men, whose influence will, in due course, be described in this book; but even his direct inheritance was not one to make him whole-heartedly devoted to republic and revolution. His mother came of a family of royalist *emigrés*; his grandmother, who outlived her, is said to have been a fanatical legitimist; so fervent was the devotion of one of his old relations to Charles X that the news of that monarch's expulsion had to be concealed from him, for fear that it might kill him.[2] This was perhaps why Ollivier grew up with a remarkable freedom from party animosity and with a passion for reconciliation which was to remain a principal characteristic of his thought. Moreover, the opinions of his father (to whom he was greatly attached and who long remained

---

[1] Ollivier to Gubernaty, 29 November 1872, copy, O.P.

[2] J. ii. 32. (11 November 1861); M. T. Ollivier, *Emile Ollivier, sa jeunesse* (1918), 10–11.

his constant adviser), though republican, were formed in the first half of the century and were very different therefore from those which inspired the republicans of the next generation. Thus, for example, Demosthenes was a great admirer of Rousseau (which explains his son's Christian name), but by 1870 Rousseau was quite out of favour with the party's young men, who, brought up instead on Proudhon, Comte, and Littré, denounced him as 'a perverter of the French mentality'.[1] Again, Demosthenes' active politics were particularly shaped by his association with his three great friends, Armand Carrel, Ledru-Rollin, and Pierre Leroux, men highly respected in their day but whose ideas quickly became out of date during the second empire.[2] Yet Emile Ollivier throughout his life clearly bore the imprint of their influence: his idiosyncrasies are thus (in part) explained by his precocious entry into politics, which had the curious result that he derived his inspiration from the prophets of a previous generation. He was in fact essentially a 'man of 1848'; the 'deviationism' of his liberal empire was not really a breakaway from republicanism, but the very contrary, an obstinate loyalty to traditions by then almost entirely forgotten. This will be seen more clearly if some of the ideas of these men are briefly examined.

Armand Carrel has long been little more than a name, for he was killed in a duel at the age of thirty-six and never actually held political office; but in the reign of Louis-Philippe he was considered to be the most brilliant journalist of the republican party and he might well have been its candidate for the presidency in 1848 had he lived. Now his republicanism had three

---

[1] Deluns-Montaud, 'La philosophie de Gambetta', *Revue politique et parlementaire*, 10 February 1897, ix. 248–9; Gambetta's speech of 5 April 1870, in *Discours et plaidoyers politiques de M. Gambetta* (1881), i. 222: 'Rousseau is wrong... The theories and doctrines of this great mind do not suit the theories, the doctrines and the hopes of contemporary democracy.' Cf. René Hubert, 'Rousseau et l'école positiviste, *Archives de philosophie du droit et de sociologie juridique* (1932), 407–27; J. Jaurès, 'Les idées politiques et sociales de J. J. Rousseau', *Revue de métaphysique et de morale* (1912), xx. 371–81; Harald Höffding, Rousseau et le XIXe siècle,' *Annales de la société J. J. Rousseau* (Geneva, 1912), viii. 69–98.   [2] J. i. 346–7 (7 October 1858); ii. 102 (March–April 1864), but cf. i. 288 (26 June 1857); E.L. iv. 22.

special features which link it with that of Ollivier. First, he was not a revolutionary; he objected to the use of violence and he urged that the monarchy should not be forcibly overthrown but instead be persuaded to reform. Secondly, he was in no way absolute in his loyalty to the republican form of government; he declared that if he had to choose between a republic without liberty and a monarchy with partial liberty, he would prefer the latter. He was finally a great admirer of Bonaparte—not the emperor but the first consul of the republic—and his ideal was a strong president with a constitution modelled on that of the United States. His great regret was that Bonaparte had not remained consul, that he had not been re-elected for a second term in 1804 and then laid down his office in 1808, gloriously, 'like another Washington'. Carrel fought with Napoleon II's regiment on the liberal side in Spain in 1823, dressed in the uniform of the Imperial Guard. In 1840, his disciple Demosthenes Ollivier is reported to have struck an Englishman who failed to raise his hat before the procession bearing the body of the great man back to France. It is interesting that Carrel's moderation earned him accusations of treachery to the republican cause, rather similar to those made against Ollivier thirty years later. At a banquet organized in his honour at Marseilles by the Pytheas Club (of which Demosthenes was president) he caused great indignation by rebuking the members for singing songs of the Terror, and men asked on whose side he really was.[1]

Pierre Leroux is remembered as the first man to introduce the words socialism and solidarity into France, but what in fact particularly distinguished him was his conciliatory spirit, his

---

[1] Œuvres politiques et littéraires d'Armand Carrel, ed. Littré and Paulin (1857), iii. 58, 122, 176, iv. 137, v. 366; L. Petit de Julleville, Histoire de la langue et de la littérature françaises (1899), viii. 622; R. G. Nobécourt, La Vie d'Armand Carrel (1930), 173–5, 185, 273. J. S. Mill said that Carrel and Tocqueville were the only two Frenchmen for whom he had a real admiration: A. de Tocqueville, Œuvres Complètes, ed. J. P. Mayer, vi. part 1, (1954), 299. Jules Simon, in his memoirs of the 1830's and 1840's talks of Carrel as 'all powerful over the minds of the youth' of those days; Premières Années (n.d.), 181. Napoleon III quotes Carrel with approval in his Œuvres (1856), i. 22–3, though Carrel rejected his advances.

desire to evolve a new order which would find room for everybody and which would reconcile all hostilities. He, too, opposed the use of violence; he called himself a 'pacific revolutionary'; and he urged his followers to take no part in any insurrection which might break out against the monarchy. He was on the side of the republic, but also on the side of religion (though of a reformed religion): he and Demosthenes at one time thought of becoming Protestant pastors and going out to preach a 'New Christianity'. Emile listened to their conversations as a child, growing up, as he said, with the words God, Humanity, Plato, and Jesus reverberating above his head. From Leroux he thus inherited an attitude which made it difficult for him to believe whole-heartedly in three of the republican's major doctrines of later years: the republic at all costs, no compromise with its opponents, and the annihilation of the influence of the church.[1]

Ledru-Rollin, the minister of the interior under whose patronage Emile Ollivier entered political life in 1848, had less influence on him, for they soon quarrelled. However, he illustrates how the republicans of the early nineteenth century had a great deal in common with the Bonapartists, not only in their opposition to the old monarchy, but also in the institutions with which they planned to replace it. He advocated first universal suffrage and then social legislation, with the aim, not of establishing the dictatorship of the proletariat, but of securing the abolition of that whole class: when all workers were made owners of property, he said, they would be 'more tranquil and more moral'. After 1849 he became an opponent of parliamentary government; he demanded the abolition of elected representatives and instead sought the 'direct government of the people by the people', voting their laws themselves by referendum. The two foundation stones of the liberal empire were precisely the denial of parliamentary government and the use of the plebiscite, and

---

[1] P. Felix Thomas, *Pierre Leroux, sa vie, son œuvre, sa doctrine* (1904); Henri Mougin, *Pierre Leroux* (1938); P. Leroux, *Projet d'une constitution démocratique et sociale* (1848); D. O. Evans, *Le Socialisme romantique* (1948); Armand Cuvillier, *Hommes et idéologies de 1840* (1956).

these derived from the same tradition that inspired Ledru-Rollin. 'Direct government' had indeed a considerable following among republicans in 1848, counting among its partisans even Littré, but all—except Ollivier—abandoned it when Louis Napoleon turned it against them.[1]

An upbringing among this highly heterogeneous party, over-rich in vague ideas, necessarily produced a complicated effect. In addition, Demosthenes' long service in the republican cause paradoxically did not increase Emile's loyalty to it. Demosthenes was a man who suffered repeated disappointments. Throughout his life he underwent much privation and hardship. He was too idealistic and selfless a man to achieve worldly success; he was too absorbed by his dreams of reform, too little a calculating business man, too given to generosity to be any good at trade; his shop of novelty goods went bankrupt and one may guess that it was more a rendezvous for his political friends than a commercial establishment. After a period of unemployment he got a job as a foreman in a mine, but was dismissed for preaching socialism to the workers. He naturally brought up his children (of whom he had six) to be politically and socially conscious, to devote their lives to improving the lot of the masses, but he was also determined that they should not be failures like himself. He instilled into them ambition, determination, self-reliance, passion for success. 'Allow nothing to distract you', he used to say, 'from the sole and great aim you must hold before you, self-improvement. . . . Become shoemakers or masons, providing you are the best among the shoemakers and the masons.' The effect of this teaching on Emile seems to have been to produce not a deep-rooted loyalty to the party but on the contrary a firm resolve, as he himself wrote, not to be 'the victim of the stupidities of [the] party' as

[1] A. Ledru-Rollin, *Discours politiques et écrits divers* (1879), i. 4–5, 20, 46, ii. 420–9; R. Schnerb, *Ledru-Rollin et le suffrage universel* (1948); A. R. Calman, *Ledru-Rollin après 1848* (1921), 54, 262; Jammy-Schmidt, *Les grandes thèses radicales* (1931), 68, iii. Cf. *Le Moniteur* of 25 October 1848, p. 2956, which shows Demosthenes Ollivier voting with the small minority which demanded that the people should be asked to approve the constitution by referendum.

his father had been. Instead he developed a distinct inclination to seek out new paths for the attainment of his aims; and the puritanism implanted in him in the course of time fostered that attitude of aloofness towards his fellows, that almost contemptuous independence of them which was at the root of his individuality.[1]

Emile Ollivier, who was born at Marseilles on 2 July 1825, was educated first at a country school near Riez (Basses-Alpes), run according to the theories of Rousseau, and then at the most fashionable boarding establishment of his native city, the Pensionnat Speiss, to which *la gentry commerçante* sent their children.[2] When his father went bankrupt, he won a scholarship to the Lycée de Sainte-Barbe in Paris and in his final year did without tuition altogether, in order to save on fees. He joined the Paris School of Law at the age of sixteen, meeting part of his expenses by giving private lessons. In 1846, after a stormy *viva* in which he obstinately contradicted his examiners, but was nevertheless passed by all of them, he emerged as a licentiate in law, qualified to practise at the bar.

However, he was not anxious simply to embark on a respectable professional career. He illustrates well how Guizot's advice to 'make money' was unacceptable and irrelevant to many of the generation of 1848. He put at the head of his thesis for his degree this motto (in Latin): 'They who strive for the highest goals shall go further than those who, despairing from the beginning of realizing the object of their wishes, remain at the bottom.'[3] He was determined to do greater things than simply earn his living: 'In the [mere] struggle for material interests . . . where is life, where poetry, where love?'[4]

He planned to devote himself to a cause, as his father and grandfather had both done. 'Life', he wrote, 'is but perpetual

---

[1] J. i. 212 (11 July 1857).

[2] M. T. Ollivier, *Emile Ollivier, sa jeunesse* (1918), 18. This book, by his widow, is the principal source for his childhood.

[3] E. Ollivier, *Du mariage considéré dans ses effets a l'égard des époux, des enfants et des parents, soutenue le jeudi 30 juillet 1846.*

[4] J. i. 2 (4 August 1846)

suffering and ineffectual yearning for an ideal which is not of this world. The only way to bear it is to impose on oneself an elevated mission, a generous role. God grant that mine be to succour misfortune, to defend and to protect disregarded rights. I hope that my heart will never forget the sorrows and humiliations in which adversity placed my youth and that this memory will be the guardian angel, the helpmate of my efforts. . . .'[1]

Ollivier obtained his inspiration not merely from the circle in which his father moved but also from the voracious reading which was his principal relaxation. 'My insatiable curiosity extended to every new publication, whatever its subject.'[2] He came to believe, in common with many others, that the great problem of the day was social rather than political. 'There is but one sole question, that of Pauperism.'[3] 'Reformers ought to have but one aim', he wrote in the language of Leroux (itself frequently borrowed from Saint-Simon), 'the alleviation of the miseries which torture and sterilize the major part of the nation.'[4] 'There must be no more such maxims as these, "The poor will always be with us", "Justice is not of this world." The people must be raised up, women must be educated, poverty must be reduced, and there ought to be no miserable men except those who have not done their duty.'[5] However, he looked forward to the achievement of his aims not so much by economic reforms as by a wholesale moral regeneration of mankind.[6] A new religion was needed, blending Christianity, socialism, and democracy, to replace the present 'religion of love of money'. He wrote to Pierre Leroux, 'We are thirsty for truth, we demand but a belief to lead to triumph, an ideal to proclaim. . . . You

---

[1] J. i. 1 (11 July 1846)

[2] E.L. iv. 23; volume of 'extracts' copied from the books he read, O.P.

[3] There is no evidence that Ollivier ever read Louis Napoleon's *Extinction du paupérisme* (1844); both men were expressing ideas widely held at the time.

[4] J. i. 10 (1 July 1847).

[5] Ollivier to Séguier, 7 September 1847, copy in D.

[6] Ibid., and Ollivier to Eugène Guiter, 14 March 1847, original in the possession of Guiter's descendants.

are performing a sacred task when you search to formulate the faith, the credo of the modern man. Too many generous instincts are offended by the present order, too many hearts bleed from their own miseries or from those of their brothers, for unanimous acclamation not to greet whoever comes, without hate and without anger, to show the way he has discovered by the sweat of his brow.'[1]

He condemned the monarchy of Louis Philippe both for its domestic and for its foreign policy. It 'had not satisfied the public conscience nor even come near to the ideal of government'. It had allowed France to 'fall from the elevated position into which the Revolution and its hero had placed her', whereas he longed for a firmer diplomacy to safeguard 'our interests and our dignity'.[2] However, it was not for an insurrection that he hoped. He was more and more convinced, he wrote on 3 November 1847, of the need for a revolution in the social mechanism, but he was equally certain that this revolution must be accomplished peacefully. The enemies of change must not be intimidated into submission by violence or by threats; they must be converted and won over through a change of heart. His ideal was to bring about the agreement of all parties, to produce a synthesis of all philosophical systems, to establish fraternity, peace among men, the 'democracy which Jesus practised'.[3] He wished to replace the monarchy not simply by a republic, but by a mixed form of government, uniting the virtues of all possible constitutions.[4] He copied into his diary this passage from the New Testament: 'Thou shalt love the Lord Thy God with all thy heart, and with all thy soul, and with all thy mind. This is the first and great commandment. And the second is like unto

[1] J. i. 12 (Letter to P. Leroux, 15 October 1847).

[2] J. i. 3 (21 October 1846); for this bellicose streak, cf. A. Carrel, 'Contre les partisans de la paix à tout prix', in Œuvres politiques et littéraires d'Armand Carrel (1857), ii. 174.

[3] J. i. 13 and i. 7, 10, 11 (11 February, 4 and 15 September 1847); cf. Pierre Leroux, D'une réligion nationale (1846) De l'humanité (1840), and his letters to Ollivier in Revue de Paris (1903), 643–8.

[4] D. 4 September 1846 and J. i. 12 (15 October 1847), basing himself on Machiavelli; see below, p. 46.

it, Thou shalt love thy neighbour as thyself. On these two commandments hang all the law and the prophets.' 'O sublime teaching!' he added. 'Will men ever have the strength to understand it and to fulfil it?'[1]

The information that is available about Ollivier's ideas before 1848 is limited and fragmentary; the ideas themselves are vague and undeveloped. Enough can be gathered however for it to be clear that the elements of a considerable number of his future opinions were already present in him, and the attitude of mind they reveal is already recognizable as his own. It has too hastily been assumed that Ollivier's early republicanism was totally incompatible with his later liberal Bonapartism. The gradual process by which the one turned into the other will be analysed in the following chapters. Meanwhile, it is important to note that Ollivier did nothing to bring about the revolution of 1848. Its outbreak came to him as a complete surprise.[2]

---

[1] J. i. 9 (16 April 1847).
[2] J. i. 16–17 (14 and 27 February 1848).

CHAPTER 2

THE SIGNIFICANCE OF OLLIVIER'S WORK IN 1848

S UDDENLY, at the age of twenty-two, in February 1848, Ollivier was appointed to govern the second largest city of France and two departments of her territory. He was thrown into a hectic life full of picturesque incidents, in turn sentimental, grandiloquent, violent, and hysterical. His romantic adventures have been frequently narrated, but the comments passed on them have generally consisted either in attacks against him or in declarations that 'his conduct appears absolutely irreproachable'.[1] The language of Ollivier's speeches and proclamations do indeed appear to mark him out as a typical representative of this revolution of good intentions. 'Remember,' Saint-Simon had told his disciples, 'that to do great things it is necessary to be passionate.'[2] Ollivier overflowed with determination to do great things and he was passionate too. He was very much at one with this generation 'intoxicated by [the words] liberty, equality, and fraternity', assured that the reign of absolute justice was at hand.[3] However, what more precisely is the significance of Ollivier's individual participation in the revolution, in what way did he distinguish himself in it, and what was the real meaning of his seemingly commonplace words and deeds?

As soon as the revolution broke out Ledru-Rollin, who became minister of the interior, offered his old friend Demosthenes the post of commissary-general of the republic in Bouches-du-

[1] P. Dubosc, *Quatre Mois de République à Marseille* (1848); P. Saint-Marc, *Emile Ollivier* (1950), 49.

[2] *Le Globe* 30 December 1831, quoted by D. O. Evans, *Social Romanticism in France 1830-1848* (1951), 11.

[3] Ranc, quoted by I. Tchernoff, *Le Parti républicain au coup d'état et sous le second empire* (1906), 166.

Rhône and Var; but Demosthenes, with characteristic modesty and idealism, made him appoint Emile instead, so that the régime should start fresh with new men. Ollivier thus entered public life simply through the influence of his father, without preparation or experience of any kind. In 1870 likewise he became head of the government without ever having held ministerial office before. It is important to remember that he was, to a large extent, always an amateur in politics.

The year 1848 first of all won Ollivier a reputation in his own right as an eloquent orator of unusual power and promise. As soon as he arrived in Marseilles, he undertook a speaking tour of his department which was an astounding triumph. Huge crowds came to hear him in every town and responded to his rapturous harangues with wildly emotional scenes. At Toulon the admiral in command of the port burst into tears and flung his arms around him. At Arles he excited 'transports of enthusiasm' and 'tears were seen on every face'. 'By his vibrant and noble eloquence,' said the local newspaper, 'by the expressions of love risen from his ardent breast, by his evangelic words, he has won more hearts to the republic than ever did the abuses and iniquities of past governments.' Daniel Stern confirms the extraordinary power he acquired by 'his happy gift for effusive and persuasive utterance, which won him access even to those who were most hostile to him'. 'You would laugh,' said Ollivier twenty years later, 'were I to recount all the pathetic, grandiose scenes.'[1]

The speeches which sent the Provençaux into such ecstasies were variations on a single theme: 'Let us be united,' he repeated,

---

[1] E. Ollivier, Le 19 janvier (1867), 16; Courrier des Bouches du Rhône (Arles), 1 April 1848; D. Stern, Histoire de la Revolution de 1848 (1851), ii. 260–8. The main source for Ollivier's life in 1848 is his own private papers, a small collection of MSS. and a bound volume of Imprimés 1848. The departmental and municipal archives of Marseilles, and the local press also have useful information about him. Cf. also Paul Raphael, 'Fortoul et la Seconde République', La Révolution de 1848 (1931), xxvii. 185 ff.; idem, 'Emile Ollivier et la suppression du recteur d'Aix en 1848', La Révolution de 1848 (1928) xxv. 6–15; and the works cited in the course of this chapter.

'let us be brothers . . . [Let us] love one another: that is all the republic means.'[1] These sentiments, which might at first sight appear to be banal and empty verbiage, had in fact a definite political significance. For the revolution of 1848 did not represent the triumph of any one party but rather the collapse and abdication of the old monarchy before deep-rooted forces which it had long ignored and which finally it had dared not oppose. The men who proclaimed the republic came not from a single party but from innumerable little cliques with widely divergent aspirations, ranging from Jacobin conspirators on the one hand to socially conservative notables on the other. The victors of the revolution moreover were not only the republicans but also the clergy and the legitimists, who were equally enemies of the Voltairian, Protestant régime of the usurper Louis Philippe. In and around Marseilles this fact was very much in evidence, for the south of France was a legitimist stronghold second in importance only to the west. There were not many large landowners here, but instead a numerous petty nobility thrived, with the leisure to organize secret societies even more efficiently than the republicans themselves; and the church perhaps enjoyed greater influence still. In France as a whole the republicans were a minority: here in the south they were a very small one.

The republicans were broadly divided into two schools on the question of how they should act to secure the triumph of their principles. On the one hand were those who frankly recognized that they were a minority and who believed that it was their mission to lead—indeed to compel—France to follow the path of progress. They should not allow their work to be delayed by the benighted peasantry who were still slaves of an out-dated

[1] Proclamations of 1 March and 11 April 1848 in O.P.; *Courrier des Bouches du Rhône*, 1 April 1848. Cf. Pierre Leroux's similar words in *his* proclamation as mayor of Boussac: 'We are all brothers; we must all be happy together, each through the other.'—P. F. Thomas, *Pierre Leroux* (1904), 91. Saint-Simon put this motto at the beginning of his *Du système industriel* (1821); 'Love one another and help one another.' *Œuvres choisies de C. H. Saint-Simon* (1859), iii. 1. On the other hand cf. L. and W. D[agusan], *Récit historique des événements des 22 et 23 juin à Marseille* (Marseilles, 1848), 29, objecting to 'scoundrels' being called 'brothers'.

conservatism: they should postpone the elections until they had time to 'educate' the nation, rather than allow the old ruling class to re-emerge triumphant. 'What makes a republic', Saint-Just had said, 'is the total destruction of those who are opposed to it': these men were the inventors of the doctrine of the dictatorship of the party. On the other hand, however, force had so often failed to achieve any lasting results that a reaction against using it had grown up in the republican ranks. Some of their utopian theorists, as opposed to their active politicians, were more ready to believe in the obvious appeal of their teaching and in their own powers of persuasion. They urged that the sterile divisions of the past should be ended, that 'fraternity' should replace 'exclusiveness' and that all men of good will, of whatever party, should be invited to unite in a universal reconciliation.[1]

Ledru-Rollin was the leading advocate of the first of these schools, of the policy of immediate and radical change. The instructions he sent to Ollivier and his colleagues laid it down that power should be concentrated exclusively in the hands of the old party workers. 'Take it as a rule,' he wrote, 'that public offices at every rung in the hierarchy should be entrusted only to tried republicans . . . to men who were republicans before the revolution' and not those who had simply joined the winning side. 'The assembly [soon to be elected] must be animated by revolutionary sentiments . . . Take note that those who solicit the honour of sitting in it must be pure of all the traditions of the past.'[2]

Emile Ollivier did mere lip-service to these orders.[3] In fact he pursued an exactly opposite policy and from the very beginning of his career he revealed an attitude of independence and

[1] A. Bonnard, Les Modérés (1936), 60; P. J. Proudhon, Correspondance (1875), ii. 316; G. Woodcock, P. J. Proudhon (1956), 91–93. Ollivier had read Proudhon and might well have been familiar with his views on the use of force and on exclusive party dogma. Cf. P. Haury, 'Les Commissaires de Ledru-Rollin en 1848', in La Révolution française (1909), ii. 438–74.

[2] Circulars of 8 and 12 March 1848, quoted by Elias Regnault (Ledru-Rollin's chef de cabinet), Histoire du gouvernement provisoire (1850), 199, 203–4.

[3] A. D. Bouches-du-Rhône, M (6) 25, Ollivier's proclamation of 11 March 1848.

indifference towards his party and a contempt of the notion of absolute loyalty to it. Though he owed his appointment to Ledru-Rollin, he appears to have been carried away by the rhapsodic idealism of Lamartine, the leading exponent of 'sentimental politics'. 'M. Lamartine liked to be magnanimous and tolerant towards the supporters of the monarchy. What he found most seductive in holding power was the ability to forgive, to be generous, and to show fine sentiments. Less interested in founding the future than in conquering the past by disinterestedness and abnegation, he transformed politics into a sort of . . . poetical . . . chivalry.' Lamartine had been a diplomat under Charles X; he had rallied in turn to Louis-Phillipe and to the republic, but he had always kept aloof from parties. The enormous and nation-wide popularity he had won as a poet had led him to imagine that 'in the very depths of the people' there existed a fund of goodwill and benevolent aspiration, with which in some mystical way he communed and to which he was destined to give effect. He was determined to be not a mere politician but a prophet and a hero. Emile Ollivier, wrote a contemporary, 'seemed to take Lamartine as his model; like him . . . he imagined that eloquence and honesty suffice in all things, that kindness is the best method of governing, and that fraternity fills men's hearts as soon as it is inscribed on the walls.'[1]

Ollivier therefore inevitably and immediately found himself at loggerheads with the republican politicians of Marseilles. For them the victory of 1848 meant that they would at last emerge from their protracted obscurity and exile to enjoy the fruits and spoils of victory. They besieged him with demands for jobs and favours, for the wholesale expulsion of the monarchists from the civil service, as just rewards for their stalwart service to the party.[2] To their immense surprise Ollivier turned a deaf ear to them all. When an old leader of the Marseilles party, a

---

[1] Regnault, op. cit. 133; V. Pierre, *Histoire de la République de 1848* (1873), i. 152–3. Cf. Joseph Salvarelli, *Les Administrateurs du département du Var 1790–1897*. (Draguignan, 1897).

[2] A.D. Bouches-du-Rhône, M. (6) 24, letters of complaint; also 33 V. 1.

family friend whom Ollivier admitted had been almost a father to him, asked to be appointed mayor of a city, Ollivier sententiously replied, 'Your name has, rightly or wrongly, become the symbol of a policy of violence and terror, and this cannot be my policy.' Instead of arresting the bishop, as the rabid anti-clericals demanded, he hastened to pay him a visit, assured him of his 'respect for religion', impressed him with his 'very great politeness', and arranged for him to hold a service for the victims of the revolution.[1] Not only did he decline to purge the administration of non-republicans, but he even enlisted a legitimist and an Orleanist on to the 'municipal commission' he formed. He stipulated that the banquet given in his honour at Toulon should be held on the field where the executions of the Terror of 1793 had taken place: 'Let us meet', he said, 'in the very place where the blood flowed, there to seal a pact of reconciliation between us.' It was in vain that the radicals summoned him to a party meeting and accused him of being a 'reactionary' in a furious and stormy debate which lasted a whole night. He insisted that he did not mean the republic to wreak vengeance on the vanquished, but to establish harmony between all parties. He believed this to be desirable on principle and he claimed that in any case, simply from a practical point of view, no other policy was possible: only by compromising with the legitimists, who were clearly dominant in Marseilles, only by making concessions to them and so preventing them from attacking the republic, could the existence of the new régime be safeguarded. As early as 1848 therefore Ollivier was an advocate of a policy of compromise with the powers that be, even at the expense of his own party.[2]

His conflict with the local party became public in the elections held in April. He now made speeches declaring that representatives of all opinions and of all parties should be elected, including

[1] Extracts from the diary of the bishop in Achille Rey, *Histoire de Monseigneur C. J. E. de Mazenod* (Marseilles, 1928), ii. 269; their correspondence in the Archives of the Diocese, file 142, and Registre du Correspondance 1844–51.

[2] Municipal Archives of Marseilles, i D 73, p. 392; E. Ollivier, *Le 19 Janvier* (1869), 13–56.

even Berryer, the legitimist leader;[1] but the central republican committee of local politicians published a list of candidates of its own, composed exclusively of men who were at once 'radical, republican, and revolutionary'.[2] Then, when only one of its nominees scraped in at the bottom of the poll, well behind three legitimists, a Catholic and four republicans whom it considered too moderate and unreliable, the committee laid all the blame on Ollivier, because he had failed to purge the constituency of reactionary influences. Nevertheless, at a by-election soon after, Ollivier not only again abstained from co-operating with the committee but this time actively opposed its list with candidates of his own. He officially supported three men of the school of Lamartine (whom the radicals abhorred because 'he lacks revolutionary sentiments'.) The roots of the liberal empire can thus be traced to this early attempt to create a 'third party' to end factions and to unite 'all honest men'.[3]

Ollivier sought to win the support of the people by an active social policy, which was urgently called for by the acute economic crisis.[4] Trade was declining drastically, unemployment rife, bankruptcy widely threatened. In the past year, the number of ships docking in the port of Marseilles had fallen by half; the city's import of cotton, which in 1847 had been 45,000 bales, was now only 19,000; but the cost of living remained one of the highest in Europe.[5] Ollivier appointed a consultative committee

[1] The government approved Ollivier's policy of co-operating with the legitimists and of supporting Berryer, but urged him to oppose Thiers and the Orleanists.—Jules Favre, Secretary-General, Ministry of Interior, to Ollivier, 17 March 1848, draft, in Archives Nationales, 43 A.P.

[2] P. Dubosc, Quatre Mois de République a Marseille (Marseilles, 1848), 22.

[3] P. Masson, Les Bouches-du-Rhône, encyclopédie départementale, vol. v. (1929) chapter on politics in 1848; P. Dubosc, Quatre Mois de Republique a Marseille (Marseilles, 1848); Gazette du Midi, 1 June 1848; Le Sémaphore de Marseille April and 1–2 June 1848; Le Progrés Social of Marseilles, 21 April 1848; A.D Bouches-du-Rhône (Aix), 15 U 1, 3 and 5; A.N. BB (30) 358, Procureur Général Aix to Minister of Justice, 8 June 1848.

[4] A.D. Bouches-du-Rhône, M (6) 24, Mayor of Marseilles to Ollivier, 23 May 1848.

[5] P. Guiral, 'Marseille [in 1846-51]', in Aspects de la crise et de la dépression de l'économie française au milieu du XIXe siècle 1846–1851, edited by E. Labrousse (1956), Bibliothèque de la Révolution de 1848, vol. 19, 200-25.

of workers, composed of two delegates elected by each trade, to meet under his presidency 'to discuss all questions of wages and labour conditions'.[1] He announced that he himself would give a course of lectures for the benefit of the workers on 'morals and political history', every Saturday at 8 p.m. Above all he helped to organize an energetic programme of public works: the long-delayed completion of the Durance Canal, the construction of the Place de la Corderie, the upper rue Paradis, and the embankment of the Plage du Pardo were all furthered, even though the city's finances were ruined in the process. These measures, together with the organization of national workshops for 8,000 men, reduced unemployment greatly. The rapid formation of a discount house to lend money to businesses in distress contributed to keeping bankruptcies down.[2] 'Republican opinion', wrote an observer, 'has undeniably increased among the mass of the population in the past few weeks, thanks above all to the spirit of fraternal love, conciliation, and moderation of our young commissary, whose popularity has constantly waxed.'[3]

At the same time, however, Ollivier associated the old ruling class with his work; he relied heavily on their advice in commercial and financial matters; and he left the national guard under the control of the bourgeoisie. Radical complaints against his conservatism were such that Ledru-Rollin despatched, as a check to it, a 'commissary extraordinary' of left-wing views, who in order to strengthen the 'democratic' elements, encouraged the formation of battalions of republican 'tirailleurs'.[4] In

[1] Decree of 11 March 1848, O.P. Cf. André Dubuc, 'Frédéric Deschamps, Commissiare de la république en Seine Inférieure', in *Actes du Congrès historique du centenaire de la Révolution de 1848* (1948), 381–95.

[2] A.D. Bouches-du-Rhône, M (6) 5309, telegrams from Ollivier to the minister of the interior, 3 and 11 March 1848; *Le Sémaphore de Marseille*, 22 March 1848 and supplement of 9 June 1848, containing *Compte rendu des travaux publics à Marseille pendant les mois de Mars, Avril et Mai*, by M. Albrand; cf. G. Rambert, *Marseille, la formation d'une grande cité* (1934).

[3] A.D. Bouches-du-Rhône (Aix), 12U1, Rubin (procureur de la république) to procureur genéral, 20 April 1848.

[4] A.D. Bouches-du-Rhône, R4 1, Mayor of Marseilles to Prefect, 22 February 1850; M (6) 26, undated note by Ollivier to the minister of the interior.

the face of such threats, 'men of property' who had no love for the new régime could nevertheless co-operate with the conciliatory Ollivier: even the legitimists found his opinions 'irreproachable' and applauded the 'benevolence he seemed to spread about him'.[1]

However, his policy of trying to satisfy everybody, or, as he put it in the language of the time, to bring about the 'fusion of all classes'[2] ended in disaster. The central government had reduced the hours of work in Paris to ten a day and in the provinces to eleven. The workers of Marseilles agitated for equality of treatment and Ollivier satisfied them by issuing a decree (in defiance of the government's policy) granting their wish. To strengthen his hand against Paris, he urged the workers to organize a petition in support of his action. But then agitators of the left distorted the issue, turned the petitioning into a demonstration and, after clashes with the police, put up the barricades. Marseilles was threatened with revolution, at the very same time as the great insurrection of June broke out in Paris for rather more serious reasons. Now came the decisive test of Ollivier's practical ability. He responded by issuing eloquent appeals to the insurgents to lay down their arms. Fortunately for him, the National Workshops for the unemployed heeded his words and refrained from joining the revolt; but he did not convince those on the barricades, and it was some days before, with the help of troops from Algeria, he restored order by force, with some loss of life.[3]

The conservatives, terrified by the 'red menace', now had grave doubts about Ollivier. They could not understand why he had wasted time temporizing and reasoning with the revolutionaries instead of annihilating them. The bourgeois national guard immediately set about arresting the radicals. The new government in Paris under the strong man General Cavaignac ordered the declaration of a state of emergency so that they could be

---

[1] *Gazette du Midi*, 3–4 April and 18 July 1848.

[2] Report of his speech at the Athenée Ouvrier in *Le Sémaphore de Marseille*, 9 March 1848.

[3] *Cours d'Assises de la Drôme: Procès des accusés de juin de Marseille sous la présidence de M. Bertrand* (Marseilles 1849), No. 5456 in the Bibliothèque de la Ville de Marseille, especially 292 ff.

tried before military tribunals. Ollivier however refused to do this: it was entirely out of keeping with his policy of reconciliation and he released many radicals as fast as they were arrested. There was no point, he wrote to the minister of the interior, in replying to the revolt simply by repression. 'You know better than I do that a reaction never produces anything durable or fruitful. . . . I am deeply convinced that the only means of bringing back this furious mass of misguided men to decent views is to busy oneself actively in their interest, so that evil passions and dangerous theories can never use hunger and poverty as auxiliaries or arguments. . . . The masses were wrong to lend ear to the pernicious counsels of those who painted the bourgeoisie as rapacious monsters of whom it was necessary to rid mankind. If we now let the bourgeoisie do as it wishes, we shall be treating the masses as beasts of burden who are wicked as soon as they cease to be servile. Neither of these errors shall determine my conduct.'[1]

It was obvious that far from winning over the conservative classes to the republic, Ollivier had merely facilitated their return to power. Far from reconciling the parties, he was now the object of abuse from them all. The radicals attacked him for suppressing their revolt, and they did not thank him for his protection afterwards. His popularity with the conservatives vanished overnight. They began to say that since he would not imprison the revolutionaries, it was clear that he must be their accomplice, a red republican at heart.[2] The judge who tried the rioters reported that 'the conduct of M. Emile Ollivier in the days of June has been diversely appreciated and attacked with passion by the political parties. Some have reproached him with having provoked the demonstration, with having betrayed the workers whom he had encouraged [to petition], and with having in this way set a trap for them. Others have accused him of having constantly temporized with the insurrection, of having made the most culpable compromises; it has even been insinuated that he was an accomplice of the conspirators of Paris,

---

[1] E. Ollivier, Le 19 Janvier (1869), 41.
[2] L'Indépendant de Marseille, 25–26 June 1848

and that he prepared and fomented what happened in Marseilles.' These, said the judge, were 'odious calumnies and unjust accusations'. 'This administrator can no doubt be reproached for hesitations and even for weakness in the first moments of the insurrection; such things had never occurred before in the city of Marseilles and for a short period he perhaps hoped that it would be easy for him to pacify men whom he believed only to have gone astray: but when he saw that his efforts at conciliation were powerless, he took, with energy and resolution, measures which assured the triumph of order.'[1]

At the same time however the commissioner appointed by the Cavaignac government to inquire into the causes of the insurrection, while also reporting that there was no foundation for the charge of complicity, sarcastically criticized 'the inexperience of Prefect Ollivier, who is not yet convinced that evangelical words and the language of the apostles are not sufficient to charm away a storm which has broken out with some considerable force'.[2]

To this charge of relying on evangelism Ollivier pleaded guilty. 'I am convinced', he wrote, 'that the supreme law of the political, moral, and religious world is Love. In this divine sentiment I placed all my beliefs as I did all my hopes of regenerating mankind. In my opinion, he who understands the simple words, "Love one another as I love you" will be a wise man, greater than any man has been in this world to this day. It is therefore natural that I should have believed in the efficacy of the language used by our first Master and His disciples. If that language was powerless, is that my fault?'[3] A few months before, Admiral

---

[1] Archives Nationales, BB (30) 358, report by the Président des Assises de la Drôme, 20 February 1850.

[2] Report of Marquesy on Bouches-du-Rhône, O.P. Cf. J. Billioud, H. Guillet, P. Ripert, and A. Villard, *Centenaire de la deuxième république: L'époque 1848 à Marseille et dans les Bouches-du-Rhône* (Marseilles, 1948), 9; T. B. [Busq], *Notice sur le plan en relief executé par M. Lavastre, suivie d'un precis de événements des 22 et 23 juin 1848* (Marseilles, 1850); L. and W. D. [Dagusan] *Récit historique des événements des 22 et 23 juin à Marseille* (Marseilles, 1848)—in the Bibliothèque de la Ville de Marseille.

[3] Undated letter in 1848 file, O.P.

Baudin, commander of the port of Toulon, wrote, 'Whoever it is who succeeds you, will not be able to replace you. He may have faith, but will he have, as you have, charity? You have made the republic loved; he will perhaps make it feared.'[1] In Cavaignac's opinion, there was no room for charity now. Ollivier was demoted and transferred in semi-disgrace to the junior prefecture of Chaumont.

Though deeply hurt by this humiliation, Ollivier decided to accept it in a spirit of Christian resignation, and to repeat his efforts in his new post. 'What matter . . . the disappointments and griefs of this world?' he wrote. 'Let us seek the truth and the rest will be added unto it.'[2] Oblivious of the arrests and repression in Paris, he continued to preach his doctrine of fraternity, 'that the reign of hate is passed, that it is love alone that ought to fertilize the earth', that the republic meant universal brotherhood.[3] As a practical start, he did much to improve the efficiency of the prefectoral administration. Moved by the daily complaints he received about the slowness with which official business was transacted, he demanded that 'the office should not be turned into a reading-room where men find leisure for historical studies' and succeeded in getting every letter answered within twenty-four hours. He won the congratulations of the minister for the speed with which he carried out instructions and a vote of confidence from the departmental council for his 'enlightened zeal' in its service. These are hints that he hoped to make a career as an administrator, but early in January, after Louis Napoleon's election to the presidency of the republic, he was dismissed—whether because of his politics, or because of the jealousy of the local deputy at the influence he had won, is not clear.[4]

Certainly he had once again obtained considerable popularity.

[1] Letter from Baudin, 22 March 1848, O.P. Cf. Prosper Rossi, *Mes Souvenirs: 1848* (Toulon, 1888) 1–60.

[2] Letter to Séguier, copy in D., 23 August 1848.

[3] Ibid., and Proclamation of the Prefect of Chaumont, 5 August 1848 O.P.

[4] Mgr. Fèvre, protonotaire apostolique, *La Vie, action politique et œuvres de M. Emile Ollivier de l'Académie Française*, n.d. 66.

Huge numbers signed petitions demanding his retention in office; the national guard presented him with a flag as a farewell token; and a large crowd saw him off from the Place de l'Hôtel de Ville. 'Profoundly moved,' says the local paper, 'by such spontaneous and ardent testimony of affection and sympathy, M. Emile Ollivier gave an . . . address overflowing with emotion and gratitude. . . . The people of Chaumont, though accustomed to the brilliant eloquence of their young governor, had yet never experienced such marvellous language, such an irresistible flow of thoughts and feelings. His farewell was touching and solemn, without recrimination, without bitterness, but with a frankness and a sincerity of emotion which won all hearts and brought tears to every eye.'[1]

Ollivier's experiences in 1848 thus in more ways than one foreshadow his later efforts at reconciliation in the liberal empire. Do they also show how hopeless it all was and how incapable he was of profiting from experience? He remained unrepentantly proud of his efforts and even twenty years later he believed that the lesson of his period of power was that he should not be discouraged by his failure. 'After having savoured what is sweetest in the smile of the masses, I tasted what is bitterest in their wrath; after having seen the sea caressing, I saw it enraged. This impression has been decisive on me. From that day I met the enraged waves, with the same calm as I met the caressing waves, for I knew well that each would fall as quickly as the other.'[2] His attitude to public opinion was never to be clear: he both sought to base himself on it and yet at the same time he despised it.[3]

Many years later Gambetta referred to Ollivier and Lamartine as being the most striking representatives of the type of politician he execrated above all—brilliant orators with a fascinating command of language, but totally devoid of any of the qualities

[1] *Le Bien Public* of Chaumont, 16 January 1849.
[2] E. Ollivier, *Le 19 Janvier* (1869), 48.
[3] Cf. J. i. 194.

which are needed in statesmen.[1] Ollivier indeed not only resembled Lamartine in 1848, he even became his disciple and,
by his own admission, owed a considerable amount to his influence.[2] In the presidential election of 10 December 1848 he
voted for Lamartine; in 1865 he carried the law granting Lamartine a state pension; in 1869 he talked of being destined to
continue Lamartine's work;[3] in 1870 he fittingly succeeded to
his seat in the French Academy. Now Lamartine, who in his
early days had castigated Napoleon I as a tyrant and who had
protested against the *coup d'état* of 1851, ended up, like Ollivier,
by calling Napoleon III 'one of those truly remarkable men'
who dwarf all their contemporaries, 'the most serious and solid
statesman, without any exception, whom he had known in his
long life spent amongst statesmen'.[4] For several strands in Lamartine's thought were curiously akin to the ideals of Bonapartism,
such as his desire for popularity among the masses rather than
among the party politicians, his advocacy of a strong centralized
state dedicated to the improvement of the lot of the poor, run
by a great man with 'a passion for the idea of his time,' in direct
contact with the people, his contempt for parliamentary government, his ideal of a 'mixed republic', republican at its base,
monarchic at its summit. Despite important differences, the
founders of the second republic and of the second empire had
much in common. Lamartine is thus another of the men who
provide a link between the years 1848 and 1870.[5] Ollivier,
observed a local newspaper, was the Lamartine of Marseilles,
who failed to learn the lesson of Lamartine's fall.[6]

[1] Letter 219, 22 October 1874, in *Lettres de Gambetta*, ed. D. Halévy and E.
Pillias (1938).
[2] D. 1870 (typescript copy, p. 60).
[3] Letter to Marie Gravier, 28 February 1869.
[4] C. Latreille *Les Dernières Années de Lamartine (1852-1869)* (1925), 15-16.
[5] *La Politique de Lamartine*, ed. L. de Rouchaud (1878); Henry Michel,
L'Idée de l'état (1896) 327-55; E. Harris, *Lamartine et le peuple* (1932); A. de
Lamartine, *La France parlementaire* (1865).
[6] *La Gazette du Midi*, 18 July 1848.

CHAPTER 3

THE DEVELOPMENT OF
OLLIVIER'S IDEAS 1849–57

FROM 1849 to 1857 Ollivier held no public office and from 1852 to 1857 he took no part at all in political life. It is generally believed that he devoted himself simply to earning a living and a reputation at the bar, and his biographer, M. St.-Marc, has covered this period simply with a brief chapter entitled 'The Barrister'. In fact, as a study of the diary he kept reveals, Ollivier now spent a great deal of time in meditation on the problems of politics and the conduct of life. These years were of crucial importance in the history of his intellectual development. He thought out his opinions in greater detail and gave them a stronger intellectual basis. By gradual stages his youthful enthusiasm for socialism, Christianity, and the republic turned into a critical independence; instead he drew close to the views of Benjamin Constant, the protagonist of constitutional monarchy and of the Additional Act. By 1857, therefore, before he had even entered Parliament, he was already well on the road which was to lead him to collaboration with Napoleon III.

The change did not come at once. In 1849 Ollivier's first idea after being dismissed was to write a book attacking the leaders of his party, to show 'the stupidity of the old guard republicans' who could only 'hinder, slander, and kill, who had no aim but a personal vengeance to satisfy, or a job to obtain', to prove that their policy of violence could found nothing.[1] By the end of the year he was waging an active campaign against them, once more preaching his doctrine of fraternity and love. He toured

---

[1] Cf. Benjamin Constant's contempt for 'The chiefs of republican France, coarse and violent men [who] could not believe that one adopted their principles if one did not also adopt their hates in all their ferocity.'—Benjamin Constant, *Cecile*, ed. A. Roulin (1951), 65–66, referring to his experiences in 1795.

the department of Var (where, unlike Bouches-du-Rhône, he still enjoyed much popularity) in support of his father, who was seeking adoption as republican candidate in a by-election, but who was being opposed by the local party leaders. He spent several months going from village to village, 'living' as he said, 'the life of the first apostles. During the day wherever I am, I read and work a little, I see my friends; and in the evening I go to dine with the people, workers or peasants, who subscribe in order to have me at table with them. After dinner, the doors are mysteriously opened, crowds of men come in and I speak for several hours. I can,' he added, 'moreover, say this for myself, that my speeches are above all moral and religious. I teach these men their rights but also their duties.' He spoke in Messianic language of the exploitation of the people, of their sufferings and longings, and of the Kingdom of God upon earth which the republicans would establish. Above all he disassociated himself from those who were said to be demanding the abolition of property, monogamy, or religion; his ideal state would appeal to all classes, because on the contrary it would make all men owners of property, and so end the dangers of poverty.[1] When

[1] Here are some examples of his speeches:
'There are in the fields great oaks that raise to heaven their thick branches and bury their roots in the very entrails of the earth. They are so beautiful that the woodcutters respect them and the thunder of the Lord dares not touch them. But one sees some minute plants, the mistletoe and the ivy, called parasitic plants because, like so many men, they live at the expense of others, winding round their trunks, covering them, embracing them. The mighty oak busy growing its branches high takes no notice. The parasitic plant is so successful that in the end the powerful tree cannot breathe, and would have to perish if some friends of forests and of oaks, taking pity on it, did not tear off the cursed plant with compassionate hand and destroy its root. The great oak is the people, the parasitic plants are those who exploit them, the kind friend is the republicans . . . .
    You are troubled, you are persecuted, but what does it matter ? After the storm, the good weather; after the winter, the spring; after suffering, joy; after persecution, triumph.
    God besides is with you. He will cover you with His shade and you will be safe under His wings. Truth will serve you for a shield; a thousand arrows will fall on your left and ten thousand on your right but none will reach you. What do you fear from men ? Has not God ordered the angels always to protect and guard the righteous? They shall bear you up in their hands lest

his father failed to be adopted as candidate, he set an example of 'generosity' and continued his tour in favour of the mediocre but more reliable man who was chosen, urging all republicans to unite for victory.

Such was the success of his emotional appeals, at which his audiences are said to have wept and applauded frantically, without necessarily understanding him, that the prefect of the department (none other than the famous Haussmann, who had not yet been promoted to Paris) began to fear that Ollivier might win the bourgeoisie over to republicanism. He saw a danger that Ollivier might create a moderate third party between the conservatives whom Haussmann was trying to organize and the radicals whom he wished to destroy. He had him watched and then prosecuted—on the charge that he had been organizing political clubs, which were forbidden by law. It was said that he was the head of a whole network of socialist societies who were secretly plotting a revolution;[1] but in his memoirs Hauss-

you dash your foot against a stone; if need be you shall trample under your feet the lion and the dragon.

Persevere and the light from on high will light up your countenances, your hearts will be filled with joy, you will be enriched by abundance of wheat, of wine, and of oil, you will one day rest in peace. And you will watch with your own eyes the punishment of the wicked who will have no other hope but in your prayers and in the goodness of your hearts! . . .

It is because we want respect for the family that we want respect and love for woman. The ancient German poets placed her on the clouds with her feet on man's head and a crown of stars round her brow; we place her at the centre of our homes and we set on her head the chaste crown of maternity.

We ought not to be accused either of wanting to make women knitters and wanderers of the market place. We address ourselves to her, first to verify the exactness of our doctrines, for like the human species, truth has two sexes and is not complete except by their union; and then in order that in our struggles the spirit of charity and of gentleness should also be represented. We men are easily carried away into violence and injustice. Come, we have said to the women, come amongst us; be the white doves who bear the branches of peace!

Despoilers, say you! Yes, we are in fact indefatigable, intractable despoilers, but it is poverty whom we wish to despoil, from whose infernal clutches we wish to tear all those who writhe there in torment! . . . ' (Unpublished D.)

[1] A.D. Var IV M. 16, prefect [?] to minister of the interior, 11 April 1850, draft.

mann wrote: 'I recognize that his language contrasted by the apparent moderation of its content and the elegance of its form, with the brutal and unrestrained declamations of other orators of club or open-air meetings. He did not frankly urge, as they did, that the trees of liberty should be watered with the blood of the aristocrats, the rich and the exploiters of the people; he never asked for anybody's head nor incited men to take up arms, but I do not know that he ever resolutely disavowed those who did. His manner of preaching liberty, equality, and fraternity discouraged no form of zeal. I say "preaching" on purpose because I see that in one of my reports to the minister of the interior written at the time, I call the speeches of this popular orator "homilies". In fact I knew ladies of the republican middle class (of the Cavaignac type) who seized every opportunity to go with their daughters to hear him, as they would have followed the sermons of a fashionable preacher.'[1]

Ollivier had no difficulty in disposing of the charge that he had organized political clubs, for he showed that he spoke only once in each village. The prosecution, he said, could really only accuse him of being a perambulating club all by himself. What he could be accused of, he went on, was preaching socialism, which was another matter. 'I preached it because socialism means goodness, truth, beauty; it means that poverty disappears, that tears dry up, that hate is reconciled, that the blind see, that the lame walk; it means that God exiled from our materialistic society returns to it bringing His blessing upon it. Socialism means that the horizon lights up, the clouds melt away, the storms move off: it means God's kingdom on earth.'[2] He was acquitted and

---

[1] G. E. Haussmann, *Mémoires* (1890–3), i. 362; cf. Maurice Agulhon, 'Le Baron Haussmann, préfet du Var 1849–50', in *Provence historique* (Marseilles April–June 1956, vol. vi, fasc. 24, 142–62; J. M. and B. Chapman, *The Life and Times of Baron Haussmann* (1957), 44.

[2] *Le Démocrate du Var*, 17 April 1850. For the trial, see Marcel Fourniol, 'Epilogue des journées marseillaise de juin', *La Révolution de 1848* (1929) xxvi. 356–77, and A.D. Var 7 U 29–2, Tribunal Correctionnel de Draguignan, affaires politiques 1850–65. Maurice Agulhon, Emile Ollivier, 'Son voyage en Provence et sa pensée politique en 1850', in *Les Conférences de l'Institut historique de Provence*, Oct.–Dec. 1957, 34th year, 55–57—brief but very perceptive.

carried away in triumph by the huge crowds his trial had attracted. He received, he said, the greatest ovation he had ever had.

Now, however, a succession of private and political disasters
shattered Ollivier's optimism and faith. First, the government
of Louis Napoleon, becoming increasingly reactionary, systematically repressed and silenced the republicans, until finally, in
carrying out the *coup d'état* of 1851, it arrested Demosthenes and
banished him from France.[1] It would probably have done the
same to Emile had he not, a few days before, by chance gone
to Montpellier, and his whereabouts become unknown to the
police. His brother Aristides, who had been editor of a republican newspaper in that city, had recently been killed in a duel
by a legitimist, to Ollivier's enormous grief. The authorities
were now prosecuting the paper, for which Ollivier had often
written.[2]

All these shocks came, moreover, at a time when he was
plunged in despair by the death of Marie Chargé, a girl with
whom he had fallen in love in Marseilles, and who was, significantly enough, the daughter of a staunch and wealthy legitimist.
His health gave way: 'My misfortune has exceeded anything
that could be foreseen,' he wrote. 'In no year of my life have I
ever had so many sorrows and afflictions, so much despair all
at once. Everything has failed me at the same time: family,
ideas, love, health, hope.'[3] He felt absolutely helpless. 'Alone,
separated from my father and from my old friends, I am

---

[1] Demosthenes escaped a worse fate through the influence of Prince Napoleon, the 'republican Bonapartist'. Pierre Leroux was hidden by Mme d'Agoult
after the *coup d'état* and then obtained permission to leave France through his
friend the St. Simonian magnate Pereire. (P. Leroux, *La Grève de Samarez*
(1863), i. 287.) These instances illustrate the early links of republicans and
Bonapartists.

[2] *L'Illustration* (1851) part 1, 402. It is interesting that the three departments
of France in which most arrests were made after the *coup d'état* were Seine,
Var, and Hérault (each over 2,000), in all of which Ollivier had been active.—
Archives Nationales, BB (30) 403, No. 608 P; Baroche Papers, Bibliothèque
Thiers, 1112, f. 605; Eugène Tenot, *Etude historique sur le coup d'état* (new ed.,
1877 and 1880, 2 vols.); A.N. F (1c) III Hérault 14, prefect to minister of the
interior, 22 October 1860.

[3] J. i. 142 (1 January 1853).

agonizingly tormented by the need to love, to believe, and to act, and yet I cannot satisfy any of these wishes. . . . To love! I dream of it for a moment, but then I stop. Who would wish to take on the task of consoling and of refreshing a creature like myself? To believe! I do not know what to believe in once and for all. An eternal tempest agitates my brain. Catholicism, philosophy, socialism, now united, now hostile, contend and clash in my head, which can feel the concord between them and yet cannot formulate it in precise terms. To act! How, when my heart is empty and my thought vacillating? Besides, despotism binds our hands and closes our mouths.'[1]

A new phase now begins in the history of Ollivier's ideas. Living largely by himself, in enforced retirement from all political activity, separated from his former mentors, and with a great deal of leisure for reflection, he began to think for himself and independently. 'None [of my ideas] were destroyed,' he noted in his diary, 'but all were turned topsy-turvy, all were called in question. I underwent what often happens to people who, having always been unthinking travellers through life, suddenly receive hard blows from it: they withdraw into themselves and for the first time understand the truths which they had till then rejected. Under the sinister light of 2 December, I scrutinized afresh all my beliefs, all my ideas; I searched myself, I probed in all directions; I re-examined the deeds and words of my past; and I sought the rule which must guide my future as I had never done before. . . .'[2]

A striking change now took place in his methods and in his attitude to life. 'I give little attention to politics,' he wrote to his father while on holiday in the country. 'I simply keep myself informed and reflect on events. I read little. I find that I gain a lot by this new method of working. My ideas become at once more firm and more original. Other people's ideas become as it were my own and I discover additional ones independently. I have finished extinguishing in myself all that was declamation

[1] J. i. 110 (4 May 1852).
[2] Letter to Léon Marès, J. i. 114-15 (6 June 1852).

and sentimentality, so as to replace it, in my language as in my thought, by mathematical strictness and reason. I was so disgusted to see how since 1848 actions have been inspired by words whose meaning no one understood, that I made the resolution that, at least as far as I was concerned, I would free myself from this tyranny and would not use terms whose exact sense I could not state very precisely. As you may guess, I am therefore very far from our Jacobins and our socialists, or those of them at any rate who live on phrases.'[1]

He had been wrong, he now said, to abandon himself to passion and emotion. 'It is reason, intelligence, knowledge which determine what duty is.'[2] The 'love' which he had preached as the sovereign solution was not enough. 'Love,' he wrote, 'is but the second good thing in this world. The first is the search, the cult, the apostolate, the defence, the realization of truth. It is by this that we are really sons of God, superior beings animated by an immortal breath. It is not love that distinguishes us from animals. . . . Animals are inferior to us entirely because they have no reason, that is to say the instruments by whose aid truth is sought and found.'[3] 'Profit from the rest which is given you in the battle of life,' he wrote to his friend Guiter, 'to submit your mind to a strong discipline. Enough of poetry, of vague reading, of Michelet, &c., &c.; take something substantial, hard, precise, arid. Undertake some difficult, unattractive work, which accustoms your mind to continual effort. We have gathered in our souls enough images, sentiments, aspirations, too many perhaps! In order that they might be useful to us, we must fill ourselves with practical facts. As a man of parts whose maxims I am reading, Joubert, says, He who has imagination without erudition has wings but has no feet.'[4]

Ollivier now ceased to preach an imminent millennium or to expect the world to be put to rights by some magic formula.

[1] J. i. 195 (24 September 1854).   [2] J. i. 181 (7 December 1853).
[3] J. i. 209–10 (31 December 1854); cf. J. i. 191–2.
[4] Letter to Guiter, 13 June 1852, copy, O.P.

He decided that a clear distinction was necessary between political philosophy and practical politics. Political philosophy was all very well, but he thought that its recent concentration on the ideal had rendered it worthless. It was not simply that there were quite enough utopian books advocating theories which might appear highly desirable though they had no earthly chance of being applied in the foreseeable future; it was rather that failure to consider their practical application meant ignorance of the whole purpose of politics. 'If you are to act with effect in politics, you must fulfil two conditions; first you must have a sense of what is possible and secondly from among these possible things, you must aim at those to which our nature can adapt itself. . . .' It was idle, for example, to talk of the complete emancipation of the people, when all that was possible was their gradual emancipation. Men must give up the habit of listening 'only to their own ideas and hardly ever to those of others. That is why so many politicians act in a way contrary to what circumstances require. Their principles, they say. Agreed: but pay a little attention to those of others. You need not modify the essential parts of your beliefs which you have acquired by meditation, but you ought to modify their form, add or subtract this or that nuance. . . .'[1]

Ollivier suggested that the next revolution, if it did not wish to share the fate of that of 1848, should treat its philosophers as Plato treated the poets—crown them with laurels and send them away; it must introduce flexibility into its statesmanship; it must show itself ready to come to terms with the world as it was. This increasing belief in the need for compromise marks an important step in his movement towards collaboration with the empire.

Ollivier now rejected the claims of the Catholic Church. For a time, during his period of depression after the death of his first love, he had thought of joining it, 'giving up the world and escaping into some deep solitude. What matter my disagreements

[1] J. i. 164 (22 August 1853), i. 209 (20 December 1854), cf. i. 61 (19 November 1850).

with Catholicism? They will subside. Like so many others I shall understand its dogma as I please and I shall at least be able to find an outlet for my affectionate nature: I shall be able to console, to heal, to comfort, to fortify, and to dedicate myself to all, since I cannot dedicate myself to *her*.' He had assured himself that the Catholic Church was not necessarily hostile to the revolution. It deserved attack only as a political institution and it had always contained a movement rejecting absolute dependence on grace, favouring liberty and free human will. 'The Protestants, the Gallicans, Port Royal, were the precursors, the preparers, the accomplices of the revolution: the only thing that is radically incompatible with it therefore is the papacy's interpretation of Christianity.' However, on further consideration, he decided that the Catholic Church was fundamentally 'too narrow and exclusive', because it condemned everybody outside its own fold; since he found a great deal of truth in many of the religions and philosophies which were its rivals, he could not accept its claim to a monopoly of truth. He felt himself, he said, to be too much of an individualist to make 'that abject renunciation of his own will and conscience without which there is no orthodox Catholicism'. In any case he believed that Catholicism gave too much scope for egoism by encouraging men to concentrate on their own salvation and to resign themselves to the evils of this world. He maintained that the present life was 'legitimate' and 'worthy of respect', that the promise of a better future life was not a sufficient remedy for the misfortune to be found here below, arguing, like Cartwright, the reformer of the 1780's, who, when Wilberforce said to him that he hoped they would meet in a better world, replied that he hoped they would first mend the world they were in. However, Ollivier did not become an atheist, or an enemy of religion. He always remained a Deist and not simply an abstract believer in God, but one passionately conscious of His presence and closely linked to Him. Thus he could still make fun of the phrase in the Lord's Prayer, 'Lead us not into temptation' with the comment: 'What an idea they have of God! My father is much better: he has never dreamt of leading me into temptation.' But he frequently prayed to God, in a form such as this: 'O, my God, supreme Intelligence whom I cannot conceive but whose being I affirm more than ever, I do not invoke You to support [my resolutions]: I alone can by persevering will-power realize my aims. I offer You my meditation only to unite myself with You, to draw myself to You. I give myself up for an instant to the contemplation of Your ineffable beauties and Your inexpressible perfections. How learned in human wisdom are those who love You. O my God, I wish to speak to You often so as to become one of the intimates of Truth and a consoler of souls. . . . '

He considered the Catholic Church to be an enemy of liberty, but he did not become an anti-clerical and he would never therefore have much sympathy for Gambetta's famous cry, 'Clericalism is the enemy', which was to be the basis of the republican creed for thirty years. He said that he could accept no existing religions and he had none to substitute in their place, but his attitude to religions would be neither hostility to them nor a weak acquiescence in the supremacy of the religion under which he happened to have been born, nor simply indifference to the whole question. The right course was to work constructively to obtain tolerance and equality for all religions.[1]

He came to the same conclusion in politics. He ceased to hope for the 'political and social accomplishment of the laws of the Gospels, the disappearance of poverty and of the proletariat'.[2] He stopped using the language of Leroux or that of Saint-Simon, whom, like Napoleon III, he had for a time held in high esteem.[3] He rejected in fact all the utopian systems with which he had flirted. He saw in them the same cardinal fault he criticized in the Catholics, that of seeking to establish what would now be called closed societies. The socialists, he said, recognized only

[1] J. i. 103-4, 154, 158, 180-1, 206, 272, 277, 279 (14 January 1852, 23 April, 12 May, and 2 December 1853, 13 November 1854, 27 April, 18 and 22 May 1857.
[2] Article in Le Suffrage universel of Montpellier, 29 March 1851; cf. Letter to Ernest Ollivier, J. i. 41 (7 December 1849).
[3] J. i. 77 (15 February 1851).

their own form of truth and beyond it they did not foresee the possibility of further discoveries: once their ideal was achieved, there would be nothing more for men to do. They were therefore not really on the side of progress: 'I do not wish to be chained by tradition', wrote Ollivier. 'I wish to develop it, to improve it.'[1]

The final result of his reasoning was 'an inflexible affirmation of the right of the individual, a profound dislike of all "cities of the sun" and an absolute faith in liberty.' He was now certain that 'all resides in the improvement of the individual and that this improvement cannot be obtained except by liberty, and not by any one form of liberty, but by many forms'. He wanted liberty not simply for the opposition, nor liberty to impose some new tyranny in the place of that which already existed, but liberty for all men to develop to their best capacity each in his own way. It was impossible to prescribe a medicine or a political formula which suited everybody in a whole nation: 'That is why liberty alone can satisfy everybody.'[2]

Henceforth, Ollivier concentrated on the search for liberty, on political rather than economic or spiritual reforms, and the change was to a certain extent natural. The July monarchy had so neglected social problems that it had encouraged men of conscience to seek socialist solutions, and so likewise the second empire's suppression of individual rights inevitably made these same men turn now to the problem of liberty. Ollivier however developed views on the method of achieving liberty, which placed him in direct opposition against the republican party on two fundamental questions. First, he agreed that the republic was ideally the best form of government, but he would not grant that it was an end in itself. The primary aim was to win liberty and his party should not therefore work blindly for the establishment of the republican form of government, mistaking the means for the end. Limited concessions of liberty were worth

---

[1] Letter to Guiter, 21 November 1855, copy O.P.; J. i. 272 (27 April 1857).
[2] J. i. 195–8, 278, 294 (24 and 26 September 1854, 18 May 1857, 29 July 1857).

having even from the existing government; gradual progress should be welcomed, whatever régime was in power. He began to think increasingly that his party's leaders were too absolute in their attachment to theoretical principles, which rendered them unfit to hold office. Government, he said, was 'the science of the relative': it required not simply mastery of theory but also knowledge of 'the art of life, which consists in knowing how to deal with men and how to act upon them when one wants to lead them to a certain goal'. It was ridiculous of the republicans to refuse to have anything to do with all governments which were not republics, even when they were promoting reforms of which the republicans approved. He contemptuously dismissed their attitude as absurdly purist.[1]

Secondly, he objected to their seeking to establish the republic by revolution. He insisted that no stable régime could ever be founded by violence. A revolution would involve fighting the monarchists and so dividing the nation in two, producing a reaction against the republic sooner or later. All past régimes in France had been weak for this very reason, that the country had been repeatedly divided; a permanent government must result from reconciliation and not from a new division. Moreover, it was impossible to carry out reforms by a stroke of the pen as the revolutionary method supposed. To be effective, reforms must be gradual: the state of society into which they were introduced must be borne in mind and due concessions made. Revolutions destroy, but the purpose of government is to build. 'I understand that in days when the temperature is close and oppressive, men should call for a storm; but what regrets there are on the morrow, if the fields are ravaged and the harvest destroyed.' Successful revolutionaries, he argued, could never become successful statesmen, because they acquired the habit of violating the law: they would end up by becoming as arbitrary as those whom they had overthrown, persecuting the defeated as they themselves had been persecuted. 'My whole being feels horror

[1] J. i. 214, 219, 261, 274, 280, 292, 294 (11 May and 10 June 1855, 25 November 1856, 1 and 25 May, 13 and 29 July 1857).

at the idea of placing the law in the brutal hands of soldiers, of making the success of truth depend on the fortune of a sudden attack, on whether a rifle is well or badly discharged'.[1]

Ollivier was aware that he differed on many points from the republicans, just as he found a great deal wrong in the doctrines of other parties. What ought he to do? Ought he to refuse to join any party, because he could not agree with all its views? 'The theorizing egoist thinks so,' he decided, 'but one's duty is to join that party whose fundamental principle is true, except that one should fight against any tendency by any party towards exclusiveness and that one should try to enrich it with elements of life which are to be found in other parties.' The 'conservative principle' or 'authority' or 'order' was, he insisted, essential to all societies, and yet this principle was particularly supported by the monarchical parties and opposed by the republicans who stressed instead the 'liberal principle'. Ought he to abstain from the struggle, therefore, since both sides had something to be said for them? No, he concluded, he must seek 'to make the republican principle as conservative as it is progressive and to remove from it its purely revolutionary element'. To be able to criticize both sides was no doubt all very well, but it was not enough: practical politics required that he should work within his own party to influence and modify it along the lines he considered right. 'There is but one role in politics which is worth attempting', he wrote, 'that of the moderator of the revolution. With one hand to crush the anarchists, with the other to draw the moderates and the indifferent towards liberty.

'Neither Danton, nor Robespierre, nor Napoleon,
But Lamartine and Cavaignac, plus resistance to reaction,
But Washington.'[2]

The history of Ollivier's thought before 1857 thus first of all

---

[1] J. i. 35 (Letter to Ernest Ollivier, July 1849).
[2] J. i. 214 and 274-5 11 May 1855 and 1 May 1857. Washington was frequently held up as an ideal; cf., e.g., A. Delvau, *Les Murailles révolutionnaires* (1851), 177.

disposes of the charge that he shamelessly abandoned his republican doctrines out of ambition for office. He had no idea in this period that he would be re-entering politics so soon, or at all, and while he was developing these views there was no question of his co-operating with Napoleon III—though that was to be their logical conclusion. It is now possible, secondly, to place Ollivier more accurately in the context of his generation. The republic of 1848, as is well known, marks an important break in the character of French political life. Utopianism was now, generally speaking, displaced by positivism; the mystic belief in the virtue of the people and the hopes for a spiritual regeneration gave way to a more guarded pessimism about mankind. Men began to look on the world in a different way, for splendid illusions had been shattered before their eyes, and their very style of talking and writing changed. Ollivier's attempt to reject sentimentality and the whole romantic approach, his determination to base his conduct instead on a rational study of the facts as they could be observed, is thus typical of the widespread intellectual movement which took place as a reaction to the disasters of 1848. However, as with so many other romantics, his transformation was very far from complete. His old self in fact remained as a substratum, on which he merely superimposed his new ideas and approach. A curious book he published forty years later, entitled *Marie Magdeleine*—which is of little merit as a novel but of considerable psychological interest for what it really is, a disguised autobiography of these years—makes this revealing confession: 'In him in fact co-existed two opposed beings, the first impetuous . . . effusive . . . given to highly coloured language, frequently overstepping the bounds of prudence, imaginative like a poet, in love with the absolute like a philosopher; the second, on the other hand, quiet, master of his emotions, industrious . . . with a feeling for realities [and] an intuition for what was possible.'[1] This underlying duality explains to a considerable extent the paradoxes of Ollivier's career.

[1] E. Ollivier, *Marie Magdeleine* (1897), 71-72, 87, 207.; cf. J. i. 182 and 205 (10 December 1853 and 13 November 1854).

He may today appear to stand between two distinct and different epochs, but this was in fact highly characteristic of the men of the second empire as a whole. A recent writer on positivist thought in the reign of Napoleon III has stressed how almost every one of the intellectuals with whom he deals was 'the victim of a divided mind . . . attempting . . . to reconcile aspirations and convictions that are incompatible'.[1] Ollivier was well aware of this, but he was not troubled by it. 'Our century', he wrote, 'is not that of criticism. . . . It is that of synthesis.'[2]

Ollivier is not an original political thinker, but he is significant for this very reason. He quite obviously obtained the ideas described in this chapter from Leroux, Lamartine, Saint-Simon, and Benjamin Constant, among others.[3] His interest lies on another level. He is an example of how men of his generation were reacting to the writings of the political theorists of the first half of the nineteenth century. When these theorists published their works, they were at most leaders of small sects and more frequently simply voices in the wilderness; but after twenty or thirty years their once unusual views were becoming, in diluted form, almost commonplace. Ollivier's amalgam of ideas, precisely because they were derived from such diverse sources, were in many ways representative of very widespread aspirations. He may have been out of date to the leaders of advanced Parisian thought, but for this very reason he was typical of the great mass of ordinary men who lagged some decades behind them. Viewed in this light, Ollivier's liberal empire must be accorded a deeper significance than it generally is.

[1] D. G. Charlton, *Positivist Thought in France during the Second Empire* (Oxford, 1959), 2.

[2] J. i. 275 (1 May 1857).

[3] See particularly C. H. de Saint-Simon, *Cathécisme des industriels* (1823-4) in his *Œuvres* iii. 72; B. Constant, *Cours de politique constitutionelle* (1818), iii. 60; G. Woodcock, *P. J. Proudhon* (1956), 75, 92-93.

CHAPTER 4

THE POLITICAL CONSEQUENCES OF OLLIVIER'S PRIVATE LIFE

OLLIVIER'S private life has more than usual relevance to an understanding of his political career. His conversion from socialism to liberalism coincides, first of all, with his transformation from a penniless student into a successful and well-to-do barrister. Until the age of twenty-eight he was very poor indeed: how he lived at all in his early years is not clear, but there are suggestions that his principal resource was coaching dull pupils for the bar examinations. His own beginnings in the law were at first very slow. He had made his mark during the republic defending his co-religionists in some important politicial trials, and notably in one at Lyons, where a large group of them were accused of organizing a widespread plot to overthrow the government of Louis Napoleon; but the *coup d'état* had suddenly put an end to this kind of work and he was thrown back on his teaching. He had some difficulty in changing over to civil practice, until his friend Ernest Picard obtained for him some unpaid work in the chambers of Liouville, a well-established republican. In 1852 Ollivier earned a mere £44 from his few cases, which was very far from being enough to support himself and his father. The crisis he underwent in this year was thus deepened by poverty and financial worries.

Gradually, however, more clients came and increasing success. By 1855 the great lawyer Duvergier was heard to say of him: 'He will certainly reach the first rank. There are barristers who are elegant, but nothing else: there are others who are logical, but dry. Ollivier's speeches are planned with strictness and accuracy, but he also knows how to introduce ornament and passion into them.' As he became increasingly well known he began accepting only a few important cases, where the effort

D

required was great, but where the rewards and the opportunities were proportionate. In 1856 he won success in an important suit in which he defended a mother whose children were trying to shut her up in a lunatic asylum. The court was apparently carried away by his peroration demanding for his client 'the peace and that internal discourse which is the supreme joy and right of old age', and the judges openly congratulated him. Finally, in 1857, his accession to the first rank of the bar was confirmed in a case in which he appeared against Berryer, the leader of the legitimist party and perhaps the most esteemed orator of the century. Ollivier could not be faced with a more redoubtable opponent: it was, as he said, his 'Austerlitz campaign', and he won it.[1]

His rising legal reputation and assured financial independence brought with it a striking new maturity in his manner and in his style of speaking. His over-florid eloquence became more disciplined and more substantial, more practised in factual argument and logical analysis. In appearance too he was now no longer the pale, lanky, and dreamy youth of the romantic age recorded in the painting of 1848: the photograph taken ten years later shows him with a broader chest and a firmer stance, which proclaim a man of considerably greater physical strength. One can now see clearly his two most notable features: an unusually large protruding upper lip, which was said to resemble that of the Greek Demosthenes and to be an aid to powerful speaking, and the unusually small steel-rimmed glasses, which almost seem to restrict the vision of the eyes behind them. On closer inspection however he was not the man of the world which a first casual glance might suggest. His self-confidence was in fact of so intense a nature that it curiously resembled Louis Napoleon's faith in his star: like him Ollivier was really a visionary, who lived very much with his own thoughts. In his habits

[1] J. i. 117, 120, 156, 220, 264 (9 June and 30 August 1852, 1 May 1853, 5 July 1855, 21 February 1857); Mgr. Fèvre, *La Vie, action politique et œuvres de M. Emile Ollivier* (n.d.); J. Sabbatier, *La Tribune judiciaire: receuil des plaidoyers et des requisitoires les plus remarquables des tribunaux français et étrangers* (1855–61) vols. vi and vii, contain examples of his pleadings.

he was aloof and ascetic and indeed almost made a cult of his asceticism. He continued to lead the frugal life of his days of poverty: he refused to move to a more fashionable address so as to attract wealthier clients and he was proud that he formed his cabinet in 1870 in the same house he had first rented as a penniless socialist.[1] Ollivier was not only independent in his politics—in his private life too he revelled in his own individuality. He gave much time to introspection, he analysed his beliefs, his emotions, his character over and over again, as his diary bears witness, and he even sought to recreate or remodel his personality in accordance with his ideals. He wrote to his brother, 'Like the potter who fashions his clay, fashion your soul on every side, work on it, render it supple. It is tender, poetic, enthusiastic: make it magnanimous, heroic, indomitable. Tear it away every day from what holds it to the things that deceive and pass, and turn it to the things that last.'[2] A colleague, in the late 1860's, was to tell him that with a character like his he ought to have become a monk and not a politician—which he had of course thought of doing.

His choice of friends was significant. He appears to have been inclined to practise the maxim of John Stuart Mill that men with intellectual aspirations should associate with 'at least their equals and, as far as possible, their superiors in knowledge, intellect, and elevation of sentiment'.[3] He did not mix greatly therefore with young republicans of his own age, and had very little to do with the party leaders, who were to be his future colleagues in parliament. His favourite companions were rather the theorists or intellectuals of the party, not its politicians. He

---

[1] However, the *Annuaire général du commerce et de l'industrie ou almanach de 500,000 adresses* (1853), published by Firmin-Didot, p. 1196, shows that his house, 27 rue Saint-Guillaume, contained the following tenants: Brig.-Gen. Piobert, member of the Institute, Boula, 'rentier', Abbé Vidalenc, Godefroy 'propriétaire', Hoffman 'avocat', and Olivier [*sic*] 'avocat à la cour d'appel'. The Institut d'Etudes politiques, a modern building, now stands where Ollivier once lived, but no plaque commemorates him.
[2] J. i. 140 (Letter to Adolphe Ollivier, 26 December 1852).
[3] J. S. Mill, *Autobiography* (1873) 228–9.

had been devoted to Michelet, and had attended his lectures assiduously; but then their relations grew cooler as Ollivier developed different views. He was shocked by Michelet saying: 'this terrible thing—no construction without preliminary destruction. In all one must proceed as Descartes did in the *Discourse on Method*, establish a *tabula rasa* before trying to raise a new building.' This was the doctrine of violence and revolution which Ollivier abhorred. 'It is impossible to cure a man of religion,' he replied, 'except as one cures him of love: homoeopathically, by another religion as by another love.'[1]

Ollivier preferred his old patron, Lamartine, whom the new generation looked upon as a disastrous politician. Lamartine in turn regarded Ollivier as his own pupil: 'I am delighted with your success as though it were mine,' he said, 'for I prophesied it. From the moment I saw you I divined your future: it is ten years since I said, You will see what this young man will one day be; and other destinies are still reserved for you.'[2] Likewise Ollivier used to visit Lamennais who again was to the new generation the representative of a hopeless cause—a priest who had vainly tried to reconcile Catholicism and liberty, and who had been unfrocked for his pains—but to whose ideals Ollivier ever remained sympathetic. He sometimes visited Proudhon, whom he admired for having 'destroyed sectarianism and made fun of its intolerance', but he strongly objected to Proudhon's motto *Destruam et aedificabo* as being self-contradictory and revolutionary. 'One must choose between these two', Ollivier wrote. 'If I can, I shall not destroy, I shall build.'[3] On Sundays he would occasionally attend a little circle which met at the house of Enfantin, the leader of the Saint-Simonians (who had begun as socialists and liberals under the restoration, and were to end up as allies and inspirers of the second empire). 'If I ever write the memoirs of my private life,' Ollivier commented later, 'I

[1] J. i. 161–2 (13 July 1853).
[2] J. i. 222 (17 July 1855); *Correspondence de Liszt et de sa fille Madame Emile Ollivier* (1936), 312.
[3] J. i. 67, 72, 85, 87, 292, 372.

should begin them like Marcus Aurelius by listing what I owe to each of my masters or friends. Enfantin taught me to free myself once and for all from the most evil of intellectual faults, fanaticism for the absolute: he gave me greater mastery of the true method and he shaped my mind to appreciate all the different sides of things and ideas. This gives both the strength that comes from seeing truth entire and also the indulgence towards the errors of the less diligent and the less broad-minded who are absorbed in the exclusive contemplation of only one of its parts.'[1] The only republican salon he visited much was that of Madame d'Agoult, which was however as much literary and musical as it was political; and even there he remained rather aloof. He really preferred the company of women: he corresponded with a number of them and particularly with Madame de Sour-deval (the adopted daughter of the financier, Benoit Fould); he called her his confessor and he found relief in bad times by pouring out his troubles to her. But in an age notorious for loose living in high places, Ollivier was conspicuous for his puritan abstention from the pleasures and adventures which so attracted the two men with whom his name was to be linked, Napoleon III and Morny.[2]

Ollivier's recreations were remarkable in several respects. He now read more works by right-wing authors than by republican ones: Taine, Montalembert, Renan, Constant, and Maistre— though he did not necessarily agree with them. His favourites were the classics, and particularly Bossuet and Pascal. He endeav-oured to see both sides of all questions and his increasing in-terest in the art of writing also encouraged his eclectic choice in books. His style certainly improved in this period, gaining in richness and in restraint, in polish and in ease. In art similarly he was an admirer of the old masters; after his retirement from politics, he published books about Michelangelo and Raphael;

---

[1] E.L. vii. 265.
[2] J. i. 273 (28 April 1857). On his early advocacy of female emancipation, see his thesis, *Du mariage consideré dans ses effets a l'égard des époux, des enfants et des parents* (1846) and D., 27 October 1850, 30 May 1851, and 13 June 1852.

and he broke with Edouard Manet, a family friend with whom he had toured the galleries of Venice as a young man, when that painter 'raised his technical ignorance into dogmas'.[1]

He was passionately fond of Italy and spent several months on holiday there almost every year. Florence was his 'adorable city', 'the immortal city where lived the first free people of the modern world'.[2] He was 'pained and preoccupied' by Italy's subjection to the Austrian yoke and looked forward to her resurrection. The fate of France, he said with Lamennais, was indissolubly linked with that of Italy, for the latter's fortunes would determine 'whether the Latin race is decidedly finished'. Ollivier had the greatest possible sympathy for Italian independence—which was common enough among republicans, but in addition his interest in Italy produced two distinctive political ideas in him. First, he formed the conclusion that the history of the Renaissance in Italy, about which he read a good deal in Machiavelli and Varchi, showed that simple governments (for example pure democracies), never lasted and that the best government was that of Venice, which was a mixture of democracy, monarchy, and aristocracy. Applied to France this caused him to see increasing merits in the mixed form of liberal Bonapartism for which he was to work. Secondly, he developed a particular admiration for Cavour as the greatest and most successful statesman of his age; and he was to observe that Cavour achieved his aims by opportunism, by a *connubio* uniting the left with the right, by a policy of the *juste milieu* which seemed to give Ollivier a good precedent for his own alliance with the Bonapartists and for the compromise solution of 1870. It is significant that the liberal whom Ollivier thus added to his galaxy of heroes, was once again a rather conservative liberal, who approved of representative institutions only 'because and in so far as they bolstered his own position' and whose idea of parliamentary government did not appear

---

[1] This phrase is used by Mme. T. Ollivier (but presumably reflects her husband's opinion) in her *Emile Ollivier, sa jeunesse* (1921), 228–9.

[2] J. i. 172–3 (4, 9, 10 October 1853).

to involve the existence of an alternative second party.[1]

It was in Italy in 1857 that Ollivier married his first wife, Blandine Liszt, who was to play an important part in winning for him the reputation of being the most brilliant young politician of the decade. It was not simply the sensation he caused by uniting himself with the offspring of the 'most striking adultery' of the composer Liszt and the blue-stocking Madame d'Agoult, after knowing her for only a month. Blandine was in fact a woman of quite outstanding intelligence, charm, and talent. Alfred de Vigny described her as 'brilliant, beautiful, and tall . . . [with] an air which was so lively, energetic, and candid all at once'; Emma Herwegh said, she was 'witty, very cultivated, and charms everyone by graces that are eminently feminine'.[2] 'She believes', wrote Ollivier to Edouard Manet's mother, 'that one can live without crinolines and without poisoning oneself periodically under the pretext of attending balls.[3] She is persuaded that life has an object other than amusing oneself and making money. . . . She does not require on the pretext that one is her fiancé, that one should visit her disguised as a hairdresser and with a bouquet in one's hand. . . . She has a heart, but she is rational; she is rational, but she is not dry; she has imagination and she employs it to idealize realities and not to realize chimeras. Admit that all this is very remarkable. What is even more so is that I am marrying her not because her father is a solicitor, nor because her mother has influence with such and such a judge, nor because this or that social consideration urges me, but uniquely for this mad reason that after having spent

---

[1] D. Mack Smith, 'Cavour and Parliament', *Cambridge Historical Journal* (1957) 13.42; *Annales des séances du sénat et du corps législatif*, 1870, iii. 50–51; *Journal des débats*, 4 January 1870; E.L. iv. 567–78. Cf. J. ii. 298 (28 July 1867): 'I shall be a Cavour or a Bismarck, but not a Rouher.' We know less of Ollivier's attitude to Bismarck; he appears to have admired him for unifying Germany, but to have deplored his autocratic domestic policy. See below, pp. 171–2.

[2] J. ii. 125–6; E. Newman, *Life of Richard Wagner* (1933–47), iii. 285–6.

[3] Cf. Gladstone's similar views on balls (P. Magnus, *Gladstone* (1954), 28) as 'indulgences not essentially linked with sin, but opening up many channels of temptation.'

twelve days with her I saw that I loved her, that after having spent thirty I was convinced that I adored her, and that after a month and a half I know that I can no longer live without her.' 'I feel,' he told Liszt, 'that in uniting her with me, I am completing myself and not weakening myself.'

Blandine had a horror of 'ordinary marriage as it is vulgarly understood', which would simply give her social position; and in Ollivier, she declared, she had at last seen 'what I had never hoped to find'. They were married at midnight on 22 October 1857 in the church of Santa Maria del Fiore, Florence, in the presence only of Ollivier's father and uncle, his friends Herold (son of the composer) and Edouard Manet, Madame d'Agoult, and two others. Blandine, however, unlike Ollivier, was a believing Catholic, and he was anxious that she should be not simply 'one of the followers of Jesus, but also one of those of Plato, of Seneca, of Buddha, of Mahomet, &c., or rather . . . that being a follower of all, she should be one of none in particular, but uniquely yours, O God'. Soon after their marriage she submitted: 'God cannot demand from me that I should torture a being I adore', she said, and she promised in tears that since he wished it, she would no longer confess, though it cost her a great deal not to do so. 'I accept your sacrifice,' said he. 'From this day our union is complete.'

Liszt had brought up his daughter to 'learn to make life soft and smooth for those who surround you, for that is woman's destiny'. She not only succeeded in giving him a happy home life and in supporting him in the important political decisions he made—but she also contributed a great deal to establishing him as the leader of a new school of liberalism. She attracted many bright young men to her drawing-room, who began to form a circle of admirers around Ollivier. Among them were Gambetta and Jules Ferry, both to be Prime Ministers also: the latter was in fact attracted by Blandine to the point of having 'a profound affection, a sort of exalted cult' for her.[1]

[1] Jean Dietz, Les débuts de Jules Ferry, *Revue de France* (1932), 516; Charles Limet, *Un Vétéran du barreau parisien; quatre-vingt ans de souvenirs, 1827–1907* (1908), 250; M. Reclus, *Jules Ferry* (1947), 29.

Liszt came to stay with them and they were friends with Berlioz and Wagner. Ollivier was one of the few Frenchmen who from the beginning welcomed Wagner's music with enthusiasm and with admiration, though 'without thinking that music began and ended with him'. He looked after Wagner's copyrights in France and helped to arrange the translation of the libretti into French. At the first performance of *Tannhauser* in Paris, which was greeted with much hostility, he and Napoleon III were in the minority which applauded. Wagner seems to have respected Ollivier, but was never greatly attracted by him, finding him 'dry and superficial'. It was Blandine who brought him into their salon and who was the animating centre of what became an increasingly distinguished circle. These contacts were important, for they stimulated Ollivier's sympathies for Germany, which were to have a considerable influence on his foreign policy when he came into office.[1]

It was with Blandine's dowry that Ollivier bought some fifteen acres on the Mediterranean coast, near St. Tropez, which was to be his country retreat and where he was to find a new constituency when he was defeated in Paris. The house on it was small and rather decayed and the land in wild disorder; but the views were magnificent and they had a clear field in which to rebuild and to plant. They intended to erect an enclosed courtyard with a fountain in the middle and cloisters all around, half Roman, half monastic, in which they could sit sheltered from the strong winds that are the scourge of that coast, and grand new rooms to contain a library and dining-hall. Though they could not afford to do it all at once, they derived much pleasure simply from making plans. Ollivier worked hard on the land himself. 'The trees will be marvellous when they grow,' said Blandine.[2]

---

[1] Ollivier's favourite composer was Beethoven, and in later life Bach.

[2] J. i. 295–316, 418–19, ii. 18 and 23, 125, 138–40 (August–October 1857, 26 January 1860, 10 April and 11 June 1861, 18 May and September 1864); *Correspondance de Liszt et de sa fille Madame Emile Ollivier*, edited by D. Ollivier (1936), 65, 100, 188–9, 256; Ernest Newman, *The Life of Richard Wagner* (1933–47), ii. 494–6, iii. 74, 145, 285–6; Ernest Daudet, *Souvenirs de mon temps* (1921), 57; E.L. v. 75.

CHAPTER 5

OLLIVIER'S ATTITUDE TO NAPOLEON III, 1857–61

Ollivier's election to parliament in 1857 was not sponsored by the republican party. He was the nominee of a dissident group within it, and he stood not only against a Bonapartist but also against a prominent republican who had been a minister in the provisional government of 1848. He openly entered national politics as a self-declared heretic and as an adversary and challenger of current republican policy.

The triumph of Louis Napoleon had decimated the ranks of the party, driven many of its leaders into exile and reduced it to apparent helplessness. The new imperial constitution, moreover, seemed to give it little opportunity to regain its strength. The emperor now possessed almost dictatorial power. His ministers were simply grand civil servants, nominated by him at will. The senate was filled with loyal officials and dignitaries on whom he could rely and who were besides entrusted with nothing more important than watching over the maintenance of the constitution. The old national assembly was reduced to a mere shadow as a small 'legislative body' of some 260 members: no longer 'national', because it was the emperor who represented the nation, and only 'legislative' now, for it was the emperor who governed. It was required to meet for only three months every year to place its rubber stamp on the budget and on any laws the emperor cared to present for its approval; but it had no power to initiate bills and hardly any to amend them. It was no longer the tribune from which speeches could be addressed to the country, for its debates were published only in a brief official summary, and criticism in it could reach the public ear only with difficulty. The enemies of the empire were effectively silenced outside parliament too: there was strict government control over the press and prohibition of public meetings: opposition could neither be expressed nor organized.

There was but one slight loophole in this dictatorial system through which the republicans might protest: the legislature was elected by universal suffrage and it was open to any man to stand. In 1852 the republicans had been too stunned by their defeat at the *coup d'état* to make use of this instrument and they had retired into indignant or morose abstention. Four of them who secured election, almost *in absentia*, ostentatiously refused to take the statutory oath of loyalty to the 'usurper' and declined to take their seats. Now in 1857, however, the legislature was due for re-election and though the leaders of the party, those who had been ministers in 1848, persisted in their belief that while the empire remained impregnable they should confine themselves to registering their protest against it and abstaining from all co-operation with it, others, with greater ambition or energy, agitated for a more positive and vigorous policy. These latter, who were willing to treat the oath as a mere formality, might have remained powerless had disagreement not broken out among the party leaders. Newspapers were needed to spread electoral propaganda, but virtually all republican ones had been suppressed. The leaders therefore made a deal with *Le Siècle*, the paper with the largest circulation in France, which was controlled by Havin, a Voltairian bourgeois, the son of a regicide, a supporter of Odilon Barrot's moderate opposition under Louis Philippe and now a mild critic of the second empire. They undertook to back Havin's candidature for parliament, in return for which he would support them in his paper. However, they then allotted him a constituency he did not want: he therefore broke with them, organized his own list of candidates, and so gave a new set of men their opportunity. He selected Picard, who had shares in *Le Siécle*, as one of his candidates and Picard secured the adoption of his equally obscure friend Ollivier. Ollivier was thus unexpectedly and rather accidentally thrown back into the political arena, to begin his parliamentary career as an opponent, not only of the government's candidate, Varin, but also of Garnier-Pagès, the representative of the old republican guard. He announced the policy he stood for in a pungent electoral address.

'Every political structure,' he declared, 'must rest on democracy. No one disputes this. But there are different types of democracy. There is one which is broad and generous, which moves towards the future. This democracy knows that growth is obtained by assimilation and not by exclusion; that in the face of a new situation, it is necessary to transform oneself and not to repeat oneself. It believes that the day of phrases is past and that of science is beginning. The moral and material improvement of the lot of those who suffer, of the workers; the development of commerce, industry and credit: that is its aim. Liberty: that is its method. It converts if it can: it never uses force, it does not even excommunicate. This democracy is that of youth. Since 1848 I have been one of its representatives. Elect me if you wish to assist its progress.'

After a great deal of personal and sordid recrimination, which belies the saying 'la république était belle sous l'empire', two men on Havin's list, Ollivier and Darimon, were elected. Four other republicans were successful, but three of them resigned their seats in the same way as they had done in 1852; and in the by-elections which followed two more republicans were chosen in their place. Thus came to be constituted the famous *Five*, the first republicans to sit in an imperial legislature.[1]

It is important to keep in mind that these *Five* were neither the leaders of the republican party, nor representative of them, nor even a homogeneous group among themselves. They illustrate well in fact the variety and fluidity of aim that characterized the party at this time. Thus, Jules Favre had been a Saint-Simonian in his youth; he had defended Louis Napoleon after the escapade of Boulogne; he had voted for him in December 1848, saying,

[1] Ollivier was elected in the fourth constituency of the department of Seine, getting 6,741 votes against 2,749 for Garnier-Pagès and 9,633 for Varin. This gave no one a sufficient number of votes and in the second ballot Ollivier got 11,005 against 10,006 to Varin, Garnier-Pagès having withdrawn.— Archives Nationales, C. 1344.

'I thought the prestige and popularity of [his] great name would serve marvellously in consolidating the republic by the reconciliation of parties'; and even now he admitted that 'though the emperor has done some abominable things' he still found him personally likeable. He had been Ledru-Rollin's secretary-general at the ministry of the interior in 1848, but had quarrelled with him; he had supported the prosecution of the socialist Louis Blanc and had quickly earned accusations of treachery and the nickname of the Serpent. Furthermore, he sometimes went to church and in 1868, on his election to the French Academy, made a spiritualist confession of faith which provoked violent abuse from the young generation of unbelievers. He lived with a woman who was not his wife and (so it was said) escaped prosecution for obtaining false birth-certificates for the illegitimate children of this union only by the intervention of the emperor. His political career was thus not one of undiluted popularity; and it was to end as catastrophically as Ollivier's: it was he who, as vice-president of the government of National Defence in 1871, conceded defeat and signed away Alsace and Lorraine. Nevertheless, for all this, Favre was without doubt the republican's greatest orator. Tall and leonine, he produced an overwhelming impression of vigour, with his vehement, bitter language, and his rich voice echoing in thundering periods. Some have doubted whether Favre actually had any firm political beliefs, whether his real interest was not the form rather than the content of his speeches. He himself did indeed admit that if he had to choose between the bar and politics, he would opt for the former; but there can be no real doubt that he was, in his own erratic manner, inspired by a genuine sympathy for the suffering of the masses.[1]

Ernest Picard on the other hand was a republican not from idealism but from scepticism. Son of a well-do-do banker, he was himself a prosperous and cultivated barrister who moved

[1] M. Reclus, *Jules Favre* (1912); J. Favre, *Discours parlementaires* (1881); J. Favre, *Henri Belval* (privately printed, 1880, a mixture of fiction and autobiography); J. Favre, *Mélanges politiques, judiciaries et littéraires*, ed. with an important preface by Paul Maritain (1882).

in conservative circles and who had taken no part in the revolution of 1848. He had a bourgeois horror of disorder; but he was also an individualist, Voltairian, sarcastic, with a biting and merciless wit. He was in fact the incarnation of the Parisian, inclined to opposition by an incorrigibly independent nature. Though possessed of no qualities of constructive statesmanship, he soon revealed himself as the best debater of the Five, brilliant as an interrupter, unanswerable because he clinched his arguments with a joke, a most effective sniper beneath Favre's heavy artillery.[1]

Likewise, the two silent backbenchers of the group, Darimon and Henon, had almost contradictory aims. Darimon was a disciple of Proudhon and Girardin: he was interested in entering parliament because he believed that Napoleon might be persuaded to carry out certain parts of their economic programme and so he was willing to accept—for the time being at any rate —an emperor who could be useful to them. Dr. Henon on the other hand was a Jacobin of Lyon who made a religion of republicanism and who had firmly refused the oath of loyalty in 1852. He now agreed to take it not because he expected any good from Napoleon but because he thought it was time to revive the party, to make it an active force in preparation for the day when the country realized how vain its hopes in the tyrant were. Darimon was a second-rate journalist who was put up because Girardin and Proudhon did not wish to commit themselves by entering parliament themselves. Henon was a scholar with a passion for botany, a man entirely free from vanity or ambition: he is said to have represented, in the eyes of his constituents, the struggle for the restoration of their municipal liberties.[2]

Ollivier was the youngest of them all and the least experienced,

---

[1] M. Reclus, *Ernest Picard* (1912); E. Picard, *Discours parlementaires* (1882-90); L. de Cormenin, *Reliquiae* (1868), i. 184, 189; E. and J. Goncourt, *Journal* (edition définitive 1935), v. 15.

[2] A. Darimon, *A travers une révolution* (1884) and *Histoire d'un parti: les cinq sous l'empire* (1885); *Notice sur J. L. Henon d'après les documents conservés par sa famille* (Lyon 1874), pamphlet in the municipal library of Lyon.

but he immediately aspired to being their leader: his success swelled his self-confidence and encouraged his independence. 'I shall never be a revolutionary or a party man', he wrote to a friend a few days after his victory. 'Between democratic Jacobinism and myself, there is an instinctive aversion which has been increased by my conduct at Marseilles and by my recent battle with Garnier-Pagès. If I ever do anything, it shall be as a disinterested moderator of the Revolution. I shall attempt what Cromwell or Napoleon did (minus their infamous *coups d'état* and usurpations), what Washington accomplished with so much nobility and purity. To be one of those who found and restrain —that is the only role I desire, the only role for which I am fit. . . . I do not wish like my father to be all my life the victim of the stupidities of a party.'[1]

When the Five came to take their places, they were immediately shown to isolated seats on the highest benches of the left; they were avoided by all other members as though they were infected with plague; even old school-fellows—now staunch conservatives—turned their backs upon them. Republicans in fact were regarded as dangerous demagogues whose re-appearance meant that the 'red menace' had revived again and must be suppressed with vigour once more. When therefore on 14 January 1858 Orsini made his famous attempt to assassinate Napoleon, a diehard general was at once made minister of the interior and a Draconian bill of public safety was introduced into the legislature to give him wide powers to arrest and expel political suspects without trial, to crush, in effect, whom he wished. For the Five this was an admirable opportunity to make their debut on really strong ground and to explain their attitude to a nation once more, though momentarily, intent on politics. Jules Favre defended Orsini at his trial with a brilliance which caused this to be remembered as one of his greatest cases; but Ollivier characteristically declined to appear for the other accused, Pieri, because he could not agree to the latter's wish to defend himself by attacking Orsini. He reserved himself instead for

[1] J. i. 291-2. (Letter to Masnou, 11 July 1857).

parliament, and made his first great speech in defence of liberty. 'Your government has been in existence for nine years,' he said; 'you are at peace with the kings of Europe; you have a numerous and seasoned army, an astute police force, an enormous budget; strategic roads cross the capital, and at intervals along them you raise veritable citadels. No liberty exists; the most redoubtable one—liberty of the press—now means only the right to say what does not displease Monsieur the minister of the interior; and yet you ask for laws of public safety! Do you not fear that the country will reply to you: I have sacrificed to you my liberties, my franchises, my traditions, all I have conquered with my blood, all that has made me glorious and illustrious among nations, in order to have a little peace and yet you return to harass me and ceaselessly demand further sacrifices from me. Where will you stop?'[1]

The speech was made with such studied moderation that it created a great impression even with the conservatives. At one point when he was ridiculing the bill by showing the absurd effects which might follow from it, a storm of interruptions broke from the right. Ollivier stopped and remained silent, but the majority was so interested in what he was saying that the hecklers were drowned by cries of 'Let him go on, let him speak'. After that he was listened to with rare attention. It was at once realized that he was no mere revolutionary and no ordinary republican. In the gallery the large crowd of distinguished liberals of former régimes were much struck by him. Montalembert, who was among them, noted in his diary afterwards. 'This young democrat will go far. By his moderation he baffles even . . . Granier de Cassagnac' (a leading ultra-right politician), and after having met Ollivier he added, 'I am very struck by the distinction and loftiness of mind of this orator in the making. He is by all appearances *a real liberal*, which is perhaps rarer in the ranks of the democrats than anywhere else.' The speech was widely reported in the English press and a Scottish M.P. wrote that 'Ollivier

[1] E.L. iv. 66. Cf. B.M., Add. MSS., 40124 f.33, Louis Blanc to Karl Blind, 26 February 1858.

brings to the discussions, or rather to the monologues of the Chamber, moderate Republican opinions, the ardent eloquence of Provence and an English spirit of compromise and party management which might have been learned from Sir William Hayter.'[1]

Ollivier was in fact at this time working, in a manner probably more English than French indeed, to find methods by which his most essential aims could be achieved in practice, and his diary makes it possible to follow the stages by which he came to believe that his best instrument would be Napoleon rather than the republican party. This new source throws unexpected light on his 'conversion'. In 1858 and 1859 he still thought that Bonapartism represented the evil traditions of French history, the despotism of Louis XIV; that though it claimed to be the incarnation of the Revolution, it was really its usurper—exploiting it and pandering to its unfortunate preference for discipline rather than liberty. He showed himself an open enemy of the empire and even refused to attend parties at the Tuileries.[2] However, the trouble was that in the course of his work as a deputy, he developed as great a distaste for his fellow-opponents of the empire, as for the empire itself. The great majority of the republicans seemed to him to be as 'Jacobin' as Napoleon, demagogues fond of glorious wars and of dictatorship, contemptuous of individual rights. He was disgusted by their systematic hostility to the régime, irrespective of the quality of its work, by their habit of determining their attitude to its policies by the sole consideration of whether those policies would hasten its fall, and by the way they were too easily content with negative criticism.

He could not agree with the maxim which was at the basis

---

[1] Montalembert's MS. Diary, 18 and 23 February 1858; *Correspondance de Liszt et de sa fille*, ed. D. Ollivier (1936), 207; E.L. iv. 66–67; *Compte-rendu des séances du corps législatif*, 1858, 56–96; 'A Few Words on France by a Scottish M.P.' [Grant Duff] cutting in O.P. Sir William Hayter (1792–1878) was Whip of the Liberal Party and patronage secretary to the Treasury.

[2] J. i. 327, 371–2, 376–8, 389, 392–3 (11 April 1858, 6 and 7 February, 14 March, 28 June, 10 August 1859).

of their action, that the end justified the means. He believed that this maxim produced the very contrary of what the men who used it hoped for: that it was at the root of all the excesses of French history, the cause of the continual see-saw of reaction and violence which had plagued the country since 1789. Men may attempt to obtain progress in one or two ways—by slow and gradual reforms or by violent and brusque revolutions. The former way was open only to governments in power, the latter the only possible resort of oppressed peoples. Yet only the gradual method could ever bear fruit, for revolutions by the mere fact that they were revolutions produced hates and divisions as undesirable as the evils they remedied: 'confusion's cure lives not in these confusions'.[1] This meant that permanent progress could be achieved only by the government.

Ollivier pursued the course of this reasoning in gradual stages, often spending a year between one position and another, and advancing only as events impressed new reflections on him. He obtained great assistance from discussion with his father who as a life-long revolutionary could not be suspected of prejudice in favour of constitutional monarchy, but who stage by stage endorsed and approved his slowly changing views.

Ollivier became increasingly convinced that it was of little consequence whether the régime which carried out reforms was a monarchy or a republic: all that mattered was the reforms themselves. Like Oliver Cromwell, he was 'not wedded or glued to forms of government'; or as he put it himself, 'republic or monarchy is but a secondary question, to be thought of exactly as a binding is when a book is judged or as a setting is when a diamond is valued. Liberty in all its forms, the guaranteeing of individual rights, that is the supreme question. Republic means but one thing, the abolition of the hereditary principle in the government, but if this cannot be effected except by the sacrifice of more precious aims, it becomes bad. The Belgian monarchy for example is far preferable to Cavaignac's republic: it can provisionally serve instead of the true republic

[1] *Romeo and Juliet*, Act IV, scene v.

and it will prepare for it far better than Cavaignac's.'[1]

He took his oath of loyalty to the empire seriously; and at the very beginning of his parliamentary career he realized where it might lead him. In 1857 he wrote to his father, 'You mock me for thinking that these people [i.e. the government] are capable of doing anything liberal; you consider them to be condemned for ever to despotism. Certainly what has happened till now justifies your opinion. . . . It is not likely that the emperor will issue an Additional Act, but it is not impossible. Its possibility is enough for me to take it into consideration before deciding [on whether to swear loyalty]. If he remains despotic, nothing will be easier than to know how to decide my conduct. I shall attack him without mercy and my blows will be all the more formidable because I shall be moderate and because I shall not say a word about overthrowing him. But if he transforms himself, I shall be obliged to help him, even if my help consolidates the very throne which has risen amid our curses. That is where the oath must inevitably lead and as I never stop half-way that is where I shall go if events take such a turn. . . . '[2]

By 1860, as a result of this train of thought, he came to wish that Napoleon should in fact turn liberal. In an extremely revealing entry in his diary for 17 June of that year he wrote: 'The only hope we ought to have is that he will grant liberty of his own accord, which, far from weakening him as people think, will in fact consolidate his throne. The treaty of commerce and my reading of his work on William III[3] make me think that he will grant liberty if he is pressed. "I ask nothing better than to grant liberty when they ask me for it," he said to someone, "but the country does not want it." (He was not altogether wrong.) He will wait for the opposition to be successful at the elections before granting it, or for some other defeats which he must redeem. Then he will not hesitate, but till then he will

---

[1] J. i. 396–7 (24 September 1859).

[2] E.L. iv. 55.

[3] Napoleon III's *Fragments historiques 1688 et 1830*, reprinted in his *Œuvres* (1856), 235–350.

not take the initiative in something which will cost him too much and which is repugnant to him. As personal rancour does not trouble me for long and as I am moved above all by truth, I have come to wish very much that he should not die and that he should complete his work. Liberty, even with him, will give me more joy than a Paris revolution carried out by generals or a popular revolution which might well end only in another despotism. We need time to educate universal suffrage. May God inspire this resolution in him. Then I shall forget his origin and all the harm he has done us in the past ten years. . . . If instead of being the dictator and the corruptor of democracy he should wish to become its founder and its educator, nobody could have a role comparable to his. Nothing has contributed to bringing me to these ideas more than my contact with the legitimists and the Orleanists. The sight of their hateful, systematic, and narrow opposition disgusts me. . . . If the emperor enters upon the liberal path, I shall break absolutely with them. If he moves away from it, I shall move closer to them. I want before all, in the company of no matter whom, liberty without epithets, neither sober liberty nor true liberty but just liberty. The republic will follow from it sooner or later as a necessary consequence, for it is the maximum of liberty. To wish to obtain it without previously having obtained the recognition of all the rights of liberty seems to me to be as unreasonable as to wish to show someone who says two and two make five that he is wrong, before having first explained and got him to accept the rules of addition.'

In this analysis of the situation Ollivier showed quite extra-ordinary appreciation of the workings of Napoleon III's mind. Napoleon did not believe that either liberalism or despotism were absolutely and always good. His work on William III, which Ollivier had read, ends with these words: 'The history of England cries out to kings: March at the head of the ideas of your century, and these ideas will follow and support you. March behind them, and they will drag you after them. March against them, and they will overthrow you.'[1] Napoleon was

[1] *Œuvres de Napoléon III* (1856), i. 342.

thus above all an opportunist who always wished to keep up with the times. He would not, as Ollivier supposed, simply yield to opposition and grant liberty if he was pressed: he would try to sense the trend of public opinion before it had actually developed into a strong force and he would seek to grant its wishes before it could demand them. Politics was indeed the art of compromise and of the relative for him. Ollivier, though he did not know it yet, had in him a monarch with whom he would have little difficulty in reaching an understanding.[1]

It is too often forgotten that even in its dictatorial period the theory of the second empire was not anti-liberal. There was a reaction at the time of its foundation against parliamentary government but not against civil liberty. Thus when Napoleon received the news of the enormous vote given in favour of his authoritarian constitution in the plebiscite of 1851, he declared, without the least compulsion, that 'To give satisfaction to the needs of the present by creating a system which reconstitutes authority without harming equality and without closing any door to improvement, means laying the true foundations of the only edifice capable of later supporting sensible and beneficent liberty'. Napoleon had after all spent his youth in the ranks of the advanced opposition to Louis Philippe, except for the periods he spent in England moving in the society of Holland House and Woburn Abbey, Sir Edward Bulwer, Disraeli, and country gentry who succeeded in instilling into him a lasting admiration for the English constitution. He must surely be the only ruler of France who has risked hurting her pride by publicly holding up England as a model for France to follow, praising England's 'unrestricted liberty given to the expression of all opinions as to the development of all interests . . . the perfect order maintained in the midst of the vivacity of debates and the perils of competition . . . individual initiative acting with indefatigable ardour', and urging France to imitate her example. For England

[1] Compare Napoleon's opportunism with Charles II's belief that 'yieldingness . . . was a Specifick to preserve us in Peace for his own Time'. *The Complete Works of George Savile, First Marquess of Halifax*, ed. Walter Raleigh (Oxford, 1912), 207.

was then the richest country in the world and few doubted that the reward of her constitution was not only liberty but also wealth.[1] Ollivier's hopes therefore were justified and realized sooner than he expected. Only six months later, on 24 November 1860, a decree was published in the *Moniteur*, granting the first instalment of a more liberal constitution: 'Napoleon, Emperor of the French, &c., wishing to give the great bodies of the state a more direct part in the formation of the general policy of our government and a striking testimony of our confidence in them, have decreed and decree . . .' that the two houses should every year vote an address to the throne to express their wishes, that their debates should be published in full, that ministers without portfolio would be appointed to represent the government in parliament and that 'in order to facilitate the expression of the legislature's opinion in the making of laws' its powers of amending them be increased.

Ollivier was delighted. 'A decree issued yesterday', he wrote, 'has justified my policy and fills me with joy. My friends congratulate me upon it as though it were a personal victory. The abstentionist cause is lost, and a step forward has been taken. It is a small step, but with time it will have decisive results. . . . I do not think that this measure or any others of the same type that may follow it weakens the empire: far from it, it will consolidate it if the empire perseveres in this wise habit of making more and more liberal concessions. When a government has an army of 500,000 men in the presence of an ignorant or exhausted nation which poverty condemns to inceasing labour, there is nothing to be feared from liberty, far from it. Besides, it must never be forgotten that our master's ideal is William III and that if he can he will govern with liberty, especially when

[1] Napoleon's speech of 31 December 1851 in *Discours, messages et proclamations de l'Empereur* (1860) 202; and speech reported in *Moniteur Universel* 26 January 1863, p. 115; see also Ivor Guest, *Napoleon III in England* (1952); and for a fuller discussion of Napoleon's views, T. Zeldin, *The Political System of Napoleon III* (1958), especially Chapter 7. Even the supposedly extremist Saint-Arnaud, who carried out the *coup d'état* in 1851, wrote ; 'Only by passing through a period of despotic and absolute rule can we return to moderate and constitutional government.'–Q. L'Epine, *Le Maréchal de Saint-Arnaud* (1929), 2, 3.

the nation will want him to. He is above all anxious not to place himself in opposition to it. This will be his system of government so long as he possesses his faculties, and age does not weaken or extinguish them. It is moreover the only system which can save him from being sooner or later *overthrown*. Although the empire is strengthened, I rejoice if this is a beginning, for I maintain that a man must obey his principles more than his desire for revenge. I rejoice also if this is but an expedient, for we have conquered yet another weapon of war and nothing is more dangerous than to wish to play with liberty or to employ it as a ruse.'[1]

The government's policy now produced a reaction in certain sections of the political world which clinched Ollivier's support for it. Napoleon's assistance to the movement for Italian independence and his approval of the annexation of part of the pope's states to the new kingdom of Italy unleashed a violent campaign against him by the Catholics and the clergy. His treaty of free trade with England produced noisy protests from a great many industrialists prophesying ruin for their factories. Napoleon III ceased to stand at the extreme right wing of politics: further right still there now came to be constituted a reactionary party of diehard Catholics and protectionists. A new dividing line cut across the political scene.

The Decree of 24 November rather oddly produced a veritable volcano of abuse against the empire. The politicians it was supposed to placate were on the whole far from thankful for it. They were infuriated by a remarkable harangue in the senate by the emperor's left-wing cousin, Prince Napoleon, rejoicing in Italy's new unity, congratulating the emperor for his part in it, and declaring that 'We are the representatives of modern society'. The emperor, said the Prince, was a parvenu who stood for 1789, for popular rights against divine rights. When the legislature reassembled on 11 March, therefore, one after another the clericals got up to read enormous speeches attacking this view, insisting that France was 'Catholic or nothing', that having been the accomplice of the revolution in Italy there was danger

[1] J. i. 444-5 (25 November 1860).

that Napoleon would be so at home too. They claimed that the second empire had been founded as a protest by the 'monarchical, conservative, Catholic, spirit of France' against the 'revolutionary spirit', saying, as it were, that the empire belonged to them, that it was a reactionary rather than a progressive force. Even the free trade treaty with England was sneered at as being revolutionary, (for had not England allied herself with the revolutionaries in Italy?) and as being a cunning invasion of France by new-fangled foreign propaganda.

They spent three days attacking in this manner. On the first Ollivier merely noted their violence. On the second he went home 'very indignant at this counter-revolutionary manifesto.' On the third, after a particularly powerful speech by the Catholic Alsatian Keller, he could bear it no longer, for the reactionary views were being received with considerable enthusiasm by the house. 'I go out of the Chamber absolutely distraught', he wrote in his diary, 'and my night is sleepless. A host of veils are torn from before my eyes. I reflect with horror on how the counter-revolution would invade the world if this man were overthrown and for the first time I understand and I excuse the Bérangers and the liberals of the restoration [who had been Bonapartists]. I understand also how, when the republic showed itself to be powerless, revolutionary France threw herself blindly into the arms of the first Bonaparte. Bonapartism has till now been the only organized obstacle which the revolution has been able to oppose to reaction, and hence its popularity. If my country's integrity were threatened, I would support the government. The moral integrity of my country is menaced, my principles are insulted, I array myself behind him who is defending them. I do not know when, nor how; but this debate will not end before I manifest these sentiments.'

On the following day, 14 March, Favre rose to speak for the republicans. He declaimed for two hours while Ollivier sat chafing that his own thoughts should be so ill-expressed by his spokesman, but holding himself back from publicly proclaiming his disagreement. When, however, the conservative Baroche,

minister without portfolio, replying for the government, likewise played down the importance of the new liberties, Ollivier
could contain himself no longer. It was five o'clock: the lamps
were being lit and Ollivier thought he felt a tense and expectant
silence fill the house. Moved by an impulse he rose to speak
despite the late hour. So troubled was he by the thoughts which
had been agitating in his mind on the previous night, that he
threw aside the speech he had prepared and gave himself up to
the inspiration of the moment. He declared with deliberate
moderation that although he hoped that the new decree would
soon be extended, yet he recognized its 'courage, generosity,
and values'. He held himself back from pursuing this subject
and tried to deal with particular points of the last speech, but he
felt himself drawn irresistibly to the topic uppermost in his
mind. Then seeing that his words were being so well received,
he threw prudence to the winds and let himself go. Napoleon
on St. Helena had said, 'Tell my son to give France as much
liberty as I gave her equality'. 'That, gentlemen,' declared Ollivier, 'is what we ask the emperor, and if our words can have
any influence on him, we would say this to him: When one
is master of a nation of 36 million men, when one has been
acclaimed by it, when thanks to the magnificent power of this
nation, one is master of the world, in the sense that one brings
victory to whichever side one joins; when one is the first amongst
sovereigns, when fortune has no more favours to give one, when
one's every wish has been granted, when one's life is a legend,
when one has emerged from prison to ascend the first throne
of the world, when one has known all sorrows and all joys,
there is still an ineffable joy one can experience which will sur-
pass all those one has known, and which will give one eternal
glory. It is to initiate a great people to liberty courageously
and voluntarily, it is to reject pusillanimous counsels and to put
oneself directly face to face with the nation. I answer for it, the
day this appeal is made, the country may still have some people
who remain loyal to the memories of the past or who are too
absorbed by the hopes of the future, but the majority will approve

it with enthusiasm. And as for me, *who am a republican*, I shall admire, I shall approve, and my support will be all the more efficacious because it will be completely disinterested.'

The house was filled with confusion. A republican had openly declared his willingness to accept the detested régime he had been elected to oppose. On the one hand the ultra-Bonapartists jumped up to object to the phrase 'I who am a republican', which they construed as treasonable, only to be appeased by the tactful president, the duc de Morny, who had it omitted from the published reports. On the other hand the legitimists, the Orleanists, and the diehard republicans were equally furious: they declared he had been moved by ambition, that he wished to be made a minister, that the government would distribute his speech. Picard was all in a flurry and Favre gravely rebuked him. Behind his back abuse was poured out against him. He was guilty of an unforgivable enormity, of asserting that his enemies would carry out the reforms he demanded better than would his own party, of offering to support the empire which decent republicans could hardly mention without spitting blood. They smiled bitterly at the sight of Bonapartists applauding him, of senators running down from the gallery to congratulate him, and of an intimate friend of the emperor exclaiming, 'It is a speech worthy of a minister.' What was the son of Demosthenes Ollivier doing in such company?

'I expected all this uproar,' wrote Ollivier, 'and I am neither astonished nor sorry. It will not, thank God, be the last time I shall cause it. When a man appeals to reason and not to rancour, when he acts according to his ideas and not to his passions, is it surprising if those who harbour rancour and passion revolt? When one puts oneself above parties, is it not natural that the parties should throw one out? I accept the consequences of this position. To be a politician, a deputy, is not an aim in itself for me but only a means, the means of serving my convictions. If I must sacrifice these, I prefer to become once more simply a barrister.'[1]

---

[1] *Annales du sénat et du corps législatif*, 1861, i. 74–98 and 229–337; E.L. v. 142–4; J. ii. 11–15 (11–17 March 1861).

CHAPTER 6

OLLIVIER'S CONSTITUTIONAL AND SOCIAL AIMS, 1861-4

DESPITE the liberal concessions of 1860, the second empire continued to be a régime which was the very negation of parliamentary government. How then could there be a reconciliation between it and the republican ideal of democracy? Rather paradoxically, it was precisely Napoleon III's reluctance to grant omnipotence to the legislature that drew Ollivier to him. For it had been a republican tradition to view parliamentary government with contempt, as a system inextricably linked with monarchy and irrevocably discredited by its corruption under Louis Philippe. To the republicans of 1848, democracy meant universal suffrage, but beyond that they could not agree. They were certain that they had no wish to copy England's aristocratic 'feudal' constitution (which appealed much more to the Orleanists).[1] Those among them who thought parliaments necessary generally wished, as the constitution of 1848 revealed, to balance them by a strong and independent president. Blanqui, Comte, Littré advocated dictatorships of various kinds, Ledru-Rollin preached direct government by referendum, while Fourier and Proudhon wanted no government at all but an anarchist federation of Communes.[2] It was only in the second half of the century that the republicans gradually became the defenders of parliamentary government, as a new body of political thought developed in reaction to Napoleon III's despotism. It was very reluctantly that they accepted the constitution of

[1] A. A. Ledru-Rollin, *De la décadence de l'Angleterre* (1850); T. Zeldin, 'English Ideals in French Politics during the Nineteenth Century', *The Historical Journal* (1959) ii. 40–58.

[2] I. Tchernoff, *Le Parti républican sous la monarchie de juillet* (1905); id., *Le Parti républicain au coup d'état et sous le second empire* (1906); G. Weill, *Histoire du parti républicain (1814–1870)* (1928).

1875 which has linked them indissolubly with this form of government but which was of course drawn up by monarchists with a view to a royalist restoration.

Ollivier was unusual in this matter because he was old-fashioned. It was his fellow republicans who changed their opinions, much more than he. They began to argue that the problem now was no longer oligarchy by a chatter-box parliament but despotism by an uncontrolled monarch, and that the need now was not the strengthening of the executive but its subordination to a freely elected parliament, which could alone ensure that the popular will was enforced. Ollivier, however, to their understandable surprise, refused to abandon his hostility to parliamentary government. Parliamentary government might work in England, he said, but the English constitution was unsuitable for French conditions; and it was, in any case, inescapably aristocratic. The democratic and republican ideal was 'representative government' not 'parliamentary government', the constitution of 1848, that is to say, rather than that of 1830. 'Representative government', he insisted, 'is as great as parliamentary government is despicable. Let us not forget the chambers of Louis Philippe.'[1]

In 1855 Ollivier had drawn up a short republican constitution which helps to show more precisely what he meant by representative government. A president, elected for four years, would rule personally. He would be assisted by a self-recruiting council of state, which would ensure a strong 'conservative principle', to balance the constantly changing assembly, elected for five years and annually renewed by fifths. The assembly's task would be limited to reflecting public opinion, and its functions strictly separated from those of the executive.[2] Ollivier's ideal was something very similar to the consular constitution of 1799. In old age he said that his heroes in history were St. Francis of Assisi, St. Vincent de Paul, and 'the First Consul until 13 March

---

[1] J. ii. 35–36 (27 November 1861). This entry in his diary is rather confused and it does not appear that he ever really understood parliamentary government.

[2] J. i. 214–16 (13 May 1855).

1804', that is Napoleon I before he became Emperor.[1] Bonaparte the Consul had been the idol of the left-wing opposition after 1815, of men like Demosthenes Ollivier and Armand Carrel. Bonaparte's nephew had been their ally against Louis Philippe, though he had deserted them in 1848 when he found that the conservatives and clericals could be more useful to him; but another nephew, Prince Jerome Napoleon, Demosthenes' friend, preserved the old tradition and called himself a radical and republican Bonapartist. Now, in 1860, the empire's alliance with the clericals appeared to have ended and it was reasonable to hope for a return to a more republican form of Bonapartism.

Ollivier's prejudices against parliamentary government were made systematic by his reading of the works of Benjamin Constant. This extraordinary man, brilliant novelist and remarkable political theorist, too little known in England in this latter capacity,[2] had argued that the remedy for despotism (such as France had suffered under Napoleon I) was not simply to transfer power from the monarch to a parliament, for a sovereign parliament could be just as dangerous to individual rights as an autocratic king. He urged that liberty could be safeguarded only by the division of power and that the executive arm should be entirely controlled by the king. Administration should be his concern: ministers should be appointed by him; parliament should confine itself to legislation and to giving advice to enable him to rule in accordance with the country's wishes. In Constant's eyes parliamentary government meant the uncontrolled tyranny of parliament associated with the horrors of 1648 in England and 1791 in France.[3]

Ollivier, in language borrowed almost verbatim from Constant, argued that a strong executive such as existed under the second empire was a political necessity; and that this was incompatible

---

[1] See the illustration opposite p. 288 in P. Saint-Marc *Emile Ollivier* (1950).

[2] Though recently resurrected by Sir Isaiah Berlin in his inaugural lecture, *Two Concepts of Liberty* (1958), 11, 48. See also the very interesting biography by Harold Nicolson, *Benjamin Constant* (1949).

[3] B. Constant, *Principes de politique* (1815). Note the date; it was written to defend the Additional Act. Cf. also his *De la responsabilité des ministres* (1815).

with parliamentary government. All he demanded therefore was representative government; that is to say, there should be free elections and a free press, but parliament should be a representative not a governing body: 'it must impose upon the executive principles but not ministers.' This belief, based on theoretical considerations, explains why Ollivier could be satisfied with much more moderate reforms than the other republicans required. It will be seen however that when he actually entered upon negotiations in 1866-70 to introduce liberty into Napoleon's empire, he was made aware of the practical difficulties of imposing principles without also insisting on a change of ministry. In the end he did in fact organize parliament to impose new ministers on the emperor, but at the same time—and this is the basic contradiction of his career—he never abandoned his ideal of a half-way house between personal and parliamentary government.[1]

His moderation was strengthened by his reading of Guicciardini, 'whose ideas on the organization of government', he wrote, 'fit in very well with mine and confirm me in them.' This frustrated politician of the fifteenth century had prescribed remedies for the troubles of Florence which seemed applicable to France. He convinced Ollivier that constitutions could be stable only if they had a 'conservative principle' in them; that the best government was therefore a 'mixed' one, combining monarchy, aristocracy, and democracy; and that Venice possessed just such an ideal constitution. Guicciardini was really an advocate of aristocracy, but Ollivier failed to understand this and exclaimed: 'Let us imitate Venice, let us establish a government which has the advantage of the one, the few, and the many. To achieve this, you, constitutionalists, must abandon heredity and you, republicans, must abandon the idea of absolutely sovereign assemblies.' Ollivier was possibly unique in finding his constitutional model neither in England nor in America but in Italy, rather curiously holding up for admiration the very system which Disraeli at almost the same time was castigating, with equal inaccuracy.[2]

[1] J. ii. 35-36 (27 November 1861).   [2] J. i. 352-7 (16-20 October 1858).

In 1860 also he found in the works of Bastiat 'the positive confirmation of principles which had till now been vague in me'. Bastiat was one of the great French advocates of free trade, a liberal of the 1848 type, who believed that ministers should not be members of parliament, that the legislative should merely lay down the policy it wanted carried out, state the price it was willing to pay, and leave the government to it. Bastiat's hero, Cobden, became Ollivier's; and the ambition to influence those in power, to convert them rather than to replace them, became Ollivier's inspiration. 'To be Cobden would be greater and would suit me better than to be Robert Peel.'[1]

Ollivier in addition thought of himself as a disciple of Mirabeau, the 'democratic monarchist', as well as of Carrel and Lamartine.[2] The diversity of his political ancestry he considered to be a positive advantage. His aim was to produce a synthesis of the wisdom of the past, to create a political party which would embrace everybody, to establish a 'golden mean between tyranny and the excesses of the masses.'[3] 'My programme', he wrote, 'is becoming clearer and clearer to me. Liberty, but democracy also. Without liberty, democracy is but despotism. Without democracy, liberty is but privilege.'[4] What he wished to achieve was a reconciliation of these two traditions which had so far been antagonistic in France. He would always he said, 'prefer progress to revolution. Devoted and tied to no dynasty, but also revolutionary against none; destroying only when it is certain that a régime cannot be improved; republican, but a patient one, and more concerned with facts than with words.'[5] He was clearly moving spontaneously towards the empire, and in 1863 finally made his disagreement with the opposition public

---

[1] J. i. 424 (21 March 1860). G. de Nouvion, *Frédéric Bastiat, sa vie, ses œuvres, ses doctrines* (1905), 180–194; E. Le Senne, *Frédéric Bastiat et l'extension du rôle de l'Etat* (1906).

[2] J. ii. 64. (Letter to Demosthenes Ollivier, 19 February 1863.) 'Despite its failure, the policy of Mirabeau, purified of all that sullied it, is the only one worth adopting.' E.L. vii. 566.

[3] J. i. 260, 274–5, 277–8, 353 (18 October 1856, 1 and 18 May 1857, 18 October 1858).

[4] J. ii. 18 (10 April 1861).   [5] J. i. 25 (25 July 1861).

when he denounced Thiers' famous maxim, 'The King reigns but does not govern'.[1]

That he actually went over to the empire was due to the duc de Morny. Did these two men have anything in common, or did Morny merely use his charm on Ollivier to seduce him, to make of him an instrument for his own purposes? Morny's papers have largely disappeared, but just enough extracts from them have survived to reveal his motives. He certainly deserved his reputation as a rake and speculator but, concealed beneath his dilettantism, he also had far-reaching political ambitions. Despite his worldly success he appears to have been at bottom a frustrated man. His dilettantism produced in him a longing for more solid achievements, for a permanent and glorious place in history. He had participated in the *coup d'état* because he savoured the idea 'that I should be at the head of everything'.[2] He believed that his services then were 'sufficiently great and sufficiently exceptional to justify every kind of reward';[3] but he demanded in vain the title of Prince Arch-chancellor of the empire[4] and ever after he felt that his talents were receiving neither proper recognition nor adequate scope. He had visions of succeeding Napoleon on his death, apparently as regent, because, he declared, the empress 'would not last three days'.[5] He hoped to win fame as 'the Richelieu of liberty';[6] but in modern conditions a statesman needed to command assemblies, and he was no orator. He thought he saw one in Ollivier, who would be his mouthpiece.[7] To this extent he certainly intended to use Ollivier as a tool of his own ambitions.

Yet his ambitions equally certainly favoured increased liberty. There was, in his view, no real contradiction between his

[1] J. ii. 97 (7 February 1864).

[2] 'La Genèse du coup d'état; mémoire du duc de Morny publié par son petit-fils', *Revue des deux mondes*, (1 December 1925), 533.

[3] Fragment of Morny's Memoirs in *L'Intermédiaire des chercheurs et curieux* (30 April 1904), vol. 49, columns 659–64.

[4] Manuscript life of Morny by Quatrelles L'Epine (his secretary's son).

[5] J. ii. 100 (17 February 1864).

[6] J. ii. 85 (27 June 1863).

[7] M. Du Camp, *Souvenirs d'un demi-siècle* (1949), i. 228–30.

reactionary role in 1851 and the mantle of a reformer in which he appeared in the 1860's. He had believed that the repression following the *coup d'état* had been necessary to save society from the radicals; now liberty alone, he thought, could dish the revolutionaries and render them powerless. He thus shared Ollivier's horror of the extreme left,[1] and he argued, like him, that 'obstinacy in keeping the Prince de Polignac in office led to the revolution of 1830; similar obstinacy in keeping Guizot's ministry produced the revolution of February [1848].' The situation was no longer what it had been in 1851:[2] 'nothing is more demoralizing for a country than to see men change without a change of policy'.[3] Liberal concessions were thus needed to establish the imperial dynasty on 'imperishable foundations'.[4]

Morny is remembered essentially as an aristocrat, but he was very far from being an aristocrat of the *ancien régime*. Liberals may have mistrusted him for corrupting democracy by 'introducing into France the English system of giving treats to the electors';[5] but on the other hand one finds him exclaiming vigorously in 1847 that 'we must never forget that we are a liberal power, that our government is born of a revolution, that we are the grandchildren of 1789'.[6] He had urged parliamentary and above all social reform on Louis Philippe; and under Napoleon III he declared that 'a government without control and without criticism is like a ship without a rudder'.[7] 'I was brought up,' he said, 'to admire English society [with its] complete individual liberty'; at one stage this had inclined him to agitate for political liberty, but he later decided that the French abused

[1] Morny to Montalembert, 3 December 1851, Montalembert papers.
[2] Note in Morny's hand, in L'Epine archives, copied by Quatrelles L'Epine.
[3] *Moniteur universel* (1848), 371.
[4] *Annales du corps législatif* (1863), i. 9.
[5] L. Faucher, *Correspondence et vie parlementaire* (1867), i. 305.
[6] A. de Morny, 'Quelques réflexions sur la politique actuelle', dated 24 December 1847, *Revue des deux mondes* (January 1848), 151–63.
[7] A. de Morny, 'Quelques réflexions sur la politique actuelle', dated 24 December 1847, *Revue des deux mondes* (January 1848), 151–63; and *Annales du corps législatif* (1863), iv. 247.

this and what was needed first was civil liberty: the government of France did too much and the individual needed to be protected against it.[1] He referred to his circulars, as minister of the interior in 1852, as proof of his consistency on this point; and one of them does indeed advocate individual freedom: 'bureaucracy should not think itself created to object, hinder and delay when it exists only to expedite and to regularize'.[2]

Though he talked loosely of 'parliamentary government' as his aim, he appears, like Ollivier, to have understood by it something different from the Orleanist system. He inspired a pamphlet pointing out that 'the liberal measures which the emperor has happily inaugurated will not have as their result the re-establishment of the old parliamentary régime'.[3] What he actually demanded from Napoleon was, first, power for the legislature to initiate laws and fuller rights to amend them; secondly, that ministers should appear before it to defend their conduct (so as to stimulate their efficiency); that they should have 'moral responsibility' before it, but they should not actually be members of the legislature (lest deputies become ambitious for office).[4] He looked upon himself as a mediator between Napoleon and the opposition; and he hoped to succeed by encouraging moderation and compromise on both sides.[5]

On several occasions, starting in 1861, Morny outlined his plans to Ollivier. He said that he was aiming to form a government based on the support of parliament, 'a ministry of fusion' which would work to establish civil liberty and that he hoped to invite Ollivier to join it. Ollivier, who was at first shy of even speaking to this imperial dignitary, received his advances

[1] Draft of an article written by Morny and left unfinished at his death, copy by Quatrelles L'Epine.

[2] Archives Nationales, 8 January 1852, F(1a +) 2119, no. 107.

[3] C. Latour du Moulin, *Lettres à un membre du parlement d'Angleterre sur la constitution de 1852* (1861), 5–6; for Morny's inspiration of it, see A. Darimon, *L'Opposition sous l'Empire* (1886), 72.

[4] Morny to Napoleon, 24 December 1863, draft, copied by Quatrelles L'Epine.

[5] *Annales du corps législatif* (1864) viii. 375; *Procès verbaux du corps législatif* (1858), 256; Morny to Ollivier, 14 January [?] 1864, O.P.

with caution, merely reiterating his promise that he would assist the empire if it did grant liberty.[1] When in June 1863 Morny again summoned him and definitely asked him to enter a government to 'fuse' Bonapartism and republicanism, Ollivier warily replied that his idea was a good one, that he would support it, but that he would be delighted if it were put into execution by others.

'But if you do not enter into the scheme, I shall not either.'

'We shall see when the time comes,' said Ollivier vaguely; 'but in any case it is well understood that I shall not enter it alone, but with my party.'

'Certainly, for otherwise I shall compromise myself and you will dishonour yourself.' It is important to note that initially the liberal empire was designed to be based on an alliance with the republican party.

Morny then read to him a note he had recently sent to Napoleon saying that the elections of 1863 had been a defeat for the clericals and that there now remained only the emperor and 'democracy' (i.e. republicanism) face to face. The strength of democracy would continue to increase and it was essential to satisfy it in order not to be overthrown by it. They must stop abuses like nepotism and scandalous appointments; they must give, if not political liberty at this stage, then at least religious and civil liberty; they must study social problems and solve the question of trade unions, which were still illegal. 'You see,' added Morny, 'it contains your own ideas.'

Ollivier replied noncommittally and with embarrassment. 'Here at last', he wrote in his diary the same evening, 'I am faced with the situation I feared. What shall I do? If this concerned only myself, my decision would be made at once: I should refuse. As I told Morny this very morning, I do not like power; to accept it would be a sacrifice. But from the point of view of the general interest, I am very perplexed. If, supposing the emperor sincerely consents to it, we refuse to assist him in establishing liberty and to give him an honest entourage in the place of what he now has, shall we not make ourselves responsible

[1] J. ii. 10, 37 and 52-3 (7 February and 10 December 1861, 1 July 1862).

for the evils which might be produced by a revolution or a *coup d'état*? I shall meditate on it this holiday. If I see that the interest of my country requires me to accept, I shall not hesitate. I shall be treated as a renegade inspired by ambition, but I shall know how to prove, by the way I carry out my sacrifice to the end, that in this matter as in all others, I am moved only by the public interest and by the sentiment of duty.'[1] He was perfectly conscious of the bewitching personal attraction Morny was exerting on him. 'It is impossible not to agree,' he noted, 'that he is a charming man, very seductive and also very intelligent; knowing little, but understanding well; the true image of De Marsay in Balzac.' But, he added, 'He understands the situation perfectly and I am convinced that he is the most remarkable politician of the empire from the point of view of sagacity and farseeing perspicacity. Many think he is deceiving me. I believe in his sincerity and I feel a real fondness for him.'[2] All the same he maintained his aloofness and Morny on his side exclaimed, 'This Ollivier is inexplicable. One does not know how to get hold of him. He despises money; he does not want power; one could perhaps capture him through his pride. His nature is too refined, too aristocratic for him to remain with his friends, but he is not ours. I do not know what he wants.'[3] He later added, 'He will not join us without a radical transformation.'[4]

Ollivier's relations with the republicans were indeed becoming increasingly strained. The elections of 1863 fomented personal squabbles about the candidates to be chosen, reviving and exacerbating political differences. The opposition newspapers added vituperation to the disagreements. The Five made themselves obnoxious to the rest by claiming to direct the campaign and, even worse, by declaring that in their magnanimity they would nevertheless approve the candidature of some of the old party leaders. Ollivier particularly took the policy of 'magnanimity'

---

[1] J. ii. 84–87 (27 June 1863).
[2] J. ii. 96 (7 February 1864). For Morny's similarities with Comte Henri de Marsay, see Fernand Lotte, *Dictionnaire biographique des personnages fictifs de la comédie humaine* (1952), 384–8.
[3] J. ii. 127 (1 June 1864).   [4] J. ii. 179 (26 January 1865).

as his line, supporting his enemies to show that he was not being moved by personal considerations. He even wrote in favour of the Orleanist opposition: he urged the electorate not to perpetuate 'retrospective recriminations and Byzantine discussions'. There was nothing immoral in uniting to obtain liberty; the parties need not abandon their principles and from their co-operation in opposition there might even spring up personal friendships which would be valuable after victory had been won.[1]

The Orleanist leader Thiers, who now returned to parliament, told Ollivier, 'You will be the link between us [the Orleanist and republican oppositions]. Apart from your talent you are adroit, I mean you are reasonable, conciliatory, courageous.'[2] The contact between the two men annoyed the radicals, who were in fact complaining about the behaviour of not only Ollivier but even Favre and Picard: the 'puritans' were disgusted to meet at the salons of the Five, Orleanists and men of the centre left 'on whom they seem to rely more than on us for fighting the empire'.[3] People recalled the acrimonious curse on Ollivier of old Goudchaux in 1857: 'Young man, you are but an intriguer today: later on you will be a traitor.'[4] Ollivier for his part made matters worse by his contemptuous attitude towards the left wing. Jules Simon, he declared, was a skilful and eloquent orator, but of doubtful sincerity, an actor always changing his mind: 'I shall be very astonished if he rises above the second rank'. Pelletan was 'grotesquely declamatory', even though he might possess 'true oratorical gifts'. Such statements, overheard and repeated in exaggerated form, alienated many possible allies. He was aware that he was wrong to speak of others in this harsh way, often saying more than he meant; he promised himself that he would stop the practice; but his opinions continued to escape him. In addition he now met a

---

[1] Letter to an elector of Grenoble on the subject of a candidature of Casimir Périer, May 1863, O.P.

[2] J. ii. 76 (4 June 1863).

[3] F. H. R. Allain-Targé, 'Souvenirs d'avant 1870', in *Revue de Paris* (1903), v. 14.

[4] Quoted by M. Reclus, *Jules Favre* (1912), 248.

fierce rivalry in parliament among the orators of the opposition, each anxious to win recognition of supremacy in eloquence. In debates they seemed to be struggling to impress each other as much as to convince the majority.[1]

The conciliatory tone of Ollivier's speeches was considered to be proof that he was pandering to the empire; rumours of his relations with Morny leaked out and there was talk that he would soon be offered a ministry. Ollivier, however, spoke to his colleagues about the problem of taking office under the empire in an extraordinarily tactless manner. He said that 'neither now nor later do I wish to become a minister, no more under the empire than under the republic. I tasted power when I was young and I have lost all appetite for it for life. My ambition is entirely satisfied. I have never wished to be anything but a respected representative of liberal public opinion. . . . The interests of the country could alone make me decide to accept the burden of office for a time. This could happen under the empire if one day the emperor called me and said to me: "Sir, I find your ideas just; I think that liberty is the only force capable of founding anything. I ask you to help me to establish it. I cannot do it with my present entourage. Be my collaborator." In such a situation I shall do all I can to avoid accepting office, but if my assistance is really necessary, I shall give it. In return for real and complete liberty, without epithets, I shall make this sacrifice to the emperor, I shall defend and accept his government and forget the past. I shall then be the Richelieu of liberty. . . .'[2]

This is how Ollivier reports his statement in his diary and he comments, 'No one dared to contradict'. However, the silence which followed it must have concealed something different from simple agreement. Ollivier was so certain that his was the right course to pursue, and so absorbed by the prospect of

[1] L. Halévy, *Carnets* (1935), i. 49.

[2] J. i. 77 (5 June 1863). Ollivier and Morny apparently both used this same phrase of 'the Richelieu of Liberty'. Lamartine under Louis Philippe also planned to be a Richelieu in the regency which would have been established had the King died while the Comte de Paris was still a minor.—L. Bertrand, *Lamartine* (1940), 315-16.

seeing liberty established, that he never seems to have thought it necessary to coax his party along so obviously reasonable a policy, or to offer it anything more than logical arguments to overcome very strong prejudice against the least co-operation with the empire. It will be noted that in this passage he talks simply of himself and what the emperor would say to him. But what part had he for his republican colleagues? His neglect of the problem of carrying at least some of them with him is one of his greatest mistakes.

Soon the government announced a bill allowing combinations of workers in certain cases. Ollivier, however, denounced it as unsatisfactory, for 'it gives with one hand and takes back with the other': strikes were made legal, but vague provisos in fact nullified the concession. He convinced Morny that the bill was worthless, and Morny therefore got Ollivier appointed rapporteur of the parliamentary committee which was to consider it. Ollivier was thus enabled to transform its character. He abolished the provisos and omitted the word combination (*coalition*) entirely, so that the offence of combining for the purpose of improving working conditions ceased to be known to the law. However, it was typical of Ollivier that he wished to be more liberal still, and he granted not only the liberty to strike, but also the 'liberty to work'. It was made an offence to use violence or fraud in the organization of a strike or to molest black-legs who refused to join in: there was to be no tyranny, that is, by the majority of workers over their fellows, and a man was to have the right to work on any conditions that were acceptable to himself even if others disapproved.[1] This idea derived from the English Combination Act of 1825 and from the comments of J. S. Mill, whom Ollivier quoted at length: the phrasing of the French law was in parts borrowed almost verbatim from these sources.[2]

[1] E. Ollivier, *Commentaire de la loi du 25 mai 1864 sur les coalitions* (1864).

[2] 6 Geo. IV c.129; J. S. Mill, *Principles of Political Economy* (8th edition, 1878), 552; the intermediary between Mill and Ollivier was probably F. Bastiat, *Discours sur la repression des coalitions industrielles*, 17 November 1849, reprinted in his *Œuvres complètes* (1854), v. 504-6.

Whatever the merits of his reasoning, Ollivier was basing his law on abstract principles rather than on the actual demands of the people involved. Inevitably he once again offended both sides. The protectionist manufacturers declared that it granted the workers far too much power, that strikes would follow without measure, and that industry would be ruined. Such was their opposition that Napoleon considered withdrawing the bill;[1] Ollivier in vain sought to console them with the argument that his bill was an inevitable corollary of the industrial revolution and universal suffrage. However, the left wing at the same time rejected it as inadequate, and demanded the simple repeal of the prohibition of combinations, without any of Ollivier's modifications and reservations. Favre and Simon denounced the bill as a mere snare: it pretended to grant liberty, but its punishment of 'fraudulent manœuvres' rendered it worthless, since this phrase was so vague as to make it capable of any interpretation. They refused to accept Ollivier's definitions and they declared that the bill was in any any case useless because associations and public meetings remained illegal. The law, that is to say, would allow temporary combination for strikes, but not permanent association in trade unions.

Ollivier appears to have been so carried away by the grandeur of the task on which he was engaged—his first experience of legislation—that he completely neglected the question of its tactful handling. He was certain that Simon was opposing simply out of pique at not being made rapporteur himself. Simon had indeed published books on working-class conditions and on the nature of liberty, which may have seemed to him to give him a better title to this appointment.[2] Ollivier however made no attempt to mollify him or his colleagues, but instead attacked them vehemently for obstructing him. 'It is wrong', he said, 'to refuse some progress under the pretext that it is incomplete. Oh! I know this theory and I have seen it described in

---

[1] E.L. vi. 540, quoting Marshal Vaillant's unpublished diary.
[2] J. Simon, L'Ouvrière (1863); idem, La Liberté (1859). L. Seché, Jules Simon (1898), casts no light on this episode.

the Memoirs of Mallet du Pan on the first revolution. It is the theory of pessimism: it consists in this, that when you dislike a government on principle, or when you disapprove its general policy, instead of doing what every man of honour and good sense ought to do, approve what is good and blame what is bad, you criticize everything, attack everything, especially the good, because the good may benefit those who accomplish it. It is thus that *émigrés* act when, instead of remaining in their countries, attending assemblies and voting to prevent the domination of the wicked, they go abroad to make that domination easier so that excess of evil might give them victory. It is too often thus that political parties have acted. And so, gentlemen, what is there left in our country after so much agitation? Many ruins, fine and great speeches—but no liberal institutions. Whatever our views, we have all of us regretted that instead of allowing ourselves to be obsessed by sterile quarrels, we did not at some time or other help those men of good will such as Roland or Martignac and others like them, that we did not accept the partial reforms they offered us, and that we sacrificed too much to the implacable satisfaction of our personal grudges. I, gentlemen, am not of this school: I am not a pessimist; I accept good from whatever hand it comes to me; I never say "All or nothing", which is a factious and terrible maxim. I say, "a little each day" and I never forget the great injunction, "Sufficient unto the day is the evil thereof": today the law of combinations, tomorrow that of associations. And since the honourable M. Jerome David asked me to, I do not hesitate to declare that in this gesture of the government, I do not see only what is missing from it—the right of public meeting and the right of association—but I see also what is contained in it— the right of combination. I do not confine myself to criticizing what we still lack, I express thanks for what is given to us.'[1]

Having failed to consult with his republican colleagues it was not surprising that he was treated as a traitor. 'His rallying to

[1] *Annales du corps législatif* (1864), vi. 171; the copy in E.L. vi. 534-7 has numerous alterations of phrasing (though not of meaning).

the empire is complete,' exclaimed Garnier-Pagès; and Favre
replied disdainfully to his accusation of pessimism. 'If it is true,'
he said, 'as we have been severely reminded, that pessimists
can impede all things, as for me, I distrust the ready yes-men
who can allow everything; and it is precisely because the bill
under discussion seems to us to be the product of such an attitude
that we cannot give it our approval. There are two schools in
politics: that of principles and that of expedients, and we know
that the public conscience does not mistake them.' On the
following day, incited to even blunter words by Ollivier's able
reply, Favre exclaimed angrily, 'We must be told how old
opinions have now come to be abandoned and a bill proposed
containing measures which absolutely contradict them.'

This was the first occasion on which Ollivier was publicly
called a turncoat in parliament. Morny rushed in with conciliatory words, but the break turned out to be irreparable. After
the debate the two met in the lobbies and Favre held out his
hand. Ollivier exclaimed 'Oh! Oh!' and did not give his in
return. Favre turned and walked silently away. Then Ollivier
had a second impulse and chased after him, but he was already
gone. When friends came to persuade him to make it up, he
replied, 'M. Favre may find it convenient to give me his hand
in the lobbies after insulting me in public: let his reparation be
as public as his insults and I shall then shake hands with him.
We are not at the law courts here.' He was painfully shocked
that even Picard, with whom he was on intimate terms, deserted
him: he could never understand the latter's point of view and
ever after considered that Picard had betrayed their friendship.
Picard, however, thought this was the very crime Ollivier had
committed. 'For me', he wrote sadly, 'Ollivier's straying from
the fold is nothing but a political illness due to the unhealthy
air and prolonged darkness of the despotism. You know how
at night objects take on the most bizarre appearances: darkness
alone explains Morny's appearing in the form of a sincere liberal
and Garnier-Pagès in that of a Montagnard. . . . What can I
say to Ollivier? I allow for all kinds of illusions in politics, for

all kinds of disagreement, but what can one say of an access of fever which hurls a man who yesterday fought on our side furiously against his friends? Can such a disease be cured?'[1]

As Proudhon rightly pointed out, Ollivier's differences with the opposition about combinations were not fundamental.[2] Had he been more tactful and less egocentric, he might well have persuaded some at least of the republican deputies to co-operate in passing the bill. Even at the cost of temporarily effacing himself, he could then indeed have laid the basis for the transformation of a section of his party into the constitutional opposition, instead of merely defecting alone into the Bonapartist ranks. The republicans were not really as irreconcilable as they made themselves out to be. Carnot, for example, to take a name always quoted for republican fidelity, had refused the oath of loyalty to the empire in 1852 and 1857, but against his personal inclination and only in order to conform with the majority decision of the party. He had in 1847 published a pamphlet saying that the Charter of 1830 contained the elements of all the liberties the republicans demanded, that it needed only to be developed further, that he hoped Guizot would follow Peel's example and voluntarily carry out the reforms advocated by the opposition.[3] He had been a collaborator of Pierre Leroux in his youth and, quoting the example of his own father who had served Napoleon I as well as the republic, he had been willing to accept Louis Philippe's monarchy.[4] Jules Simon likewise was, as he himself admitted and as later became notorious, extremely moderate in practice, however radical he may have claimed to be in theory; and he had much in common with

[1] Picard to Ferrouillat, 27 July 1864, in M. Reclus, *Ernest Picard* (1912), 113–14; J. ii. 102–27 ('Ma scission'); E.L. vi. 501–74.

[2] P. J. Proudhon, *De la capacité politique des classes ouvrières* (written in 1865, new edition 1924), 383–4.

[3] H. Carnot, *Les Radicaux et la charte* (1847); Comte d'Alton-Shée, *Souvenirs de 1847 et de 1848* (1879), 137.

[4] *Une Famille républicaine: les Carnots, 1753–1887*, par un Député (1888), 240–1; 'Notice historique sur la vie et les travaux de M. Lazare—Hippolyte Carnot, par M. Jules Simon', in *Mémoires de l'Académie des sciences morales et politiques* (1896), vol. xix, 21, 32–33, 37–38.

Ollivier.[1] The youthful Ferry and Gambetta remained loyal to Ollivier for a few months still: he had a nucleus round which to build.[2]

Ollivier looked on his law of combinations as 'a conquest for the working classes in the social sphere, equal in importance to that of universal suffrage in the political sphere'.[3] Many workers and members of the left wing protested however that its text was so ambiguous that it should really have been entitled 'law against combinations'.[4] This criticism receives some support from a comment made by the public prosecutor of Lyon, who wrote of it: 'We retain sufficient legal powers to preserve order. Experience over many years shows that it is impossible for a combination of impressive numbers to come into existence without threats, [fraudulent] manœuvres and even some violence. Repression will therefore lose none of its energy.'[5] In 1884 Waldeck-Rousseau secured its partial repeal, denouncing it as 'preventing not only felonious combinations, but even all combinations from the moment they become effective'.[6] The idea of 'freedom to work' was unacceptable to trade unionists;[7] and Ollivier has been taken to task because the number of prosecutions for infringing it almost doubled after 1864.[8]

In England, however, the *Saturday Review* wrote that it was

---

[1] 'Notice sur la vie et les œuvres de M. Jules Simon, par M. Liard', ibid., vol. xxi (1898), 621–52; cf. E.L. vi. 564.

[2] E.L. vi. 556; A. Darimon, *Le Tiers Parti sous l'Empire* (1887), 272.

[3] E. Ollivier, *Démocratie et liberté* (1867), 381, article of 29 March 1866.

[4] J. Barberet, *Les Grèves et les coalitions* (1873), 18–19, 148–85; and *Larousse du dix-neuvième siècle*, s.v. Coalitions.

[5] Procureur Général of Lyon, 3 July 1864, quoted by M. Moissonnier, *L'Opposition ouvrière à Lyon à la fin du second empire* (unpublished D.E.S. mémoire 1957), ch. 3, p. 3 n.

[6] Waldeck-Rousseau, *Questions sociales* (1900), 187; but Ollivier's article 416 was repealed with considerable difficulty and only after the senate had in vain sought its retention. Cf. E. Levasseur, *Questions ouvrières et industrielles en France sous la troisième république* (1907), 474–5; *Débats parlementaires, Sénat* (1884), 193–4.

[7] F. D. Longe, 'The Law of Trade Combinations in France', in *Fortnightly Review* (1867), 220–5, 296–309.

[8] M. Leroy, *Histoire des idées sociales en France* (1946–54), iii. 274.

'an improvement on the law then existing and as liberal a measure as could be carried and as France was likely to welcome'. Of Ollivier's open letter, giving his reasons for co-operating with the empire to pass it, it said, 'Modern France has seen few documents from which such good auguries of the future might be drawn. . . . His constituents may perhaps recognize not only the justice of his excuses but the greatness of the service he has rendered to the cause of liberty.'[1] J. S. Mill altered the text in the 1865 editions of his *Principles of Political Economy* to indicate his approval.[2] Today, it is clear that though it undoubtedly did create problems, it was, as Henri Sée has said, 'an act of major importance in the social history of France'.[3] It contributed something to the progress of militant trade unionism: though paradoxically this was disappointing to Ollivier. His ideal was that conflict between master and man should cease. He had proposed, but had been unable to carry, a clause making arbitration compulsory: by this means he had hoped to 'bring about the necessary compromise between capital and labour, the apeasement of hates, the harmonious development of industry and the end of strikes'.[4] Nevertheless, despite its limitations, he considered his achievement to be extremely important. 'One more law like the one on combinations,' he said, 'and within five years the workers will cease to concern themselves with politics.'[5]

[1] *Saturday Review* (11 June 1864), 707, 'Party Spirit in France'.

[2] Contrast the 1st–5th editions of his *Principles of Political Economy*, which make no reference to France, with the later ones, which do.

[3] H. Sée, *Histoire économique de la France* (vol. ii, new edition 1951), 342; cf. J. M. Jeanneney and M. Perrot, *Textes de droit économique et social français* (1957), 216–17; E. Dolléans, *Histoire du mouvement ouvrier* (1948) i. 286; Louis Barthou, 'Des atteintes à la liberté du travail', in *Nouvelle Revue* (1 February 1901), 321–34; P. L. Fournier, *Le Second Empire et la législation ouvrière* (1911).

[4] Conclusion of his report on the law, reprinted in *Démocratie et liberté* (1867), 211.

[5] V. Duruy, *Notes et souvenirs 1811–1894* (1901), i. 217, Duruy to Napoleon, 5 March 1865.

CHAPTER 7

OLLIVIER AND THE CONCESSIONS OF 19 JANUARY 1867

WHEN parliament reassembled in 1865 the opposition group did not invite Ollivier to their meeting, but sent word indirectly that he might be readmitted if he confessed his guilt and acknowledged that he had been mistaken. Ollivier replied by a violent attack on them in the very first debate. 'I cannot associate myself,' he declared, 'with the amendment presented by some of our colleagues of the left saying that far from moving towards liberty, the government is moving away from it. This view is no doubt based on the opinion expressed in another amendment that "it is an illusion to seek progress anywhere except in political liberty". Political liberty is but a guarantee. In a state without social and civil liberties, political liberties are useless and simply sources of danger. Political liberties, gentlemen, are the ramparts that protect a city; but if there is no city, what use are the ramparts?'[1]

The government, he maintained, was moving in the right direction: it was laying essential foundations with laws of civil liberty, like that on combinations; but it must not delay in completing the building, for the youth of the country was turning against it more and more. 'Gentlemen, you are not eternal. . . . Think about finding successors for yourselves. . . . I am convinced that governing is the art of yielding, the art of yielding without giving the appearance of capitulating, the art of yielding

---

[1] Cf. Benjamin Constant: 'Individual liberty . . . that is the true modern liberty. Political liberty is only what guarantees it. . . . ' (*De la liberté des anciens comparée a celle des modernes*, reprinted in *Œuvres politiques de Benjamin Constant*, ed. by C. Louandre (1874), 278–9. E. Laboulaye, *Le Parti libéral: son programme et son avenir* (1864) says the same, p. 12; cf. A. Bertauld, *La Liberté civile: nouvelle étude critique sur les publicistes contemporains* (1864), and also A. Otetea, *François Guichardin, sa vie publique et sa pensée politique* (1926), 228.

in time to the legitimate aspirations of a people. Had Louis XVI
not sacrificed Turgot to the egoism of his court, had he later
listened to the counsels which Mirabeau gave him in his admirable notes, he would have been able to avoid or to master the
revolution. Had the revolution itself stopped before the cursed
days of September, had it listened to Bailly or to Vergniaud,
had it not allowed itself to be carried away into excesses whose
memory still causes us sorrow, it would have ended in liberty
and not in dictatorship, and Bonaparte, for all his genius, could
not have been more than a Washington. Had Napoleon, after
having charmed and conquered France and the world, wished
to attach to himself those whom he had seduced; had he, instead
of replying as he did at Mainz and even after Bautzen that "so
long as this sword hangs by my side, you shall not have the
liberty you long for", had he granted the Additional Act before
his exile to the Isle of Elba, before the Russian campaign, then,
instead of perishing in torture at St. Helena, he would have
ended his days in Paris amidst a satisfied people.' Had Charles X
and Louis Philippe likewise accepted a measure of liberty, they
would not have fallen either. It was necessary not just to yield
but to yield at the right time: and now for the second empire
it was neither too early to yield nor too late—it was the right
moment.

An Additional Act—and that of 1815 had been, as Thiers
himself had admitted, 'the best constitution France had obtained
in its long series of revolutions'—would win over to Napoleon
most of those who were now in opposition. 'I do not hesitate
to declare it publicly today that my most sincere wish, my most
ardent wish, is that the government of the emperor should
consolidate itself with liberty. I once thought that the form of a
government was highly important, more so than anything else;
but I was mistaken. The best government is that which exists,
from the moment the nation accepts it. The vital reason that
has made me believe this with such determination is that when
you make the establishment of a certain form of government
an indispensable preliminary to progress, you are compelled

however moderate you may be to use revolutionary methods; and by revolutionary methods I do not mean only the sedition and violence which some people can never agree to use, I mean also the denigration, the exaggeration of grievances, and the disparagement of atonement made, the criticism levelled in order to discredit and not to improve, those thousand underhand manœuvres employed in all ages by those whom implacable enmity inspires. Now I am convinced that if the good cause in Europe and in France has suffered so many defeats, it is the result of this fatal habit of always opposing in a revolutionary manner. The consequence of this habit is that if the government wins, its victory leaves it irritated and inclined to fall into arbitrary ways. If the government succumbs, the victors, being unable to govern by the methods they employed to obtain their victory, are obliged to contradict themselves, to call in evil expedients to their aid to mask their weakness and to postpone for a short time their fall—which alas means also the fall of liberty.'

To show that he meant what he said, he did what he had never done before: he cast his vote in favour of the address to the throne. This gesture, he declared, would serve as a token of thanks to the Bonapartist majority for their conciliatory move in choosing him to be rapporteur of the law of combinations. It indicated not satisfaction with the government but hope in it, encouragement to it. The appaluse to his speech came from the government side of the house; on the left, where his former republican colleagues sat, there was silence.

'The great event of the other day', wrote the radical Allain-Targé, 'was the defection of Ollivier, who has thrown himself into the arms of the empire without conditions. It is more than a capitulation, it is treason.'[1] The young republicans who had

---

[1] Suzanne de la Porte, 'Autour du 19 Janvier; tiers parti et opposition républicaine (fragments inédits de la correspondance d'Allain-Targé)', *Revue historique* (1937), vol. 179, pp. 135–45, letter of 28 March 1865. Cf. the puzzlement expressed by Baudelaire; 'I have just read the long speech of Emile Ollivier. It is very odd. He speaks, it seems, with the authority of a man who has a great secret in his pocket.'—Charles Baudelaire, *Œuvres complètes, correspondance générale* ed. J. Crépet, vol. v. (1949), 76–77.

formerly almost worshipped him declared they now realized that his oratorical talents were but the attractive ornament of a hollow interior. 'He is neither a man fit to govern,' they said, 'nor a statesman, but simply an admirable phrase-monger . . . who like a barrister pleads the case in favour after having pleaded the case against. I shall never be able to think that this man has ever been sincerely convinced at any time during his political variations.' There were few who were kind enough to attribute his defection from the party to a habit of seeing everything through rose-coloured spectacles. Far more often they accused him of bloated conceit, uncontrollable ambition, and an 'excessive need to be applauded at all costs.'[1]

His conceit was in fact the characteristic which, by adding personal dislike to political disagreement, made the break irreparable. Confidence is no doubt essential to a politician, but with Ollivier this involved a haughty contempt for his opponents— the revolutionaries and the irreconcilables—which made his opinions unbearably obnoxious. He pointed out too frequently that he personally was right and that they, the whole lot of them, were wrong; he thought it a simple statement of fact and did not stop to consider how they would react. He compared himself too complacently to Mirabeau and Sir Robert Peel, both of whom had 'betrayed' their party as he had done; and appeared to consider himself their equal. 'If', as one critic observed, 'the Athenians grew tired of hearing Aristides being called The Just, how should the Parisians not become impatient when they heard Aristides perpetually addressing the same compliment to himself.' 'If only he could get his personal pronoun out of his head,' declared an English journalist, 'he would be one of the most statesmanlike and efficient legislators in France.'[2] One pamphleteer did indeed speak of the 'esteem . . . and sympathy which

---

[1] Juliette Adam, *Mes premières armes littéraires et politiques* (1904), 100; idem, *Mes sentiments et nos idées avant 1870* (1905), 153, 189, 408; J. J. Clamageran, *Correspondance 1849–1902* (1906), 235, 255, 265, 270, 273, 278.

[2] Alphonse Daudet, *Souvenirs d'un homme de lettres* (1889), p.4; Ludovic Halévy, *Carnets* (1935), i. 200–1; P. Guiral, *Prévost-Paradol* (1955), 661; [E. G. Grenville Murray], *Men of the Second Empire* (1872), 99, 103.

this deserter of our party, this apostate of his past still inspires in us. His simple grandeur, the nobility of his disposition, and even that imperturbable naïveness which makes his adversaries laugh, please us as being indications of an elevated and generous soul. . . . M. Ollivier is not a renegade of the vulgar type; he has not so much deserted as lost his way. He has wandered into the clouds, he has not fallen into the mud.' If only he would admit his mistake, they would take him back into the fold.[1] But this was no longer really possible. He would never be trusted again by them.

The attitude of the republicans towards him became not only hostile but vindictive. Morny's last act had been to arrange for Ollivier to be appointed legal adviser to the Khedive of Egypt on matters relating to the Suez Canal. This was not quite a sinecure, but it provided Ollivier with an assured regular income for many years, in return for a very moderate amount of work. The republicans replied by declaring that such a post was one which a practising barrister could not hold, and they pushed a measure through the Bar Council striking his name off the list of the order. Ollivier's relations with his old friends would never have reached such a pass had he not lost his wife so early. Blandine had died in 1862, a month after she had given birth to their only child, Daniel. With her charm and tact she might well have kept the friendship of the young men like Ferry and Gambetta, who now no longer had any inducement to frequent the rue St.-Guillaume. Ollivier underwent a period of acute depression: 'My happiness', he wrote to Liszt, 'is destroyed for ever.' How would he be able to live alone without 'that incomparable being who has given me the only years of happiness I have had in my sad existence'? Her death left him permanently affected: it accentuated his reserve and his isolation.[2]

Gambetta now replaced Ollivier as the idol of the republicans, but Ollivier began to receive new encouragement in liberal and

[1] Anon., *Saint Ollivier, ministre et martyr* (1869), 6.
[2] Letters to Liszt 8 and 9 September 1862; to his father 3 and 11 October 1862; to E. Guiter 31 October 1862; to Mme Singer 18 July and 4 November 1862, O.P.

Bonapartist circles. In April 1865, in his home department of the Var, he was elected unopposed to the *conseil général* (county council).[1] Some Bonapartist deputies offered to finance a newspaper to be edited by him, saying that quite apart from thus advancing their political views, they were certain that such a venture would be a highly profitable investment. Another one, after listening to a speech of his, sent him an anonymous present of a small bronze lion by Barye labelled, 'To the genius of M. Ollivier— a deputy of opposite opinions'. Favourable biographies appeared of him, written by such men as Ernest Daudet (brother of the more famous novelist) and Biard d'Aunet (son of Victor Hugo's mistress). The composer Meyerbeer, who had married off one of his daughters to a stupid nobleman, declared that he now saw his mistake and wanted a real man of value as his son-in-law— 'a man like M. Ollivier for example. That is what I call a man.'[2] Sainte-Beuve, talking of Mirabeau, declared, 'He was the Emile Ollivier of those days.'[3]

Most important of all, he was supported by Emile de Girardin, one of the most powerful journalists of the day. Girardin had pioneered the system on which the modern press is based: he had been the first man in France to found a newspaper which met its costs from advertisement income, which sold at half the price then normal, and which made its profit by having a huge circulation; his paper (*La Presse*, later *La Liberté*) had a sale second only to that of the republican *Siècle*. His keen business sense had won him a fortune, but his talents as a writer also made him a very influential political figure behind the scenes. He was a polemicist with a genius for journalistic strategy, choosing his ground carefully and then fighting his campaigns with the heavy artillery of perpetual repetition, so that his formulae were soon on

[1] A.D. Var II M (5) 78–81.

[2] A man who was present when Meyerbeer said this reported it to Ollivier, and arranged a meeting between them. A friendship was soon formed between them—to be ended however by Meyerbeer's death soon after. Ollivier made a moving speech in his honour at the funeral; but nothing came of the marriage idea. J. ii. 127–30.

[3] J. ii. 136 and 203 (29 July 1864 and 14 July 1865) The lion, now at La Moutte, came from Didier, a friend of Edmond About.

everybody's lips. He had few rivals for incisiveness, for clear and catching phrases, for power in hammering his ideas in with inexhaustible examples and impressive quotations. Though personally a difficult man to get on with—cold, haughty, brief in his conversation to the point of being barely intelligible, independent and uncontrollable—he was tremendously industrious, energetic, and resourceful.[1]

Ollivier gives the impression in his memoirs that Girardin was only an erratic supporter of his cause, but in fact he owed much more to him. Girardin appears to have been the first man to popularize the phrase 'the liberal empire' and to have come to the idea before Ollivier—though Louis Napoleon had advocated it even earlier in his own books. Girardin had throughout his life taken the line that he was 'indifferent to forms of government', and he quoted Mirabeau quoting Pope that the best government is that which administers best. He would never resort to revolution: he called himself a disciple of Turgot (and 'if I were an Englishman, I would be a Peelite'). He always remained outside parties, and he accepted Louis Philippe, the republic, and the empire in turn. In 1852 he had launched a programme of constitutional opposition, saying that the empire should be used for the economic reforms it could accomplish; in 1857 he had supported the election of the Five as a positive means of obtaining liberty by legal methods; and in 1859 he republished his articles on this subject under the title *The Empire with Liberty*. He quoted encouraging passages from Napoleon III's works and added: 'Let the empire mean not only peace, but also liberty (and whatever men say, it can become liberal without danger to itself), and I shall wish that it lasts, as sincerely as, before 1848, I wished that the monarchy should consolidate itself and, after 1848, that the republic should establish itself.' When in 1861, after Ollivier's speech of that year (which made exactly the same point) he hailed the event with the words 'liberty has found its orator', he was not so much declaring support of Ollivier, as welcoming a recruit to his cause. He, like Morny,

[1] M. Reclus, *E. de Girardin* (1934).

was incapable of making speeches, and Ollivier would be an invaluable mouthpiece.[1]

It is interesting that Girardin's view of liberty, like Ollivier's, did not involve parliamentary government. He had long abandoned advocating a constitutional monarch above politics and a responsible ministry and he now preferred the direct government of the people. He was a business man who believed in material progress, prosperity, railways; but he was also an individualist who wished to obtain this without increasing the government's power; he had much sympathy for the ideas of Proudhon and he hoped somehow to reconcile anarchism with modern efficiency. It has been suggested that an 'adventurer' and 'newspaper merchant' like Girardin was not a sound guide, but at least it is to Ollivier's credit that he borrowed selectively from Girardin's copiously confused mass of ideas.[2]

In 1865 finally Ollivier came under the charm of Napoleon III. In May for the first time he accepted an invitation to dinner from Eugénie (after obtaining an assurance that it would be private and no precedent for requiring him to attend official functions in the future). Here at last was the republican in the Tuileries —and he enjoyed himself. At table he was so beguiled by the beautiful lady-in-waiting, Mademoiselle Bouvet, that he had nothing to say to the great legal brain, Ravaisson, who was on his other side. Afterwards, in the drawing-room, when he stood rather isolated among the Bonapartist dignitaries, the empress came up to him, asked him to be seated, and talked with him alone for an hour. To the fears she expressed about the consequences of the law of combinations, the dangers of freedom of the press, arguing that a certain amount of dictatorship was

---

[1] Odysse Barot, *Historie des idées au dix-neuvième siècle: Emile de Girardin, sa vie, ses idées, son œuvre, son influence* (1866), 127–8; E. de Girardin, *L'Empire avec la liberté* (1859), 44, 89, 102; E.L. v. 175; A. Darimon, *A travers une révolution* (1884), 313; idem, *Les Cinq sous l'empire* (1885), 89–91; J. Vier, *Emile de Girardin inconnu*, (privately printed, 1949).

[2] E. de Girardin, *La Politique universelle* (1852) and *L'Empire avec la liberté* (1859); G. Thuillier, 'Les idées politiques d'Emile de Girardin', *La Revue Administrative* (1959), 134–6; J. Barthélemy, 'Un grand industriel de la presse, Emile de Girardin', *Revue politique et parlementaire*, vol. 159 (June 1934), 514–20.

necessary in order to effect economic reforms, he was able to
object freely and at length. He was pleased to astonish her by
concluding: 'Your Majesty will allow me to say something which
I hope she will remember. You will come to accept liberty. You
will one day think as I do.' Then, on taking leave, he added,
'I am at present attempting a considerable task. I am trying to
transform a violent democracy into a constitutional democracy.
But my work is now meeting with an obstacle: people think I
wish to become a minister This weakens me and I am obliged
to avoid everybody connected with the government. I am above
all anxious that I should be considered an honest man. . . .'

'It is enough', interrupted Eugénie, 'to have spoken with you
for a minute to be sure of that.' Ollivier was pleased when it was
reported to him that she had been impressed by him and his 'air
of profound conviction in what he says': that she had found him
charming, that he had spoken to her without embarrassment,
as one does to a woman in whom one feels sympathy and whom
one wished to please, and that she was very grateful for this. He
in turn was impressed by her, observing that she was different
from what popular rumour supposed. Her beauty was certainly
very remarkable, but she had shown a lively intelligence as well.
'At sixteen,' she had said, 'I was a follower of Fourier. I have
always been fond of political economy. I know I have the reputation of being a woman who likes reading nothing but novels,
but this does not displease me.'[1]

A month later, the empress invited Ollivier to join a committee
she had formed to examine the treatment of juvenile criminals,
and when he accepted she asked him to call on her to discuss it.
On 27 June he duly came to the Tuileries once more and Mademoiselle Bouvet 'whom I found even more beautiful than the
first time' led him to the empress' apartments. He found Eugénie
alone, sitting at a little table laden with books. After they had
talked a short while, the door was opened very slightly for a
moment. She made a sign as though to someone outside, and
continued the conversation. A few minutes later the door was

[1] D., 7 and 10 May 1865.

flung open and Eugénie rising to her feet cried in a loud voice
and in a theatrical manner that shocked Ollivier: 'The Emperor'.
Ollivier rose and moved forward to meet for the first time 'the
man of December'.

'I have often heard about you,' said Napoleon, 'from one of
my friends—from Morny.'

'Oh, yes,' replied Ollivier. 'He was a man of acute vision,
charming, tough, and I had great affection for him.'

'He also,' said Napoleon, 'greatly esteemed your talent.'

The emperor asked him about the political attitude of the
working class. Ollivier said that hostility to the dynasty had
diminished greatly, but that the demand for liberty was increasing.

'What liberties are needed, then?'

Ollivier said that first of all there should be liberty in elections.
'Thus there is for example a by-election at this moment in
Auvergne [to replace Morny]. I do not know its result. . . .'

'M. Girot [the opposition candidate] has won.'

'Well, then, what was the purpose of saying in the prefect's
newspaper that to vote for M. Girot is to vote against the emperor's government?'

'You are right,' replied Napoleon, 'but what do you want?
One cannot but use men and men are carried away by their
zeal. This is a question of degree.'

Ollivier then criticized the censorship of the press, but the
emperor defended it saying, 'All governments make mistakes
and newspapers perpetually try to make the mistakes rankle.'
Eugénie also maintained that a free press would be dangerous,
insisting above all on the dishonesty of its reporting. Ollivier
in return pointed out the absurdities of the existing system of
control; newspapers were allowed to print what they wanted,
but were then suppressed if they said anything which was personally resented by any particular minister.

'Yes, it is difficult,' said Napoleon, 'but what system can one
find?' He listened in silence, as was his habit, while Ollivier
argued in favour of ending all administrative control, leaving
slander and similar offences to be punished through the normal

legal procedure, with trial by jury. He ended by saying, 'Your government is strong enough to dare a great deal', which, as might be expected, rather struck Napoleon.

Ollivier was, as he wrote soon afterwards, 'literally charmed by the emperor. He was gay that day, easily given to merriment, not talkative certainly, but conversing enough. When he has not got a clear and decisive reply to make, he remains silent: what he does say is always just. His eye is lively, soft, acute and caressing. He appears to be cold, but I think from timidity rather than from stiffness. One feels that he has a delicate, sensitive, feminine nature. I do not think that he can be carried by assault: he must be acted on by slow and patient insinuation. The dogmatic and the impetuous will fail with him, at least usually. There is hope only for the flexible (in the good sense of the word) and the gentle. . . . His health seemed to be good. Only he appeared to be weary intellectually: one feels that one would bore him quickly: at any rate the blasé can be seen under his pleasant manner. . . . I do not know about what it was that he said: It is necessary to advance little by little. These words seemed to me to sum up his true state of mind. He does not intend to retreat but, at least at present, he will not rush forward: he will advance gradually if he does move at all. We have not yet reached the crowning of the edifice. . . . I avoided insisting on anything to him, or preaching a programme to him. I wished to show him clearly that I was not determined to make a conquest of him. I acted towards him as one does towards a woman one meets in a drawing-room. If one ever gets anywhere with these people, it is not by offering oneself: they care only for people who seem to be ready to do without them. So though etiquette requires one to wait till he grants one leave to go, I rose after an hour and took leave myself.'

Once again he was pleased to learn that Napoleon in turn had been impressed. 'M. Ollivier is not as people have tried to make me think, a mere man with ambition. It is enough to see him for a minute to be sure that he is an honest man, a convinced man. Morny was right.' He had added to Walewski, 'There is in the legislature a man for whom I have a great liking, who must be watched—Ollivier.' Walewski replied, 'You have been misled if you have been told that M. Ollivier is a man "to be had". M. Ollivier has political ideas. If you want him, consider whether you want to do what will be necessary to gain him.'[1]

It was in this way that Napoleon and Ollivier ceased to be enemies. They now lost the prejudices they had had about each other and instead developed a mutual respect which could be the basis of a fruitful co-operation. But why was it almost five years before Ollivier became Napoleon's minister? Why, that is to say, did the liberal empire come so late and perhaps too late? Part of the answer is that the accusations of ambition and treachery levelled against Ollivier made him determined to prove his critics conclusively wrong. He deliberately cultivated an attitude of disdain for the prizes of politics and sought to hold himself ostentatiously aloof from the struggle for power. He was 'weary of public life', he declared, 'of its miseries, its platitudes, the lack of good faith among its participants, and the monotony of its action'.[2] He took refuge for half the year in his country home on the south coast; he gave free rein to the fatalistic side of his nature and his favourite books now were the *Introduction to the Devout Life* and Marcus Aurelius's *Meditations*. 'I find it so hard', he wrote, 'to say whether an event is fortunate or unfortunate, that the best course is neither to rejoice nor to grieve but to give oneself up in all docility of mind to the will of Him who holds all in His hands.'[3] Determined to avoid being minister at all costs, he would remain a simple member of parliament influencing policy but taking no active part in its conduct himself. He conceived for himself, in fact, the role of *eminence grise* of the second empire, aspiring to influence it without committing himself to it. In this he miscalculated entirely and the years 1866–7 showed how impossible his plan was.

For this was the very period when Rouher reached the zenith

---

[1] D., 27 June 1865 and 7 January 1866.
[2] Letter to Girardin, copy in D., 20 October 1865.
[3] Letter to Mme Fould, copy in D., 28 September 1865.

of his ascendancy and might. Rouher had made his mark in 1848 as a vigorous, die-hard conservative, demanding the suppression of socialism and its 'baneful theories', insisting that the need of the time was 'order' and 'strong government'. Enlisting in the cause of Louis Napoleon, in whom he saw a saviour of society against the revolutionary menace, and becoming head of the government prosecution office, he had been particularly energetic in suppressing the left-wing opposition. It was he who in December 1851 had been responsible for drawing up the constitution which gave France eighteen years of despotism. After a period as vice-president of the Conseil d'Etat, he was in 1855 made minister of agriculture, industry, and commerce, in which office he worked to promote the economic prosperity for which the reign is famous. He believed that social progress could best be obtained by the government establishing political order and giving private enterprise a free hand to expand in the economic field; and he was thus the principal negotiator of the free trade treaty of 1860. His vast capacity for work, his exceptional command of detail, and his great vigour as the government's spokesman in parliament caused him to acquire enormous influence and to be nicknamed 'the vice-emperor'. Ollivier does not appear to have realized how greatly Napoleon valued Rouher, nor how strongly Rouher had entrenched himself with a network of allies during his long years of office, when 'he suffered no job, no decoration, no favour to be given without his advice'.[1]

Rouher was hostile to liberal concessions in politics and he might long have postponed them and remained impregnable but for the reverses the empire began to suffer in its foreign policy. The tragic fiasco of Mexico and the humiliation of France after the Austro-Prussian War seemed to call imperatively for some popular measure to strengthen Napoleon's waning prestige. For some time, Napoleon hesitated, held back partly by the empress but no less by his own authoritarian instincts. 'You

---

[1] H. Pessard, *Mes Petits Papiers* (1887), 227; cf. the interesting reminiscences of J. Simon, *Premières Années* (1901), 428, and generally R. Schnerb, *Rouher* (1949).

are wrong to think', Ollivier remarked, 'that the emperor has plans. If he did he would have been overthrown a hundred times already. His strength is in having none and in allowing himself to be carried along by events. He has aspirations, but not plans.'[1] But he was finally stirred into action by Walewski. This illegitimate son of Napoleon I, having succeeded Morny as president of the legislature, aspired to his mantle as leader of the liberal empire. He was jealous of Rouher's dominance and was besides a genuine liberal, who had begun his career during the July Monarchy as a protégé of Thiers and who had remained faithful to him. Unfortunately, he was a rather second-rate politician, with nothing like the ability of either Morny or Thiers. The liberal plot he and Napoleon planned therefore emerged as a half-measure, based on confused and timid thinking.[2]

On 31 December 1866 Walewski offered Ollivier the ministry of education in a cabinet which, he said, would represent the crowning of the edifice and the inauguration of a new liberal era. However, when he went into details, it appeared that the only constitutional changes he proposed were to allow ministers to defend themselves personally in parliament (though they would not be members of it), and to give parliament the right of interpellating the government on matters of policy. Walewski insisted that the emperor had great confidence in Ollivier's abilities and character as well as fondness for him personally, and that he believed his presence in the government was necessary to show that a new departure was really being made.

Without hesitation Ollivier replied: 'I cannot agree. I shall defend you in the legislature as a deputy, and this will benefit you more. I am firmly resolved not to accept a ministry.' When

[1] Letter to Princess Carolyne Wittgenstein (former mistress of Liszt), copy in D., 28 October 1866.

[2] P. Poirson, *Walewski* (1943); Comte d'Ornano, *La Vie passionnante du Comte Walewski* (1953); F. Chalamon de Bernardy, *Un Fils de Napoléon: le Comte Walewski* (Paris Univ. 1951 doctoral thesis, typescript in the Sorbonne); Bibliothèque Nationale, N. A. Fr. 20617 f. 98–99, (Walewski to Thiers, 12 October 1846) and N. A. Fr. 23066 f. 323–4 (Persigny to Napoleon, draft, 29 March 1865).

pressed, however, he agreed to think it over, and for a time inclined to the view that he would be wrong to allow his immediate reaction of personal distaste for office to hinder what might be a decisive step forward in his country's history. He wrote therefore to say that he would agree to join the government provided the emperor went further than appeared to be his intention. He must inaugurate this liberal era in a more decisive manner. Bills should be introduced at once allowing freedom of the press and public meetings, ending interference in elections, enabling ministers to be members of the legislature; Napoleon should promise a foreign policy of peace, and publicly declare that these measures meant the definite turning of a new leaf and the advent of the liberal empire.

Napoleon was, however, in too hesitant a mood to go so far, to make so complete a capitulation, and Ollivier was reaffirmed in his belief that it would be unwise for him to accept office as yet. If he did, he would be a mere appendix to a government consisting almost entirely of men who had long served the despotism, and in a helpless minority in it. He would be isolated from parliament (since he would have to resign his seat); he would lose the strength he derived from being 'the representative of public opinion'; and the accusations of ambition would be justified. He determined therefore not to accept office except at the head of a liberal parliamentary majority. That majority did not yet exist. For the time being, he would best assist progress by encouraging the existing government under Rouher to introduce liberal reforms itself.

When invited to see the emperor he found him in a good mood, as he always was when planning some new coup, but slightly hesitant also. The empress, who was the only one in the secret apart from Walewski, had agreed with him that liberal reforms were necessary, but had maintained that this was not the opportune moment for them. Napoleon was therefore wavering a little about it, for he paid quite extraordinary attention to her views; and he now interrogated his guest in the hope of finding arguments to convince himself that he was right. What did Ollivier think of the present situation?—There was dissatisfaction, came the answer: 'It seems to me that your majesty must carry out a vigorous act to show the persistence of your individual initiative, that you must resolutely affirm your intention of maintaining peace; and this is not possible except by a series of liberal measures.'

'My information is just so; but what liberal measures?' asked Napoleon, trying to draw him out. Ollivier spoke of the need, first of all, for the ministers to be members of parliament. 'But do you not fear', said Napoleon, 'that this will bring a return to a parliamentary régime, and that the assemblies will begin again to make and unmake ministers?'—The assemblies, answered Ollivier, would have neither more nor less rights than they already had. 'As it is, they can, if they think it useful, compel you to dismiss a minister.'

'How?'

'By refusing a section of the budget with a rider that they were doing so in order to obtain a change of minister. In such a case, what would your majesty do? You would be obliged to dissolve the assembly or to change the minister.'

'You are right,' replied Napoleon, as though he had not thought of this possibility before. 'But would it be opportune? Would I not appear to be doing this to obtain pardon for my setbacks in Mexico and Germany? . . . I am of your opinion. I must do something resolute and liberal. I am doubtful only about the moment. . . . And you,' he added, 'it appears that you believe that you cannot take office?'

'No. I do not wish it to be said that I am supporting you because I profit from it. Let me prove that there are still men of character left. I do not like power. . . . So many people think it is the height of bliss, whereas it is but a burden, except when one succeeds in one's task. One must prove one can live without it. The less I receive from you, the stronger I shall be in defending your liberal measures. Later, if it is necessary, I shall aid you as much as you please.'

'I find your reasons so good,' answered Napoleon, 'that I

yield to them. But it is clearly understood that I do so only *temporarily*.'

'Sire,' said Ollivier as they parted, 'I am happy at the decision your majesty is making. For your majesty it means greatness, for the country it means happiness. You can count on my help.'

Ollivier was once again charmed by Napoleon, by the gentle voice and kind manner, though he observed with concern that the emperor was obviously more interested in the effect his measures would produce 'than in what they ought to be from the moral point of view'. This was in fact a difference between the two men which remained to the end. Ollivier was the theorist, the moralist, of the liberal empire, while Napoleon took to it as a matter of opportunism, from mere empirical calculation. Their different approaches were in fact probably a source of strength to them, a guarantee that working together they would season their logic with common sense.

Ollivier now became, as it were, honorary consultant on liberal reforms, but this placed him in as false a position as actually joining the government would have done. For the reforms announced on 19 January 1867 completely failed to make any impression on the popular imagination. Ministers could now defend themselves in person before parliament, but they could not be members of it; parliament could interpellate them, but this concession was counterbalanced by the abolition of its right to vote an annual address to the throne. A relaxation in the laws on the press and public meetings was promised. Obviously, all would depend on the way these measures were actually put into practice; but the country was given little ground for optimism. Most of the ministers who had served the despotism remained in office and, more oddly still, Walewski the prime abettor of the new régime, was almost at once dismissed. The indispensable Rouher remained supreme.

The emperor instructed him to obtain Ollivier's co-operation in working out the details of the projected bills; but Rouher, conscious and jealous of his power, held it as a grievance that Ollivier had 'espoused M. Walewski's hostility against me' and ignored him.[1] Thus Ollivier who had at first greeted the letter of 19 January as a further victory for his policy, was now in turn puzzled, embarrassed, disillusioned, and finally led to proclaim publicly his disappointment. He had had a vision of reforms magnanimously self-imposed, of the government turning a new leaf, but he now realized to what an extent questions of policy were dominated by those of persons. It was all very well to be agreed in theory, but who was to put the theory into practice? How could Napoleon, convinced though he might be of the need for change, reward ministers, who had rendered long and faithful service, by dismissing them? Ollivier was no doubt right in thinking that he would be helpless if he joined a predominantly reactionary government, but it was even worse being its ignored, disowned, back-stage prompter. The episode of 19 January bore the obvious lesson that in order to fulfil his policy, Ollivier must have behind him a majority in parliament to sustain him and to compel the sovereign to accept it.

The episode was equally instructive to Napoleon. His over-subtle plot, which he expected to give him the best of both worlds, to establish liberty, but without conceding any great changes, proved to be absolutely a *coup manqué*: it was just not radical or decisive enough to make any impression on the masses. He was too obviously giving with one hand and taking back with the other. His latest petty alterations to his constitution were too reminiscent of those he had made in 1860 for men to believe that they would make much difference. It was all too like '*The Last Word of Rocambole*'—the latest volume in a best-selling series of novels about the adventures of a hero who had been killed many times but who had been perpetually resuscitated to take part in further adventures, and whose creator was now promising that this time he would be killed once and for all. Who could believe any more in this than in Napoleon's

[1] The liberal plan of 19 January was tied up with a personal intrigue by Walewski to oust Rouher, just as that of 24 November 1860 had been directed by Persigny against Fould. In both cases the intrigues failed, largely because Fould and Rouher were men with specialized economic knowledge, unlike the mere politicians Persigny and Walewski.

assertion that this last move was the final 'crowning of the edifice'? Therefore, just as after the derisory fiascos of Strasbourg and Boulogne Napoleon could not risk a third repulse, so in his liberal experiments, after the abortive half-measures of 1866 and 1867, there was now room only for a decisive and thorough transformation.[1]

[1] For this chapter generally see D., 31 December 1866–February 1867; E. Ollivier, *Le 19 Janvier* (1869) and his *Empire libéral*, vol. 9 (1904); R. Schnerb, *Rouher* (1949); J. Maurain, *Baroche* (1936).

CHAPTER 8

THE ESTABLISHMENT OF THE LIBERAL EMPIRE, 1867–70

WHY did Napoleon III eventually select Ollivier to lead his liberal empire rather than Thiers, who was richer both in experience and in prestige? What significance and what consequences did his choice of the former have? At one time it had seemed that some agreement with Thiers was envisaged. In 1840 he had been appointed prime minister in Louis Napoleon's proclamation of Boulogne. In 1857 the emperor did him the rare honour of referring to him in a public speech as the country's 'national historian', for his work on the *Consulate and Empire*. Thiers then submitted a plan of liberal reform to Napoleon through the British ambassador; Morny, Walewski, and Maupas, all of whom had known him under the July monarchy, sounded him out at various times on the possibility of his joining the government, believing that his love of power would eventually get the better of his scruples. Thiers, however, had insisted on being foreign minister and on having the title of prime minister too: he expected Napoleon, that is, to capitulate to him. The spasmodic negotiations thus came to nothing, partly because Thiers' terms were too high, but partly also because the two men disagreed too profoundly in their approach to politics. Thiers seemed to imply a return to the past in both domestic and foreign policy, the abandonment of Napoleon's championship of nationalities, and the restoration of Louis Philippe's constitutional monarchy: Napoleon flatly rejected 'the complete and immediate return to parliamentary government'.[1]

[1] H. Malo, *Thiers* (1932), 441–7; *The Paris Embassy during the Second Empire*; selections from the papers of ... Earl Cowley edited by his son, F. A. Wellesley (1928), 212.

Thiers, moreover, was essentially the representative of the middle classes, interested in a rather conservative form of political liberty but very little in social reform. Napoleon on the other hand had said, 'I want as my ministers only men who love the people: I had the misfortune to begin my career through the old rue de Poitiers; I should not like to end it in alliance with a new version of it.'[1] When Ollivier took office, the empress explained that he 'was the only democrat in the cabinet, and consequently the only acceptable intermediary between the emperor and the people. The other members of it are all conservatives who are more or less millionaires.'[2] The emperor himself told Ollivier that the upper classes 'caress me because they are afraid, but they do not like me, we are not of the same race, whereas you and I may disagree on certain questions, but basically our sentiments are identical.'[3] Thiers would insist on the upper hand in any alliance, whereas Napoleon felt he would be able to control Ollivier, and looked upon him indeed as a prospective pupil. 'Ollivier', he said, 'is certainly a man of talent: he is young still: he has a future before him and could achieve great things if he is properly guided. . . . [He] has two precious qualities which make me forget his defects. He has faith in me and he interprets my ideas eloquently, above all when I let him think they are his own.'[4] 'When Ollivier comes to see me, I find him restful. He is the only politician I have met who has faith in me and who has no ulterior motives. I wish I had known him earlier. I like him even when he is wrong.'[5]

However, it was not caprice or personal considerations alone that settled the issue. Ollivier played a decisive part in winning both the country and parliament to the idea of the liberal empire, which became associated with his name rather than with that of

---

[1] E.L. xii. 177, and 157. Cf. J. ii. 311 (11 February 1868). The rue de Poitiers was where the conservative, monarchist deputies of 1848–51 used to meet, under the leadership of Berryer, Broglie, Molé, Thiers, &c.
[2] H. Oncken, *Die Rheinpolitik Kaiser Napoleons III von 1863 bis 1870* (Stuttgart, 1926), iii. 337.   [3] D. 1870 J. ii. (446–7).
[4] Oncken, op. cit., iii. 336–7 and 350. (Metternich to Beust, 26 March and 14 May 1870).   [5] J. ii. 443 (12 May 1870).

Thiers. His disappointment with the reforms of 19 January led him to embark on a new policy. He vigorously set about attacking the great obstacle he now saw to stand in his way, the omnipotent Rouher, his works and his henchmen. In the debates of the year 1868 he acted as a full member of the opposition and mercilessly criticized the bills on the press and public meetings for being mere half-measures, inadequate and weak. Such was the power and the energy of his assaults that the old days of the Five seemed to return: there could no longer be equivocation about his attitude, and his popularity rapidly revived. The conservative Bonapartists were so infuriated by his attitude that one of their most fervid leaders challenged him to a duel. At one session such insults were exchanged and tempers rose to such unwonted heights that on the following day Ollivier went with two pistols in his pockets and a sword-stick in his hand, determined, as he unashamedly confessed, to blow Cassagnac's brains out if he dared slander him again.

All this reflected the characteristic violence that invaded almost every sphere of political life in these last years of the authoritarian empire. The press, as soon as it was freed from censorship and control repaid the government for this liberty by unbridled and virulent abuse. In some sections of it the summons to revolution became a daily routine: newspapers like the *Lanterne*, edited by Rochefort, contained the most provoking attacks, which were so extreme indeed that even that old radical Ledru-Rollin wrote to *The Times* to say that though he wanted liberty, he did not want it at the price of civil war, to which Rochefort's tactics were inevitably leading. 'Sire,' said someone to the emperor, talking of this *Lanterne*, 'the paper is read, but most of those who read it despise it.' 'I know,' replied he, 'but there are women whom one despises and whom nevertheless one does not disdain to court.' The revolutionary menace was no less dangerous in itself than because of the use to which it might be put by the conservative enemies of the régime.[1]

[1] Hector Pessard, *Mes Petits Papiers, 1860-70* (1887), 248; Robert Mitchell, *Un Demi-siècle de mémoires* (1911), i. 45.

Napoleon bore with it because, as he said, if a free press brought no other advantage, at least it gave him the power to have a newspaper of his own which would not be censored by his ministers. Soon it was an open secret that the *L'Epoque*, edited by the young Clément Duvernois, was subsidized by him, and no small source of bewilderment to the Bonapartists that it contained articles, apparently inspired, waging war against the vice-emperor Rouher and his reactionary followers. Should loyal men therefore turn liberal? If Rouher was about to fall, would it not be wise to join the victorious party in good time? All the while, however, Rouher seemed to be impregnable, backed by the empress, and returning fire with no less energy through a paper of his own.

This chaos in the councils of the government gave Ollivier his chance. He had no doubt now about the lesson of 19 January: he must either direct the government as its leading minister or else oppose it: it was no use trying to influence it without actually controlling it. He must form a party in parliament to impose his policy on Napoleon, and now this was not as impossible as had once seemed. In the early years of the reign the menace of revolution had loomed so large and the prestige enjoyed by the sovereign was so overwhelming that the legislature could not oppose a government which practically the whole nation hailed as the 'saviour of society'. It approved its measures almost unanimously, willy-nilly, and so got the reputation of being composed of mere puppets—a reputation increased by the fact that at the not very free elections its members were approved, recommended and assisted by the government. The outward impression of servility was, however, false. The legislature contained many men of independent standing, who had had experience of parliamentary government under previous régimes, whose fathers and grandfathers had often been deputies before them and whom the government had accepted as its official candidates because it had not dared dispute their power in their constituencies. These men had acquiesced in the empire from necessity, to save themselves from the 'reds'; like Morny they would have called in the Cossacks of Imperial Russia rather than have allowed a socialist victory. But now that the danger had passed they began to believe, to hint, and then to insist that a change of system was needed. They felt that although in 1852 Napoleon, fresh from his victory at the plebiscite, had represented the nation's will, now with the passage of time the frequently re-elected parliament inevitably represented it better. They did not ask that the emperor should therefore hand over his power to them, but only that he should rule 'with their advice and consent'; that instead of continuing to leave the fate of the country dependent upon the life of one sick man, he should give permanence to his work by basing it upon lasting institutions. The test of statesmanship lay, after all, in the power to provide for the future, in the power to cure diseases and not simply to remove symptoms. When the men who had personally experienced the terrors of the republic had passed away, who would there be left to support dictatorship? How could the youth of the country, which was by nature and by tradition hostile to governments, be won over except by a share in power? How indeed could young men generally be prevented from turning rebel against the old except by a share in the latter's responsibilities?

The *Saturday Review* had said in 1863 that the deputies ventured now to laugh when they were amused, 'unless the Duke of Morny looks very fierce.'[1] After Morny's death, their position was rather like that of the members of the English house of commons in the reign of James I. Country gentlemen there, as in the legislature of Napoleon III, had been bred to believe that it was their duty to aid their king, but they found themselves increasingly without that leadership from able privy councillors to which they had been accustomed under Queen Elizabeth; and leaders like Pym and Eliot could therefore rise among them in their stead. So likewise in the second empire, since the ministers were not members of the legislature, a gulf inevitably grew between ministers and deputies, who began to look for guidance from among the more energetic of their number. There were indeed

[1] *Saturday Review*, 14 February 1863, p. 190.

quite a few who had developed a mastery of technical subjects or revealed gifts of oratory and exposition which made them feel capable of doing more than simply giving advice.

This is what gave Ollivier his opportunity. He perceived that to realize his ambitions he needed to win over not only the emperor but these men too. The most successful reforms, he said, were self-imposed: 'The best plan is for us to mix as much as possible with the liberal elements in the house', to encourage them in their growing but still hesitant voicing of their demands. He cunningly saw, however, that the condition of winning them over was that they should not be made to feel that they were attacking the emperor. He therefore drafted extremely moderate interpellations suggesting as inoffensively as possible that more liberty was needed, and he got his friends to collect signatures for these interpellations among the majority. He made sure that the republicans did not sign them and he abstained from doing so himself so that they should in no way appear to be hostile acts. When members of the majority had voted for liberty once, they found new courage in the support of their fellows, they got into a habit of expressing their opinions more freely, and they lost their distaste for associating with the opposition. It was in this way that by 1869 Ollivier was successful in obtaining 101 votes in favour of a more liberal constitution.[1]

He was not of course the only one responsible for organizing this growing agitation. Thiers, Buffet, and Latour du Moulin, among others, played an important part; there were numerous divisions among the recruits; and Ollivier was far from being the undisputed leader of their coalition. Chesnelong (whose election had been sponsored by the government but who turned out to be a very independent clerical) accurately summed up the attitude of these men when he said of Ollivier that 'exposed to the wrath of his former friends, still suspect to his new allies, admired for the brilliance of his talent, esteemed for his generous

---

[1] 'La Legislative 1863-9', in *La Liberté*, 2-7 May 1869; A. Darimon, *Le Tiers Parti sous l'Empire* (1887); C. Latour du Moulin, *Autorité et liberté* (1874) preface to volume two on 'Le Tiers Parti et les 116'.

qualities, feared for the vagueness of his aspirations and the uncertain rashness of his character, he was more admired than followed. . . . He was an admirable orator, although his oratory, always literary in form and artistically sculptured, dazzled rather than persuaded. Lively, colourful, arranged with art, dignified by the beauty of its form, free of unnecessary length or bad taste, it rose high rather than penetrated deep: it thrilled the imagination rather than stirred the heart. It had, truth to tell, more brilliance than power; yet at times the vigour of the thought and the emotion of the heart widened its inspiration; it then attained the summit of eloquence.'[1] Ollivier fascinated and frightened them: a republican commented that they would prefer to do without 'this ambitious and rash personality who has more talent and principle than themselves and who would become not their ally but their tyrant'.[2] They might perhaps prefer to follow the dull, solid, thoroughly bourgeois Buffet who personified moderation and honesty, but they could neither ignore nor avoid Ollivier.

Ollivier now brought out a book entitled *The Nineteenth of January*, an address to his electors (with a motto from Benjamin Constant's *Memoir on the Hundred Days* on the cover), in which he sought to explain himself and to justify his conduct. It was a vigorous political autobiography, designed to show that he had been consistent all his life, that his conversations with the emperor (which he narrated in detail) did not represent a betrayal of his mandate as an opposition deputy, and that the time had come now for the dissolution of the old parties and the union of all lovers of liberty. Twenty thousand copies were sold in less than a month, but with what effect on the general public it is naturally difficult to say. Sainte-Beuve wrote to congratulate him: 'You have envisaged a fine ideal of union, of generously forgetting the past, of foreseeing the future. Despite the names you quote

---

[1] C. Chesnelong, *Les Derniers Jours de l'empire et le gouvernement de M. Thiers. Mémoires publiés par son petit-fils* (1932), 13–15.
[2] Allain-Targé to his father, 28 March 1865, in *Revue historique* (1937) vol. 179, p. 135–45.

to support you, you have obtained your truly patriotic and dis-interested inspiration from none but yourself; what you are attempting has an originality which I would say is unique and which is entirely honourable. In many passages you recount and explain it to us with eloquence. Your conclusion is extremely noble.'[1] Prévost Paradol on the other hand described it as 'the most naïve monument of conceit and self-admiration any man has ever raised'.[2] The book was so full of 'Je', men declared, that its publication had to be postponed until the printer could get a further supply of Js. 'It is written with a candid self esteem', wrote Ludovic Halévy, 'which is disarming. . . . Never has a man said more frankly and at the same time more proudly: "I wanted to be minister, minister at all costs, minister no matter how, minister in any ministry, with or without M. Rouher, but minister, minister, mi-ni-ster. Nothing has availed me. They did not want me, they made game of me and that is why France owes me its liberty, that is why there is no citizen purer than I." I, I, I, always I, nothing but I. And this man is convinced, per-fectly convinced . . . and he has talent. It is written with much animation.'[3] Ollivier's conceit was a standing joke in political circles. He 'makes statements', wrote Allain-Targé, 'which make one die of laughter. He says, "France is in my hands" &c. . . . He confides in his barber, and so makes the latter's fortune: everyone goes to be shaved by him to learn the secrets of the state.'[4] Even Renan, who considered him 'intelligent', found him 'always vain and self-centred'.[5]

However, the election of 1869 showed that, personal questions put apart, his policy was widely approved and substantially representative of a large section of the country. He was of course too moderate for Paris, where the irreconcilable radical Bancel

---

[1] E.L. xi. 475.

[2] P. Guiral, *Prévost-Paradol* (1955), 661.

[3] L. Halévy, *Carnets* (1935) i. 186.

[4] Allain-Targé to his father and mother, 2 February 1867, *Revue historique* (1937), vol. 179, pp. 141-2.

[5] E. Renan to Cornélie Renan, 28 July 1868, *Œuvres complètes d'Ernest Renan*, ed. H. Psichari (1947-60), ix. 1446.

defeated him by 22,840 votes to 12,848; but then even the respected republican Carnot was considered too mild and was ousted by Gambetta, the rising star of the extreme left. Ollivier, who had once been a bright young man denouncing the stupidity of old party leaders, now found the tables turned: Gambetta sadly reflected on the necessity of 'political parricide'. [1] Ollivier, however, made a valiant resistance: he offered to hold a public disputation with Bancel at a joint meeting, and when that was refused he held a great meeting at the Chatelet Theatre, despite organized obstruction. Bancel's supporters filled much of the hall and a huge crowd packed the square outside, shouting to prevent him from being heard, singing the Marseillaise and the Chant du Départ, blowing on whistles—a sackful of which had been presented by a hostile manufacturer. The police advised Ollivier to stay away; he reached the rostrum after much difficulty and at great personal risk. With remarkable skill he at length silenced the boos and the cat-calls. He pointed out that Bancel represented revolution, and 'at every period of French history, the great statesmen, of whom I am the humble disciple . . . have recognized that a revolution is nearly always a defeat for liberty', ending in dictatorship. A distinguished scientist later recounted that he had gone to this meeting as a student, determined to boo, but had ended by applauding. Half-way through the speech some of the audience jumped on to the stage and in the ensuing riot the meeting was dissolved by the police amid 'an indescribable agitation'. Gustave Schlumberger recalled how, as a medical student at this time, 'he applauded above all Emile Ollivier, whose magnificent and too hollow eloquence carried us away, so young and inexperienced were we. After that famous meeting at the Chatelet Theatre, where the partisans of his opponent, the radical Bancel, threatened him with death and devastated the neighbouring café, we acclaimed him for the whole evening with frenzied applause. On the morrow we went in a deputation to congratulate him in the name of the

---

[1] Gambetta to Dr. E. Fieuzal, 2 April 1869. *Lettres de Gambetta, 1868-1882*, ed. D. Halévy and E. Pillias (1938), letter 13.

university. He embraced two or three of us. "You were magnificent," we told him. "Yes, I was magnificent," he replied with naïve pride.'[1]

Paris was clearly hostile to the empire, but it is seldom representative of France as a whole, and in the provinces the results were very different. In the department of Var, where Ollivier's home now was, he was put up by his friends as an independent candidate, against both an official Bonapartist, Lescuyer d'Attainville (the son-in-law of the Duc de Rivoli), and a radical, Clément Laurier, friend of Gambetta. The conservatives were so terrified by the violence of the latter's polemic that they saw in Ollivier the only man who could save them from the reds, and they began cheering him with unwonted enthusiasm. There was a 'movement of public opinion'. They, who were accustomed to leaving the government to arrange the election, now spontaneously organized a meeting of some thousand notables of the department—mayors, councillors, leading landowners, and professional men—which declared in Ollivier's favour. The official candidate, Lescuyer, finding himself deserted, withdrew: Ollivier was elected triumphantly with twice as many votes as his radical opponent.[2]

The elections as a whole were a victory for his policy too. The country decidedly rejected the advocates of revolution and gave the republicans only thirty (or one-ninth) of the seats. It showed clearly that it wanted the empire, but the empire with liberty. The majority of the new house remained Bonapartist, but with this remarkable alteration: a large number of former official candidates renounced that title, issued liberal circulars, and declared in favour of a reform of the constitution. This

---

[1] G. Schlumberger, Mes Souvenirs (1934) i. 55–56; A. Vitu, Les Réunions électorales à Paris, mai 1869 (1869); L. Girard, Les Elections de 1869 (1960), introduction and chapters 1 and 2; G. Lefrançais, Souvenirs d'un révolutionnaire (c. 1902), 350; E.L. xi. 515–36.

[2] Archives Nationales, C. 1377, BB (18) 1786, F (90) 408, F (90) 591—reports of the Procureur Général of Aix and telegrams of the prefect. It is curious that Clemenceau also began as M.P. for Paris, but then, when he grew less radical, retired to represent Var instead.

conversion of a part of the majority was precisely what Ollivier had worked for, and these men were to supply the backbone of the liberal empire. Thiers, leading some forty non-republican liberals who had been elected as opposition candidates, was in a decided minority, and many of his distinguished friends had been soundly defeated. It was Ollivier who now organized the union of the liberals with the converted Bonapartists.

As soon as the new parliament met he counteracted the efforts of Thiers' party on the one hand and the right wing on the other, each of whom planned separate and different demands to the government. Instead he drew up an interpellation on which as many deputies as possible could agree, demanding simply that the government 'give satisfaction to the feelings of the country by associating it more efficaciously in the conduct of affairs', and adding that ministerial responsibility would be the crucial change in such a reform. By saying 'more efficaciously' he gave the Bonapartists credit for what had already been done; by asking for ministerial responsibility he satisfied the more advanced liberals; and by thus uniting the groups he was able to obtain 116 signatures to his interpellation. With the support of the left he could thus get a majority of nine votes in his favour. The issue was decided. Rouher resigned. Napoleon replied on 11 July with a message promising satisfaction. Ollivier in return, anxious that Napoleon should not be humiliated and so perhaps tempted to reaction, used his moderating influence once again to have the interpellation withdrawn as a sign of confidence in the emperor's intentions.

Napoleon now summoned Ollivier, together with three other deputies who had taken leading parts in organizing the new majority, and invited them to join the ministry. Ollivier, however, had learned the lesson of 19 January and refused. The 116 by themselves did not provide a clear majority, and in any case he did not wish to compromise himself by associating with servants of the despotism, by being given a few votes in a hostile cabinet. He preferred to wait until Napoleon should be willing to accept an entirely liberal ministry, to turn over an entirely new leaf. In vain did Thiers urge him to accept, saying, 'It is always honourable to be a Martignac ministry.' 'When I form a ministry,' replied Ollivier, 'it will be a Casimir Périer one.'

Napoleon therefore summoned the Marquis de Chasseloup-Laubat,[1] who had already served the empire with distinction as a minister of the navy and the colonies for many years, and whom Napoleon could therefore appoint without appearing to yield to his opponents: but Chasseloup was, as those in his confidence knew, also a convinced liberal, and he proceeded to draft a new constitution which granted even more than Napoleon had promised. He not only made it possible for deputies to be ministers but also gave them the right to initiate legislation. Ollivier was delighted. 'The senatus-consultum', he wrote, 'is excellent, complete, honest. For twelve years I have been abused because I believed that the empire was compatible with liberty. I have been proved right and the question is now decided. I have achieved my aim. The first part of my political life is over. Another is about to begin.'[2]

Ollivier had now reached a position of enormous strength. Chasseloup declared the ministry could not last without him and sent letters, emissaries, invitations after him to St. Tropez urging him to accept office. A secret meeting was at length arranged with Napoleon, to which Ollivier came disguised in the middle of the night, without his spectacles and with a muffler hiding his face. Conscious of his power, he insisted that the emperor must accept him as the head of a parliamentary ministry, with his friends and with his programme and Napoleon had no choice but to agree. However, it was not a complete parliamentary ministry that took office. The emperor firmly maintained that he would not 'charge any one person to form a ministry. This would be to recognize the existence of a prime minister, to give the Chamber full powers over the choice of ministers;

---

[1] In addition to being an interesting man he was responsible for an active policy of overseas expansion; he won Cochinchina for France, pursued an original colonial policy, and waged an exciting struggle against England for the mastery of the seas. I plan to publish a biography of him.

[2] D. 4 August 1869.

whereas by the constitution they ought to depend only on me and I exercise my responsibility as president of the council of ministers.' Ollivier agreed to compromise on this and, instead of an announcement that 'M. Ollivier has been entrusted with the task of forming a ministry', he accepted one saying more ambiguously, 'The ministers have resigned. M. Ollivier has been summoned by the emperor.' Secondly, Napoleon insisted that the ministers of war and the navy should remain unchanged, so that the security of the state should not be put at the mercy of party strife. Ollivier raised no objection; but when, thirdly, Napoleon urged that the violence of the press required repression, Ollivier stated that he could be no party to such action, that this violence required simply the application of 'the wise maxim of Walpole: *quieta non movere*', that given a few months of liberty the extremists would soon be discredited. Napoleon acquiesced.

The ministry of the liberal empire, which took office on 2 January 1870, was far more heterogeneous than is perhaps realized. It contained no less than five different elements. Ollivier, who took the post of minister of justice and religions (because, he said, it involved the least amount of departmental drudgery, but perhaps also because its adjunct title of 'Keeper of the Seals' gave it a certain pre-eminence) brought with him only two men who could be called personal allies: Chevandier de Valdrome (Interior) and Maurice Richard (Fine Arts). Segris (Education), Louvet (Agriculture), and Talhouet-Roy (Public Works) having been members of the legislature since 1852, elected with government support, had for long accepted the despotism: they represented the converted majority, the 'centre right'. Buffet (Finance) and Daru (Foreign Affairs), however, had both, until now, opposed the empire; they had entered the legislature as opposition candidates and were leaders of the 'centre left'. General Le Bœuf (War) and Admiral Rigaud de Genouilly (Navy) were Napoleon's nominees. Parieu finally (Minister-President of the Conseil d'Etat) was a bureaucrat whose presence in the cabinet even Ollivier could not explain and who appears to have been chosen by accident. The ministry did not contain a single man who could be called a convinced Bonapartist and Ollivier was probably the nearest approach to one. Daru had actually, as vice-president of the legislative assembly in 1851, led the opposition of that body to the *coup d'état*. The ministry could thus well lay claim to being essentially a ministry of reconcilation.

Ollivier's triumph took place while he was on his second honeymoon. He had in 1869 married a girl of twenty, saying (rather curiously, in view of his imminent political union with the empire) that 'I am actually incapable of falling completely and headlong in love, of abandoning myself entirely except with a young unmarried girl, for purity alone captivates me, attracts me, subjugates me and holds me'. Marie-Therèse Gravier was the daughter of a cotton manufacturer of Pondicherry and a great grand-niece of Admiral Suffren. Like Blandine, she combined fair-haired, blue-eyed beauty with exceptional ability and a serious mind. She had agreed with his views on dancing and had promised never to go to a ball again. '. . . To make some loved being happy', he had written to her, 'was the sole ambition, the sole hope, the sole desire of my austere youth. But it seems that fate used indefatigable efforts to foil my ambition, to deceive my hope, to mock my desire. I raise my eyes to Marie Magdaleine: fate removes her at eighteen. I meet her sister Blandine: fate leaves her to me for five years and then takes her away. So I throw myself into politics, which I hate, to escape, to distract myself. Shall I now ask a gentle being to come to me with open heart to restore to me the sweet joys I have lost? I was tempted to do so, I am still tempted sometimes, but when I reflect I say to myself: it would be unpardonable egoism not to resist such an idea. No matter that she should agree from generosity: I must protect her against her own enthusiasm. In a few months there will be not a hair on my head which is not white, and she will still be as fresh as the dawn: my soul is already heavy and hers is light. Besides, do I know what vicissitudes the future has in store for me? I have not been able to create for myself an independent financial position to shelter me from misfortune, and who knows into what poverty or wretchedness the blows of fate or the fatigues of life may throw me? No, the charming singing bird ought not to be dragged into the turmoil. . . . '

At once came her answer: 'The very renunciation to which you resign yourself out of kindness to my tender years, will in fact turn my youth into despair. You have judged me to be very vain then, very selfish, and very much of a wretch if you suppose that I care so much about questions of age and fortune. If you do not judge me so, have confidence in me as I have in you, and if happiness must come to you through me, accept it. Above all, do not think that I am making a sacrifice. O no, for I have such need of love myself, and who can love me like you? Take me therefore: I give myself to you, but with what humility!'

They were married quietly at the very time when the emperor was sending emissaries to La Moutte. She became his most devoted friend, his secretary when he went blind, and an energetic defender of his memory after his death. In 1870 when the wives of the new ministers were presented to the empress Eugenie in her expensive crinoline and low open neck, Madame Ollivier appeared in a very simple dress with a high collar. The contrast almost seemed to indicate a protest. It was a small but significant sympton of the new era the liberal empire was designed to introduce.[1]

[1] The source for this second marriage is Ollivier's letters to his 'confessor', Mme de Sourdeval (the originals themselves are in O.P.); and the manuscript history of it written by his wife, including copies of letters now lost. There were three children of this marriage; one died young; Jocelyn (so named in memory of Lamartine) was a barrister, who died a few years ago; and a daughter Geneviève, who married Jean Troisier, professor of medicine at Paris.

CHAPTER 9

THE WORK OF OLLIVIER'S MINISTRY

THERE is a view frequently expressed that Ollivier's ministry was doomed to failure; but did contemporaries in fact generally regard it as no more than a desperate attempt by Napoleon III to avoid imminent and inevitable disaster? There is certainly a considerable body of evidence to show that its appointment raised high and widespread hopes and that it appeared to rally to the régime large numbers of men who had formerly been hostile. The Orleanist leaders found themselves 'dished', like the Whigs in 1867: Guizot, Thiers, Broglie, and Odilon Barrot felt bound to promise the emperor their support: the legitimists, Polignac and Falloux, expressed their approval; the Catholic, Montalembert, declared himself 'rejuvenated at the sight of the political resurrection of our country'; the protectionist, Jules Brame, called the change 'the most admirable revolution of modern times'; and the normally sceptical *Revue des Deux Mondes* added that 'if it is not the greatest of all revolutions, it is at least one of the most interesting, one of the most salutary and most opportune'. The French Academy, for long the asylum of the intellectual opposition to the empire, elected Ollivier a member with rare unanimity (by 26 votes out of 28) as a mark of its support.[1] Among the republicans George Sand was almost enthusiastic; Clamageran, who had till then mocked Ollivier's efforts, admitted that this 'half-liberalism' was better than the revolution which was its only alternative; even Picard and Favre hinted, though with many conditions, that they might support the government if it fulfilled its promises. To crown it all, two authoritarian Bonapartists who had been principal agents of the

[1] E.L. xii. 331–47; Hector Pessard, *Mes Petits Papiers 1860–1870* (1887), 291 and 307; P. Guiral, *Prévost-Paradol* (1955), 663 ff.; Letters received by Ollivier during his Ministry, O.P.; *Revue des deux mondes*, chronique of 31 January 1870, 779.

coup d'état, announced that they were converted to the new cause, because only liberty could save the empire.[1]

In the face of this 'fusion of the several societies', the British Ambassador in Paris wrote optimistically that he fancied he saw 'signs of the success of the present ministry'.[2] *Punch* portrayed Napoleon in the guise of King John signing Magna Carta and *The Times* declared that 'It is hard indeed to see how the reconciliation between the Founder of "Personal Rule" and the champion of sound Liberal principles could be more sincere or more complete'. *Vanity Fair* had a full-page coloured cartoon of Ollivier in its series 'Men of the Day' and wrote that 'the Government of M. Ollivier, although its formation was a work of time, difficulty, and negotiation, appears to carry with it the elements of stability. . . . Personal government has been condemned irretrievably and for ever . . . and if aught but force can govern France, she may descend peacefully to the Fourth Napoleon endowed with free institutions. For this end M. Ollivier may be trusted to work with equal honesty to the people and devotion to the Sovereign. Personally, he is well fitted for the task he has undertaken. Deeply calculating in design, he is tenacious in action and persuasive in speech. Nor does he greatly care for criticism. "The most useful and necessary quality a politician can have," he has written, "is a readiness to be considered foolish or vulgarly ambitious when that is calculated to promote the success of a long-meditated plan." M. Ollivier has already succeeded in being thought both foolish and ambitious and it only remains for him now to be successful.'[3]

[1] J. J. Clamageran, *Correspondance 1849-1902* (1906), 325; Juliette Adam *Mes sentiments et nos idées avant 1870* (1905), 367, 373, 460; M. Reclus, *Ernes Picard* (1912), 161; M. Reclus, *Jules Favre* (1912), 304.

[2] Lord Lyons to Lord Clarendon, 18 and 21 January 1870, Bodleian MSS., Clar. Dep. 477; P.R.O., F.O. 27/1797 (18 January 1870); E.L. xii. 331-47.

[3] *Punch,* 15 January 1870 (cartoon reproduced in T. Zeldin, 'The Myth of Napoleon III', *History Today,* February 1958, 107); *The Times,* 4 January 1870; *Vanity Fair* (1870), i. 32, 36; Thibaut Lefebvre, *Adhesion à l'empire libéral* (1870); Antonin Chatel, *Napoleon III et l'opposition* (1870). *La Mère Duchêne,* 30 January 1870 had a 'poem' beginning thus:

Ollivier began on his ministry with immense self-confidence and undiluted optimism. 'Sire,' he declared flamboyantly, 'I am happy because I believe I am saving your dynasty'; and when the emperor politely thanked him, 'No,' he insisted, 'it is I who should thank you for associating me with a great deed, because what you have done, Sire, is great.'[1] Moreover, as though to blinker himself against doubt, he made it his rule never to read any newspaper articles about himself: he had, as he himself admitted, a 'contempt' for the difficulties facing him.[2]

However, if one examines public opinion at this time more closely one sees that even though the state bonds did rise by two francs on the news of his appointment, approval was loaded with reservation. The Bonapartist press mingled its congratulations with warnings that he must not go too far in his liberalism nor give too much power to the centre-left; while, on the other hand the liberal press urged the very contrary. The plaudits he won from the Catholic papers roused immediate fears among the anti-clerical ones. The *Journal des Economistes* warned him that the protectionists in the cabinet must be kept in check. *Le Charivari* printed a cartoon of two half-men labelled centre-left

A M. E. Ollivier.

> Oui, ta voix a vibré, soudain la France entière,
> Alors a reconnu son plus grand orateur;
> Consacre lui toujours ton illustre carrière,
>   Tribun dominateur!
>
> Ta place, au premier rang, fut toujours, O mon maître,
> L'amour des libertés t'a grandi parmi nous,
> La France, à tes accents, vit aussitôt renaître,
>   Son espoir le plus doux!

But cf. the music-hall song *'Emile au Cabinet'* (P. Barbier and F. Vernillat, *Histoire de France par les chansons* (1959), vii. 168) which begins:

> Sire, autrefois, j'étais de la montagne
> Un des vrais 'cinq' de l'opposition,
> Mais aujourd'hui, moderne Charlemagne,
> Je viens a vous, mû par l'ambition. . . .
>   *Refrain:* Je suis donc bon à mettre au cabinet.

[1] D. 2 January 1870. This naïve complacency was too much even for Ollivier when he re-read it thirty years later. In his memoirs he inserts a considerably amended version, E.L. xii. 221.

[2] E.L. xii. 227, 334.

and centre-right, with the legend: 'two halves do not make a whole'.[1] In view of all these conflicting pressures, Lord Clarendon was perhaps justified when he sceptically observed that Ollivier's 'task requires tact, experience, firmness, knowledge of men, and a few other qualities in which he seems singularly deficient and I cannot think his ministry will last.'[2] The pessimists were, however, very much in a minority and Clarendon reported that 'People here are much impressed with [Ollivier's] courage and ability and wish him success'.[3] But the trouble with the ministry of reconciliation was that it tried to reconcile too many interests. It was bound to disappoint some. Its weakness was that it was not partisan enough.

Now in what way precisely and to what extent did the ministry's policy and methods differ from those of the despotism of the previous twenty years? Was the left-wing opposition justified in claiming that the old order was really unchanged beneath its new disguise? Ollivier, first of all, certainly attempted to inaugurate a new approach to reform. The age of partisan legislation was to be over: he introduced into France the English system of royal commissions, composed of distinguished experts of all opinions, from whose deliberations he hoped universally acceptable solutions would emerge. He proposed to tackle the most fundamental problems at their roots, to complete what the Revolution of 1789 had left undone, to introduce liberty, which still existed only superficially, into the very life of the nation. He therefore appointed one commission to examine the best method of ending centralization (which Tocqueville and many others had revealed as a survival of the *ancien régime*); a second to devise a system of self-government for Paris; a third to study the question of freedom for higher education and the monopoly of the university; a fourth to discuss technical education, the new need of the age; a fifth, to consider public works,

---

[1] *Le Charivari*, review of the press, 5 and 24 January, 12 February 1870; *Journal des économistes*, January–June 1870, p. 166.
[2] Quoted by G. P. Gooch, *The Second Empire* (1960), 183.
[3] Bodleian MSS. Clar. Dep. C. 474, 19 January 1870.

and the improvement of communications in keeping with industrial advance; and a sixth to revise the criminal code, to end the inquisitorial system which placed the onus of proof on the defence.[1] Ollivier assumed the presidency of this last one himself, and in addition planned a seventh, of 'social peace', which was to be slightly different, in that it would be a permanent body. He envisaged it as a sort of arbitration tribunal for industry and agriculture, working actively to promote understanding between master and man, studying the condition of labour both at home and abroad, encouraging improvements in it by adult education, libraries, factory hygiene, the regulation of female and child labour, the establishment of savings banks, insurance, pension schemes, and trade unions. It was to be composed in equal proportions of workers, employers, and economists or lawyers, with himself again as president.

Ollivier was not of course original in thinking that the matters with which these seven commissions were charged needed reform; they had for long been demanded by a great number of people. The only one which reflects a personal interest was the commission of social peace. The preamble to the decree appointing it declared that the antagonism between capital and labour was not inevitable, and that 'harmony established by justice and mutual goodwill' was 'the real law of human work'. This reveals not simply Ollivier's inextinguishable sentimentality of 1848 but more particularly the influence of Le Play, the founder of 'social peace unions'. Ollivier submitted the decree to him and received some amendments from him. It is doubtful, however, whether this source of inspiration would have commanded wide approval. Le Play was an excellent sociologist, and his descriptive work is of permanent value, but his political ideas were essentially backward-looking and have since found favour only in the régime of Marshal Pétain.[2]

---

[1] *Journal officiel*, 22 and 28 February, 4 and 20 March, 25 May 1870; E.L. xii. 537–41.

[2] E.L. xiii. 247; cf. *Recueil d'études sociales à la mémoire de Frédéric Le Play* (1956) viii; Dorothy Herbertson, *The Life of Frédéric Le Play* (Le Play House, Ledbury, 1950); draft of decree in O.P.

Nevertheless, great things might well have been expected from these commissions, for the men whom Ollivier was successful in persuading to sit on them were the most distinguished of the age: Broglie, Guizot, Rémusat, Thureau-Dangin, Chambrun, Léon Say, Drouyn de Lhuys, Saint-Marc-Girardin, Dupont-White, Freycinet, Odilon Barrot, Franqueville, Léonce de Lavergne, Prévost-Paradol, Viollet Leduc, Waddington—representatives in fact of most shades of opinions and of every learned institution, though politicians of the left, like Grévy, Picard, and Jules Simon, who were also invited to join, declined. It is known that the commission of decentralization drew up a plan which placed local government in the hands of the *conseils généraux*, leaving the hitherto omnipotent prefect as simply an executive officer under them, though it rather curiously counterbalanced this by simultaneously transforming him into a regional or provincial prefect, with authority over a group of several contiguous departments.[1] The commission on university education likewise worked out a bill which was much more liberal, said the duc de Broglie, than anything proposed since: 'in this matter', he wrote, 'we have certainly declined in breadth of mind in passing from the liberal empire to the republic.'[2] The war broke out, however, before any of the commissions' proposals were complete and nothing actually came of it all. Nevertheless, it was an experiment which might justifiably be called interesting and even promising.

On the other hand the idea of royal commissions produced unexpected difficulties, over which Ollivier in his memoirs glosses silently. What would happen if they proposed measures with which the government did not agree? The commission on decentralization in fact voted, by a majority of one, that mayors should be elected—whereas it was the government's official policy that they should be nominated by the emperor from among members of the municipal council, and Napoleon adamantly insisted on retaining this power. The minister of

---

[1] C. de Freycinet, *Souvenirs 1848–78* (1914), 96.
[2] Albert de Broglie, *Mémoires* (1838–41), i. 348–54.

the interior was so taken aback by this unexpected development that he asked for the vote to be taken again, and then declared that the government would not feel bound by this recommendation.[1] It is very likely that Ollivier would have come to loggerheads with his commissions on many other subjects and it is by no means certain in any case that parliament would then have agreed to give effect to their wishes. For it was soon protesting that a parliamentary government's duty was to carry out the demands of parliament, and that this method of seeking wisdom elsewhere was an insult to it. The cynics mocked that the commissions were really designed to keep busy the many ambitious men for whom there was no room in the government[2] and it was perhaps a mistake on Ollivier's part not to have kept busy instead the members of parliament, who could be far more dangerous to him. The system of commissions, moreover, resulted in a postponement of all radical reform until their deliberations were complete, so that the enthusiasm for the liberal empire not unnaturally began to wane. 'The ministry,' complained *Le Charivari*, 'resembles the barber's shop with the legend on its door: Free Shaves Tomorrow. When will this tomorrow come?'[3]

Nevertheless, in the meantime the government was able to bring forward a significant amount of liberal legislation. Its principal work was to reduce its own power. It moved one bill to repeal the law of Sûreté général of 1858, which gave it rights of arbitary arrest; a second to establish trial by jury for press offences, and a third to repeal the stamp duty on newspapers, so giving far greater freedom for the expression of opinion; a fourth to transfer the right to authorize great public works from the emperor to parliament; a fifth to abolish the hated *livrets* which workers had to carry; a sixth to give local councils, in departments and arrondissements, the right to elect their own presidents, to make their own standing orders and to publish

---

[1] C. de Freycinet, *Souvenirs 1848–78* (1914) 97–98.
[2] M. Du Camp, *Souvenirs d'un demi-siècle* (1949) i. 249.
[3] *Le Charivari*, 12 February 1870.

their debates; and a seventh establishing the rule that mayors must be nominated by the emperor from members of the municipal council.

These bills would certainly have increased the liberty of Frenchmen, and Ollivier, with considerable justification, remained very proud of them; but close examination reveals that some of them were prepared in such a hurry, that, incomplete or ill-thought out, they diminished Ollivier's prestige quite as much as further delay would have done. The fact that commissions were debating many of the subjects they touched on, compelled him to limit their scope, to make them temporary measures, to be supplemented at a later stage; inevitably the impatient parliament found them inadequate. It protested, it sought to amend, it presented counter-proposals. Ollivier had rashly, in his enthusiastic early days of power, invited 'all those who believe they have a useful reform to suggest [to] come to us: we shall welcome them and study their project'.[1] No less than 128 bills were presented by the deputies and the machinery of the legislature became clogged. Ollivier, forgetting that he had asked for it, attributed this to the deputies' malicious desire to win easy popularity by forestalling him with all sorts of desirable but impracticable reforms.[2]

He met with far more resistance than he had foreseen and soon revealed that he had limitations as a parliamentarian. He sat through a great many of the debates and answered questions like a true constitutional minister, taking the principal load in this work, and he frequently made very eloquent replies. His speeches were however delivered too much like beautiful arias in an opera; they were delightful to listen to, but they seldom contained the tact and conciliatory spirit that were needed. The absence of Morny, who possessed these very gifts, was a great handicap.

[1] Speech of 17 January 1870. E. Ollivier, *Mes Discours* (1875), 47. This was used as a motto by Comte de Mac-carthy, *Les Assemblées départementales devant la France parlementaire* (1870).

[2] *Travaux de la session extraordinaire de 1869 et des sessions ordinaires et extraordinaires de 1870* (1870).

The government thus lost control over a certain amount of its legislation and a number of its bills were amended to an extent never known earlier in the reign: the liberal empire certainly meant that parliament participated actively in the making of laws. Thus Ollivier's bill on the *conseils généraux* had added to it, in the committee stage, an amendment widening it so as to give these bodies the right to express opinions on matters of general interest, including politics; and then in the course of debate, two further ones, that judges of the peace should no longer be eligible to sit in them and that their debates should not only be published but held in public.[1] Ollivier's bill that senators should receive a salary of 15,000 francs was rejected and one substituted that they should be paid the same as members of the lower house.[2] Again, his bill providing trial by jury for press offences was heavily criticized for being incomplete: it did nothing to abolish the many crimes for which writers could be convicted (like that of 'outrage to public and religious morals' for which Vacherot had been punished) and it left the composition of the jury unreformed. The legislature tagged on to the bill a clause that political cases should also be tried by juries, and insisted that the ministry should at once bring in a bill abolishing the stamp duty on newspapers, which it had postponed for budgetary reasons. When it was accordingly offered one hastily prepared, which replaced the stamp duty by a tax on advertisements, it rejected it because the change would take place only in 1872: a compromise had to be agreed on, reducing the duty at once and leaving the method of finding compensating revenue undecided.[3]

Moreover, the senate vied in demonstrating its own independence, and rejected two of the legislature's amendments to the bill on the *conseils généraux*. It might have worked greater havoc

---

[1] *Annales du corps legislatif* (1870), iv. annexe 31–34, vi. 214–15.

[2] Ibid., iv. annexe 11, v. 5–6, v. 278.

[3] Ibid., iii. annexe 93–101, iii. 328–55, iv. 60, iv. annexe 123, iv. 499, v.3. Cf. Irene Collins, *The Government and the Newspaper Press in France, 1814–1881* (1959), 161–3.

had the declaration of war not caused it to postpone consideration of the bills sent to it.[1] Only a small proportion of the government's proposals therefore actually became law.

The pressure for immediate action in every sphere caused Ollivier to placate it with means which in fact increased the criticism. Algeria was subject to a military régime: but the plans for changing this were not ready. Ollivier, therefore, as a temporary alleviation, issued decrees freeing the prefects from subordination to the generals and authorizing elections for the *conseils généraux*, which had formerly been nominated. He was, however, at once accused of being content with half-measures, for Algeria still had no representation in parliament; and of acting improperly, for a parliamentary minister had no business issuing decrees like his despotic predecessors. Ollivier was certainly right in arguing that good laws took time to prepare; but it was in vain that he pleaded with the deputies: 'Gentlemen, you must not ask of human strength beyond what human strength can do.'[2]

His desire to reconcile all antagonisms meant that, as in 1848, he satisfied no one completely. Thus his minister of agriculture and commerce declared that the government favoured neither free trade nor protection; it stood for a 'juste milieu' between them; it would work for the establishment of free trade, but by gradual stages. Nevertheless, it yielded to the pressure of the industrialists (who, according to Rouher, threatened it with workers' risings) almost as soon as it came into office, issuing decrees ending the admission of cotton textiles and iron without duty if they were to be re-exported after further manufacture. The free traders sarcastically commented that it was curious that a government which called itself liberal should begin by increasing protection, and by decree. But on the other hand Ollivier refused to denounce the 1860 free-trade treaty with England, as forty-seven protectionist members of the legislature demanded.

---

[1] *Annales du corps législatif*, (1870) vi. 214–15; cf. J. B. and J. Duverger, *Collection complète des lois, décrets, etc.* (1870), vol. 70, p. 219 n.

[2] *Annales du corps législatif* (1870), iii. 32, iv. 528.

He thus succeeded in annoying both sides.[1] Again, the great financiers hoped that the advent of the liberal empire would mean the destruction of the monopoly of the railway companies, the throwing open of new building to free enterprise, and the inauguration of a great era of improved communications: but there was also the old contradictory pressure for balanced budgets and conservative finance. The ministry promised that the abuses and delays of the old régime would be ended, but also declared itself hostile to any 'untimely innovations'.[2]

The budget contained several indications of good intentions: the allocation to education was raised; the salaries of the lowest paid teachers, government employees, and parish priests were slightly increased and those of the highest officials slightly reduced. Duties on the sale of land were diminished for agricultural plots exchanged with the intention of creating larger and more efficient holdings. These were, however, all very slight modifications. The government concentrated on restoring order in finance; its reassuring but perhaps over-sober budget contained nothing spectacular—neither reduced nor reformed taxation.[3] The personnel of the despotism's administration was purged only to a slight extent. Haussmann was dismissed, together with another dozen prefects and sub-prefects who seemed to be more particularly representative of the golden age of prefectoral autocracy; but the majority were left unmolested, with optimistic instructions that they were no longer to interfere in politics. In his own department, Ollivier proposed to end the French system by which judges are chosen in the same way as other civil servants and to adopt, at least in part, that of England: in future he would fill half the vacancies direct from practising barristers. Since barristers were often men of the opposition unable to get jobs, this measure was designed to help end the

---

[1] *Annales du sénat* (1870), i. 194–211; *Annales du corps législatif* (1870), i. 400; J. B. and J. Duverger, *Collection complètes des lois, décrets etc.* (1870) vol. 70, pp. 9–10.

[2] L. Girard, *La Politique des travaux publics du second empire* (1952), 388–94.

[3] *Annales du corps législatif* (1870) ii. ann. 49 ff.; v. 384, 433, 437; M. Marion, *Histoire financière de la France depuis 1715* (1928), v. 502–6.

division of the nation into 'ins' and 'outs'. It was of course a long-term undertaking and in practice therefore the liberal empire produced only limited changes in the official relations between the masses and the government; and it did little to entrench its power in the provinces.[1]

Ollivier created an entirely new ministry to deal with the fine arts, to end the 'contempt for taste and intelligence' which had made so many artists and writers hostile to Napoleon. The minister Maurice Richard, however, met with unexpected difficulties in trying to introduce the principles of free enterprise into art. He proposed to deliver the artists from the tutelage of the state and to abandon the system whereby the state organized the annual Paris exhibition. The artists were invited to form their own society and arrange their exhibitions themselves. Much to his surprise, they refused: they preferred to leave these financial worries to the state and they informed the minister that if he was so well disposed to them, he would serve them better by buying more of their paintings. In the end it appears that Maurice Richard was reduced to giving parties and receptions for them and to disbursing some £10,000 from his own pocket (for he was very wealthy) to help meet the many solicitations for patronage that came to him and for which public funds were quite inadequate. It is interesting that this unhappy ministry, which disappeared with the empire, was revived by none other than Ollivier's chief opponent, Gambetta, in 1881.[2]

The list of men Ollivier proposed to make senators showed again how he wished his régime to be one of reconciliation. He included Bonapartists like Las Cases (son of the companion of St. Helena) and Pietri, prefect of police, a stout defender of 'order,' but also the liberal Girardin, the Orleanists Barbet and Saint-Marc-Girardin, and great national figures like Pasteur, Ferdinand de

---

[1] For a witty criticism of Ollivier's tolerance of the old prefects, see Dr. E. Ordinaire, *Du perfectionnement de la race préfectorale* (1870).

[2] M. Du Camp, *Souvenirs d'un demi-siècle* (1949), i. 246; Ollivier to Wallon, December 1872, copy, O.P. The restoration monarchy appointed a 'Director-General of the Fine Arts' in 1824, who was remembered only for his decree fixing the length of dancers' skirts at the Opera.

Lesseps, Viollet Leduc, the archaeologist Rougé, the playwright Emile Augier and, with less certain judgement, the mediocre Maxime Du Camp.[1]

'The essential thing at the moment,' wrote Ollivier to Napoleon on taking office, 'is to reassure and to win to your side the intelligent and middle classes.'[2] Many of his liberal measures were designed to appeal to them, but he was quite right that they also needed to be 'reassured'. The freeing of the press, the relaxation of censorship, the revival of political life, in short the successful realization of their demands, had let loose the forces of revolution, which had been silenced for twenty years and which they seemed to have forgotten. The red menace had been resurrected and the hydra-headed agitation of the professional revolutionaries had suddenly revived the tense atmosphere of 1848 and its uneasy wavering between optimism and fear. The radical newspapers freely slandered respectability and openly threatened violence: *Le Père Duchêne*, for example, wrote in December 1869 after having had an issue seized by the police, 'They have broken our pens. When the revolution comes, we shall break their heads.'

'For some months,' the *Daily Telegraph* reported, 'the Press of France has been the freest, or at least the most licentious, in the world. Even the journals of New York would not dare to fling at President Grant, or at the meanest public functionary, one-tenth of the abuse with which the writers of the *Rappel* and the *Marseillaise* have pelted the Emperor, the Empress, the Prince Imperial, the Prince Napoleon, and all the members of the Imperial house. Had such words been used in England against the Royal family, the offending journals would have been snuffed out in a week. . . . Were any Ministry in this country to tolerate the existence of an English *Marseillaise* it would be ignominiously dismissed from office. Such a Ministry would

---

[1] A. Poulet-Malassis, *Papiers secrets et correspondance du second empire* (1880), 59–60; Notes in O.P., Ollivier to Cardinal de Bonnechose, 12 February 1870, draft in O.P. In fact the ministry fell before he could make the appointments.

[2] D. 1870, letter of 2 January 1870.

be told that if the liberty of the Press implied the freedom to invoke rebellion and massacre, the sooner newspapers were sunk in the depths of the sea the better would society be served.'[1]

Ollivier had been in power for little more than a week when he was in fact faced with a revolutionary challenge. The attacks on the Bonapartes (accusing them of being 'cowardly Judases . . . beggars, vagabonds, traitors', 'scratch a Bonaparte and you will find a ferocious beast') had caused an obscure member of that family, Prince Pierre Bonaparte, to challenge the leader of this movement, Rochefort, to a duel. The latter's seconds, two journalists called Fonvielle and Victor Noir, called on the prince; insults were exchanged; Victor Noir struck the prince on the cheek; the prince, who was a fiery Corsican always carrying a revolver, and even placing one by his side when at table, took a few steps back, drew out his gun and shot Victor Noir dead.

Ollivier, without even consulting Napoleon, at once ordered Pierre Bonaparte's arrest and summoned the High Court for his immediate trial. But the extreme republicans thought this incident would be just the right kind of spark to set a revolution alight. 'Vengeance' became their watchword. Rochefort published an undisguised appeal to arms: 'I was weak enough to believe that a Bonaparte could be something other than an assassin', he wrote. 'People of France, do you not find that you have really had enough?' The revolution was fixed for the day of Victor Noir's burial. All the faithful of the left were summoned to join the procession: 'Tomorrow', wrote Flourens, 'the republic's flag must be triumphant.'

'We are the law,' replied Ollivier, 'we are justice, we are moderation, we are liberty; but if you compel us, we shall be force.' Determined to avoid the mistakes of 1830 and 1848, he ordered a division of cavalry to prevent the funeral from entering Paris, believing that a show of force would stop the insurrection from taking place at all; and indeed, though a crowd of 100,000 men, many of them armed, came out on that day, Rochefort saw that he had been out-manœuvred and told them to disband

[1] *Daily Telegraph*, 24 January 1870.

quietly. They returned home singing revolutionary songs, 'brutally dispersed by the police' according to one witness. It was a great relief to the terrified conservatives. The emperor gave Ollivier and his colleagues generous credit for their triumph: 'Without my ministry,' he said, 'I should not have been able to meet this crisis.' 'The agitators of the press and the clubs', remarked Ollivier, 'are dangerous only if one is afraid of them.'[1]

Although this success over Rochefort strengthened Ollivier's hand, the menace of revolution also produced an increasing clamour for strong government and for the repression of the left-wing extremists. Most people, wrote the procureur général of Lyon to Ollivier, congratulated him on his firmness, but thought that he ought now to 'clean all this up thoroughly' for 'if the chassepots are not put to use, the agitators will not stop their violence'.[2] It was not only the government or the empire that was being attacked but religion and the whole economic order. Terrified by the radical press which respected none of the established values, Bishop Dupanloup warned against the dangers of *Atheism and the Social Peril*.[3] The Workers International had been expanding fast and now had a quarter of a million members in France. Strikes, in which it frequently had a hand, grew increasingly numerous, spreading now from the mines to the iron and textile industries, revealing national solidarity and growing political activity among the workers. There were prolonged stoppages of work at Le Creusot, Lyon, St.

---

[1] E.L. xii. 396–487 and D., notes in the volume of 1870; G. Lefrançais, *Souvenirs d'un revolutionnaire* (c. 1902), 374. The prosecution did not accept the prince's plea of self-defence, though it admitted provocation. The prince was acquitted by the jury largely because of the disgust aroused in the court by the violent behaviour of Noir's friends. Rather oddly soon after (13 March) the duc de Montpensier, son of Louis Philippe, killed don Henry de Bourbon in a duel at Madrid—for which he was fined a little over £1,000.

[2] M. Moissonnier, *L'opposition ouvrière à Lyon à la fin du second empire* (Typescript thesis for the diplôme d'études supérieures of Lyon, c. 1957, kindly lent to me by Professor Fugier), chapter 6, p. 5. The British Ambassador in Paris reported the same thing, 8 March 1870, Bodleian MSS. Clar. Dep. 477. Cf. also *Journal des débats*, 15 and 16 January 1870.

[3] F. Lagrange, *Vie de Mgr. Dupanloup* (1884), iii. 12.

Etienne, in Normandy and in Alsace. This was not a period of economic depression, though political uncertainties did check business to a certain extent; but between 1850 and 1870 wages had risen by only 45 per cent. and real wages by only 28 per cent., whereas on the other hand profits had gone up by 286 per cent. There was an inevitable demand by the workers for an increasing share in the improving standard of living, particularly since prices continued to rise: though the men in skilled occupations and in new industries were doing well (and agitating to do better), the smaller artisans were frequently in distress. There was a vast mass of misery and poverty in Paris alongside the new wealth: over half the working population there was in debt and only a quarter managed to save: according to Haussmann, the city contained over a million souls in a state of 'poverty verging on indigence': the gulf between the classes was pregnant with danger.[1]

The employers looked on strikes almost as a form of rebellion and clamoured for troops to maintain 'order', to protect the blacklegs who wanted to work. Ollivier's law of 1864 of course provided for just this situation, ensuring 'the liberty to work', but the minister of the interior Chevandier de Valdrome, who was himself an employer on quite a large scale, was understandably rather embarrassed. He tried to steer a middle course, instructing the prefect to 'be at once very firm and very prudent, and if you have to resort to force, take great care that the summons to disperse, prescribed by the law, is first read out'. The strikers attacked the blacklegs whom the government tried to protect, and the prefect spent his time composing posters guaranteeing the freedom to work, which the strikers then tore down. Twenty-five men were convicted at Le Creusot after the strike petered out from lack of funds, the judge adding that they had shown 'the blackest ingratitude' to their beneficent employer. Here therefore the government failed to satisfy either the workers,

[1] E. Labrousse, *Le Mouvement ouvrier et les idées sociales en France 1815–1900* (1949), 99; E. Dolléans, *Histoire du mouvement ouvrier* (1948) i. 349; G. Duveau, *La Vie ouvrière en France sous le second empire* (1946), 216, 404; M. Dommanget, *Blanqui et l'opposition révolutionnaire à la fin du second empire* (1960), 220–1.

who declared that it had reverted to the brutality of Rouher and Forcade, or the employers, who demanded active repression.

In Alsace, however, the Protestant employers were generally hostile to the second empire and so the workers looked to the government for support against them. The prefect here went to negotiate with the employers on behalf of the workers: when the employers' attitude hardened, the strike leader sent a telegram to the emperor, whose answer, delivered the next day by the prefect, 'moved him to tears'. The employers were so dissatisfied that they even accused the administration of fomenting unrest, with the assistance of the Catholic clergy. The latest and most thorough historian of these strikes believes that this last year of the empire shows signs that the government was on the road to winning the working class. The latter was not, as a whole, republican here and the strikes were not generally hostile politically; the emperor who stood for the extinction of pauperism still made an appeal to them.[1]

Ollivier certainly carried out a certain amount of repression, determined to be firm as well as liberal. At the end of April he ordered the arrest of the leaders of the International, some of whom were condemned to a year's imprisonment. His failure to purge the administration meant that the police frequently revived the methods they had used under the despotism. Varlin, for example, was arbitrarily put in prison in February and released a fortnight later without trial, explanation, or even interrogation.[2] The Paris police is said to have broken up the hostile crowds in the Latin Quarter with indiscriminate violence, marching in squads through the streets, swinging their clubs wildly at those who resisted, to the accompaniment of boos from the students and wailing from the women, while respectable citizens ran for their lives at their approach.[3] A newspaper called *La Libre Pensée* was suppressed for 'insults to religion' and individual issues of

---

[1] F. L'Huillier, *La Lutte ouvrière à la fin du second empire* (1957); cf. A. Scheurer Kestner, *Souvenirs de jeunesse* (1905), chapter 9.

[2] E. Dolléans, *Histoire du mouvement ouvrier* (1948), i. 345–6.

[3] G. Schlumberger, *Mes Souvenirs* (1934), 73.

many others were not infrequently seized for attacking the emperor.[1]

Ollivier, however, insisted that he was working 'in an inexperienced and perhaps unskilful manner, I concede, but . . . at least with a sincere and ardent heart, to bring about social peace and union. What it [the ministry] does not want, is to sacrifice the people to the bourgeoisie, to bend him who has nothing under him who has. Oh, no! It wants to effect a work of appeasement and conciliation and to bring together, by justice, the man who has not and the man who has.'[2] This revival of the dreams of 1848 probably stood no more chance of success in 1870; there is no evidence that Ollivier's ministry did anything to improve the relations of master and man; but there is some that he strengthened the links between the masses and the emperor. It is interesting to note that he had a policy to win the peasants also. In a conversation with Lord Lyons he said that his ministry 'depended . . . principally on the great agricultural population of France for support against socialism and revolution. It was essential therefore that they should do something for that population. To conciliate them, either taxes might be remitted or the call upon them for recruits be diminished. There were great difficulties in the way of remitting taxes; and when a reduction of the army was proposed, the ministers were met by the emperor and the Military Party with a declaration that it would be unsafe to diminish the forces of France while those of Prussia were on their present footing; that the effect would be that Prussia would make some attempt on Southern Germany, and war would be the consequence. If, however, Prussia would make a simultaneous disarmament, all would, M. Ollivier thought, be well.' Conscription, and therefore taxes, could then be reduced.[3] He made considerable efforts in favour of European disarmament,

---

[1] I. Tchernoff, *Le Parti republicain au coup d'état et sous le second empire* (1906), 314; G. de Molinari, *Le Mouvement socialiste et les réunions publiques avant la révolution du 4 septembre 1870* (1872), 92–95.

[2] E. Ollivier, *Mes Discours* (1875), 47.

[3] Lyons to Clarendon, 30 January 1870, Bodleian MSS. Clar. Dep. 477.

and did in fact reduce the army's intake in 1870 from 100,000 to 90,000 men.

Allain-Targé was not justified in asserting that Ollivier had become reactionary.[1] Ollivier's government was known in its day as 'the ministry of honest men', and it would perhaps even more appropriately be called the ministry of good intentions. 'Never since 1789,' it has been said, 'had such ardour [in reform] been seen'; with the aim, as Prévost-Paradol put it, of 'remodelling in a liberal sense all the institutions of France, as established by the Revolution, the Consulate, and the Empire'. La Gorce has judiciously commented that 'this work, though interrupted at its very start, though a little spoilt by some excesses of optimism and some inexperience, deserves not to be forgotten. It was one of the best attempted in the nineteenth century.'[2]

---

[1] Allain-Targé, *La République sous l'empire: Lettres 1864–1870* (1939), 204.
[2] P. de la Gorce, *Histoire du second empire* (1894–1904), vi. 20 and 31.

CHAPTER 10

THE CONSTITUTION OF 1870

THE constitution of 1870 is the only one, among the many France has had, which has never been studied in detail. No doctoral thesis, not even a single learned article, has been written about it. There are only brief references to it in the standard text-books, and these are by no means agreed on its interpretation. Esmein dismisses it as a bundle of contradictions, whose real purpose was to restore the personal power of the monarch.[1] J. J. Chevallier looks upon it as a 'short-lived liberal deviation from an essentially authoritarian régime', in which, however, the authoritarian element continued to predominate, as in the unequal marriage of the hare and the carp.[2] Pierre de la Gorce says firmly that it was the 'negation' of parliamentary government.[3] On the other hand Gabriel Lepointe declares with equal directness that it established 'veritable parliamentary government'.[4] Maurice Duverger finally classifies it as something in between, a revival of Orleanism.[5] No one in any case thinks it has much significance, except as a transition between the despotism of the second empire and the democracy of the third republic.[6] Can closer investigation clarify its nature?

[1] A. Esmein, Eléments de droit constitutionnel français et comparé (fifth edition, 1909), 248.
[2] J. J. Chevallier, Histoire des institutions politiques de la France de 1789 à nos jours (1952), 286.
[3] P. de la Gorce, Histoire du second empire (1894–1907), vi. 94.
[4] G. Lepointe, Histoire des institutions du droit public français au dix-neuvième siècle, 1789–1914 (1953), 135.
[5] M. Duverger, Droit constitutionnelle et institutions politiques (third edition, 1958), 436.
[6] M. Prelot, 'La Signification constitutionnelle du second empire', in Revue française de la science politique (1953), 31–56; cf. M. Deslandres, Histoire constitutionnelle de la France (1932–7), ii. 666–70.

Originally, Ollivier did not intend to produce a new constitution at all. 'My natural inclination', he wrote, 'is to do things in the English manner, little by little and not in great *coups*';[1] and he was satisfied to make slight constitutional changes, as and when the need for them arose. However, the constitution in force at the time of his accession to office seriously restricted the power of the legislature to carry out reforms, for important reforms usually involved constitutional changes, and these could be effected only by the senate. The legislature began to agitate against this limitation, and to urge that instead of having preliminary 'Senatus-Consulta' for each individual law, the whole system should be revised. Daru particularly showed himself a keen advocate of a totally new constitution because if the government produced one, 'men would not be able to say that we are doing nothing'.[2] It was as a result of these pressures that the constitution of 1870 was drawn up.

Napoleon remained the head of the government,[3] appointing the ministers, presiding over their deliberations,[4] retaining his veto,[5] and remaining responsible to the French people, with the right of appealing to them by plebiscite;[6] but two innovations now restricted these wide powers. He was required, first, to rule 'with the co-operation' of the ministers and parliament, instead of using them simply as 'instruments',[7] to give parliament, that is, a certain share in the executive power; and secondly, the initiative in legislation would in future be exercised not only by him but by both houses of parliament as well.[8] His ministers, moreover, no longer 'depended only on the emperor', but were declared 'responsible'.[9] The importance of the legislature was thus greatly increased, but it was at the same time held in check by two other provisions. First, the senate (which was nominated by the emperor) had to approve all legislation, being transformed

[1] D., 10 April 1870.   [2] D., 7 March 1870 (J. ii. 427).
[3] Article 10.   [4] Article 19.   [5] Article 17.   [6] Article 13.
[7] Article 10; 'avec le concours' instead of 'au moyen de' (Art. 3. of 1852 constitution).
[8] Article 12.
[9] Article 19. Ministers could be members of the legislature since 1869.

in fact into a non-hereditary house of lords, with the power
to veto the bills of the lower house.[1] Secondly, the constitution
could not in future be altered except by a plebiscite held on
the emperor's initiative.[2]

This is an unusually confusing constitution. It combines plebiscitary government (by an emperor responsible to the masses)
with limited monarchy (power residing in a sovereign who
must, however, work in accord with an elected but not omnipotent assembly), and also parliamentary government (through
responsible ministers). How can this hybrid concoction be explained? One answer is that Ollivier was driven into a series
of compromises by the pressure of circumstances. Napoleon
would not yield up his right of appeal to the nation. The senate
insisted on a share of the legislative power in return for surrender-
ing its control of the constitution. It is certain that the constitution
of 1870, like most of Ollivier's legislation, was drafted in a
great hurry, inadequately thought out and presented quickly
in order to placate a public opinion clamouring for action of
some sort.

However, there are also indications that the constitution was
intentionally hybrid, that it was a conscious attempt to carry
out that reconciliation between the ideals of all parties which
was always Ollivier's ambition. Its purpose was not to revive
any previous constitution but to draw on all of them so as to
unite their merits. It was to be imperial, monarchical, and
republican all at once; and it is for this reason that it contains
striking echoes of the Hundred Days (a compromise between the
empire and the restoration) and of 1848. Ollivier in fact stated
that the primary maxim on which he based it was that the best
form of government was a mixed one. 'When one consults the
written testimony which observers of politics have left us,' he

---

[1] Article 30. Napoleon, moreover, could not pack it, since a new provision
was introduced forbidding him to create more than twenty senators in any
one year (Article 26). The senate now became a legislative body, but the
name of the lower house, *Corps législatif*, was not changed.

[2] Article 44.

said, 'one is struck by the unanimity with which, from Aristotle and Polybius down to Benjamin Constant, all declare against simple governments. Whatever these latter may be, monarchical, aristocratic, or democratic, they quickly perish. . . . Democracies particularly . . . quickly degenerate into licence and dictatorship. . . . [For them to become durable] they must be tempered by the introduction of a conservative element or a monarchical element. The government of Venice has seemed to these publicists, as well as to Paruta, to Fra Paolo Sarpi, and to the whole Italian school, the best government of those that existed not only in their time but even in antiquity, because with its ducal throne, its grand council, and its senate, it participated in all forms of government, and by this combination the defects of each were mutually corrected.'

The most perfect form of mixed government, he said, was 'constitutional government'. As practised between 1815 and 1848 in France, it had not been a balanced mixture, for the monarchic or conservative element had been preponderant over the popular element, and it had therefore failed. In the constitution of the Hundred Days, however, the democratic principle, strengthened by universal suffrage, had been as powerful as the others and there had been a real equilibrium. 'It is for that reason that it deserves to be considered an original work which will be imitated.'[1]

The equilibrium was to be ensured by three peculiar features. First, the democratic principle required that government should be based on popular approval. Taking this to its extreme limit, 'the democratic party', said Ollivier, 'at one time agitated for direct legislation by the people', by referendum, for, according to Rousseau, the people could not alienate their sovereignty nor be represented. Such methods were now generally discredited, but Ollivier nevertheless thought they had some merit: the referendum was 'chimerical for ordinary laws, but it was justified in so far as constitutional laws are concerned, for these are capable

[1] Speech of 28 March 1870, in *Annales du sénat* (1870), iii. 50–51 and *Mes Discours* (1875), 152–4.

of being summarized in a few simple points, easy to formulate and to understand.' The Napoleonic plebiscite represented the democratic element in, as he thought, a suitably moderated form.[1] Secondly, Ollivier, following Constant, was very anxious that no one, neither parliament nor the emperor (nor even the people) should have absolute power. The constitution thus provided for the division of power, and for checks and balances. The emperor was kept in check by parliament, the lower house by the upper house, and all three by the people acting through elections and plebiscites. The constitution was original in Ollivier's view above all because, thirdly, it was the shortest France had ever had. That maker of the catch-phrase, Girardin, had already supplied the idea: 'The constitution of France', he had written, 'ought to be brief enough to be inscribed on a hundred-sous coin.'[2] The less there was in the constitution, said Ollivier, the less there would be to quarrel about and to revolt against; and he quoted de Maistre to the effect that written constitutions are in any case powerless against public opinion.[3]

The constitution of 1870, for these reasons, appeared to Ollivier not to represent a surrender on his part but to be, by its very ambiguity, a triumph for his policy of the *juste milieu*. Those aspects of it which others thought despotic seemed to him, as a man of 1848, to be entirely republican. The idea indeed of making a head of state responsible to the people, and at the same time having a cabinet responsible to parliament, dates from the second republic, because the 'irresponsibility and inviolability' of Louis Philippe had been considered an offence to democracy.[4] Strong government had been a major aim of the constitution of 1848, which had given the president 'all the powers of a king and even more'.[5] The inalienability of the people's sovereignty was laid down in it as a primary maxim and it declared also that

---

[1] *Annales du Sénat* (1870), 48 ff.

[2] Quoted by P. de la Gorce, *Histoire du second empire* (1894–1907) vi. 90.

[3] *Annales du Sénat*, ibid.; E.L. xiii. 321.

[4] Cf., e.g., *Exposé des principes républicans de la société des droits de l'homme*, quoted by G. Weill, *Histoire du parti républican* (1925), 94.

[5] Jacques Cohen, *La Préparation de la constitution de 1848* (1935), 65 ff.

'the separation of powers is the first condition of a free government'.[1] The demand for the limitation of the powers of parliament was very much in the air at this time: Tocqueville, one of the authors of the constitution of 1848, popularizing the arguments of Benjamin Constant and Royer-Collard, had inveighed against the tyranny of assemblies and majorities. J. S. Mill likewise, in his treatise on *Representative Government*, devoting a chapter to 'the proper functions of representative bodies', urged that these should neither govern, nor appoint all ministers, nor even work out the details of legislation.[2] The direct government of the people through plebiscites derives originally from the great revolution: Condorcet had the same distinction as Ollivier, that the people should vote on fundamental and constitutional questions, but not on ordinary laws; Sèchelles in drafting the constitution of 1793 had attempted to create a similar compromise, combining 'democratic' with 'representative' institutions; and the whole idea had been widely canvassed again in 1848.[3]

It is worthy of note that one of the leading influences in the making of the constitution of 1848, Cormenin, who came top of the poll in the election of the constitutional committee of that year, held views remarkably similar to Ollivier's. He too wanted a short constitution (and actually produced one of four articles): a strong executive, centralization of the Napoleonic type, a popularly elected president and a constitution approved

---

[1] Constitution of 4 November 1848, Chapter I and Article 19.

[2] A. de Tocqueville, *De la démocratie en Amérique* (1835–40), especially vol. i, part 2, ch. 7, and vol. ii, part 4; P. de Barante, *La Vie politique de M. Royer Collard* (1861), ii. 132; B. Constant, *Principes de politique* (1815) (Edition de la Pleiade (1951), 1126); J. S. Mill, *Representative Government* (1861) (Everyman edition (1948), 228–41).

[3] M. Fridieff, *Les Origines du referendum dans la constitution de 1793* (1931), 185–90, 274; A. Sarraut, *Le Gouvernement direct en France* (1899); J. Signorel, *Le Referendum législatif* (1896); J. Godechot, *Institutions de la France sous la république et l'empire* (1951) 241–54; A. Soboul, *Les Sans-Culottes parisiens en l'an II* (1958), 504–41; V. Considérant, *La Solution, ou le gouvernement directe du peuple* (1850); C. Renouvier and C. Fauvety, *Le Gouvernement direct* (1851); H. Rittinghausen, *La Législation directe par le peuple* (1850).

by referendum, the separation of powers—his ideal being the direct government of the people as opposed to the rule of an assembly.[1] He had rallied to the empire even before Ollivier, declaring that Napoleon was 'more republican in the audacity of his ideas than the republicans suppose'; and as early as 1861 had urged the Five to follow him, to 'lay aside their wrath' and to carry out the fusion of Bonapartism and republicanism which they ought to have attempted before 1851.[2]

But why then did the republicans of 1870 greet the new constitution of 1870 with such hostility? The answer is that for them these ideals of 1848 were totally out of date. The constitution of Tocqueville and Cormenin had ended in disaster and had produced not the democracy they had hoped for but the autocracy of Napoleon III. Vermorel's book denouncing *The Men of 1848* (1869) and old Quinet's remark that the republicans now used 'a new language which I do not know and which I cannot learn'[3] showed how the new generation had entirely broken with their elders. The curious characteristic of Ollivier's politics is that he, almost alone, remained faithful to the past, resuscitating the ideas of 1848 and 1815 in the hope—to be proved vain—that they might be successful if given another chance.[4]

Ollivier did not intend to establish parliamentary government or to copy the Orleanist system,[5] but his theory differed from his practice. Though he said that 'constitutional' or 'representative' government was his ideal, he also frequently made, in his speeches of 1870, the entirely contrary assertion that he had established parliamentary government.[6] The practical need to

---

[1] P. Bastid, *Cormenin, précurseur et constituant de 1848* (1948), 202, 204, 222, 236, 246, 261.

[2] Louis (Vicomte) de Cormenin, *Reliquiae* (1868), i. 129–30.

[3] I. Tchernoff, *Le Parti républicain au coup d'état et sous le second empire* (1906), 364.

[4] See the condemnation of the constitution of 1848 in P. Bastid, *Doctrines et institutions politiques de la seconde république* (1945), ii. 312.

[5] Cf. a note by Napoleon III printed by Ferdinand Giraudeau, *Napoléon III Intime* (1895), 169.

[6] E. Ollivier, *Le Ministère du 2 janvier: mes discours* (1875), 120, 123, 139, 153, 161, 169, 205, 215, 300.

win the support of the legislature in fact compelled him to concede it wider rights than he wished. 'I never liked the parliamentary régime much,' he wrote in his diary[1] 'even before I had experienced its inconveniences. I had been very struck by the criticisms of it made by Bastiat and Fonfrède, and by the contempt Lamartine felt for it in his later days.[2] I resigned myself to it for this reason: the revolution was threatening, the union of the forces of conservatism could alone stop it; the parliamentary system seemed to me the only one on which liberals could suitably unite. That is why I defended it.' In his memoirs, Ollivier described his constitution as an essentially plebiscitary one, reading back the ideals of the liberal Bonapartists of the third republic into it. He tried to conceal this temporary deviation towards parliamentary government: and he surreptitiously omitted an inconvenient passage from a letter of this period in which he had denounced plebiscitary government but which was inconsistent with his other writings.[3] These hesitations at any rate help to explain why the constitution of 1870 is so difficult to classify and so easy to find fault with: they added a further element of confusion to a system which was in any case open to many-sided attack. A study of the opposition to it will help to bring out the issues involved.

First, the position of the emperor was criticized as being anomalous. He was supposed to be 'responsible to the French people',[4] but there was no machinery by which the people could express their dissatisfaction with him. On the contrary, it was all arranged

---

[1] D. 1870, undated, probably late 1870, jottings, p. 60 of typescript copy.

[2] F. Bastiat, Œuvres complètes (1854–5), v. 518–61. Henri Fonfrède (1788–1841) was 'the leading provincial journalist' of his day; 'his articles were read throughout France with as much avidity as those of the great Parisian newspapers.' His essay On Royal Government and the Constitutional Limits of the Parliamentary Prerogative (1839) opposes Thiers' maxim that the king reigns but does not rule (p. 32), just as Ollivier does, and it advocates a very limited role for parliaments. Œuvres de Henri Fonfrède, edited by C. A. Campan (Bordeaux, 1844–7), 10 vols., particularly vol. vi.

[3] E.L. xii. 612, letter to Girardin; about six lines are omitted at line 8; there is a full copy of the letter in O.P. Cf. also J. ii. 253 (August 1866).

[4] Article 13.

that he should be succeeded by his son and a long line of rela-
tives, whatever the people thought of him. Since the idea of his
being responsible was taken from the republic of 1848, it was
easy to point out that responsibility and heredity were incompatible. If the nation really was sovereign, it ought at least to
be able to expel its chief of state at periodic intervals. In a pamphlet which was very widely distributed by the republicans and
from which Gambetta drew most of his arguments, Gustave
Chaudey asked the question, *Is a Parliamentary Empire Possible?*,
and categorically replied that universal suffrage could be master
only in a republic.[1] Besides, what was the emperor responsible
for? Not the conduct of government, for his ministers were
now declared responsible precisely in order to take the blame
for this. Ollivier's answer came in the form of a quotation from
Mirabeau: 'The prince is the perpetual representative of the
people, just as the deputies are its temporarily elected representatives':[2] he was what Benjamin Constant called 'the neutral
power', whose function it was to mediate between the various
powers in the state, to ensure that parliament did not go beyond
its mandate, or, it might be added, as the Constitution of the
Fifth Republic puts it, 'to watch over the maintenance of the
constitution [and] ensure, by his arbitration, the regular function-
ing of the public powers as well as the continuity of the state'.[3]
The idea of the liberal empire was not only that the emperor
should commune with the people in some mystic Lamartinian
manner, but that he should perform the functions of an active

[1] G. Chaudey, *L'Empire parlementaire est-il possible?* (1870); *Discours et
plaidoyers politiques de M. Gambetta* (1881), i. 221, speech of 5 April 1870; E.
Laboulaye, *Le Parti libéral: son programme et son avenir* (1864), 205–8.

[2] Napoleon I had scornfully asked the members of his legislature, 'Are you
the representatives of the people? It is I who am this, I; four times I was summoned by the nation and four times I received the votes of five million citizens
cast in my favour. I have a right to call myself their representative and you
have not; you are only the deputies of the departments of the empire.' Speech
of 1 January 1814, quoted by R. Jacquelin, Les Cent-jours et le régime parlementaire, *Revue du droit public et de la science politique* (March–April 1897), 194.

[3] E.L. xiii. 329 n.; B. Constant, *Principes de politique* (1815), edition de la
Pleiade (1957), 1114; M. Duverger, *La Cinquième République* (1959), 304
(Article 5 of the constitution of 1958).

constitutional monarch. Ollivier had no wish to give the people absolute sovereignty: like the liberals of the restoration he wanted the 'sovereignty of reason', a constitution of checks and balances.[1]

The second criticism of the constitution was that the position of the ministers was ambiguous. They were declared 'responsible', but it was not stated to whom they were responsible, and the omission has been taken as a disguised preservation of imperial despotism. That, however, was certainly not Ollivier's purpose nor any one else's. An examination of the constitutions of 1814, 1830, and 1848, all parliamentary in various degrees, reveals that they used the identical unexplained phrase. Prévost-Paradol, in his highly influential book, La France Nouvelle (1868), had urged the need to end this traditional ambiguity and to state plainly that ministerial responsibility meant that parliament appointed the prime minister.[2] Ollivier, however, more old-fashioned than the new school of liberals and a pupil of Benjamin Constant, wished to avoid the 'government by assembly' which was to flourish under the third republic. Constant had maintained that ministers should be appointed by the monarch and not by parliament;[3] and Daru now publicly stated that in the event of a disagreement between the cabinet and parliament, it would be Napoleon who would decide which of the two would go.[4] In leaving the responsibility of ministers unexplained, Ollivier clearly intended that they should be responsible simultaneously to the emperor and to parliament. Such a situation had prevailed in France under the restoration and in England in the late seventeenth and eighteenth centuries, when the king played an active part in government but needed to follow a policy acceptable to parliament, and in

[1] J. ii. 42 (15 March 1862); B. Constant, Principes de politique (1957 edition), IIII.

[2] La France Nouvelle (1868), 102.

[3] B. Constant, Principes de politique (1815, édition de la Pleiade, 1179; idem, De la responsabilité des ministres (1815), 41-43, 70-71; cf. J. Barbey, Le Conseil des ministres sous la restauration (1936).

[4] Annales du Corps législatif, 22 February 1870, ii. 364.

neither country had this arrangement necessarily involved any despotism.[1]

The Bourbons, by Article 14 of the Charter of 1814, had power to rule by ordinance in emergencies; and Napoleon III's constitution of 1852, Article 33, likewise gave the head of state (in conjunction with the senate) the right 'to do all that was necessary . . . in the event of the dissolution of the legislature'. Now, after much hesitation, Napoleon agreed to give up this right, and its omission from the constitution of 1870 marked an important diminution of his power. On the other hand, however, he retained his right to appeal to the nation by plebiscite. This was at first looked upon by liberals as simply a historical relic which would in practice fall into disuse; but when soon after it was actually proposed to hold a plebiscite to approve the new constitution in terms chosen arbitrarily by the government, its significance as a menace to parliament emerged and it became the opposition's principal target of attack.[2] It was pointed out that the emperor had a perfectly adequate method of restraining the legislature in his right to dissolve it; and that the preservation of the plebiscite meant that the threat of another *coup d'état* of 2 December 1851 would for ever hang over France. 'I am the adversary of the empire, personal or parliamentary', wrote Jules Favre to Picard, 'because the empire always keeps a reserve of despotic power which, at a given moment, can destroy the rights of the nation.'[3] Ollivier replied that new elections would not take the place of a plebiscite, because elections involved numerous personal and local issues, unlike a straightforward plebiscite requiring the answer *yes* or *no* to a single question. His opponents insisted that on the contrary the wording of the question could determine the result: plebiscites gave

---

[1] P. Duverger de Hauranne, *Histoire du gouvernement parlementaire en France* (1857–72), Preface to vol. i.

[2] See the striking change of attitude by Prévost-Paradol in *Journal des débats*, 31 March–14 April 1870.

[3] I. Tchernoff, *Le Parti républicain au coup d'état et sous le second empire* (1906), 575; M. Réclus, *Jules Favre* (1912), 308.

the people an illusory sovereignty and no freedom at all.[1] The fact that the legislature still could not alter the constitution was a further ground for complaint: in this respect, the opposition argued, Ollivier brought no improvement on 1852. He replied that it was a great democratic achievement on his part to have removed the constitution from the oligarchic control of the senate and to have 'restored the constituent power to the people'. He refused the legislature the right even to discuss constitutional questions, which, he insisted, should be left entirely to the people. In practice, however, it was the emperor who had to take the initiative in a constitutional plebiscite, and this, it was argued, made him the ultimate master.

It was indeed largely the retention of the plebiscite that discredited Ollivier's constitution in the eyes of most liberals. It was for this reason that Bagehot apparently saw nothing to distinguish the liberal empire from the old despotism. The whole régime, he declared, rested on an 'abuse of the confidence reposed by the most ignorant in a great name, to hold at bay the reasoned arguments of men who both know the popular wish and also are sufficiently educated to discuss the best means of gratifying those wishes [;] a virtually irresponsible power obtained by one man from the vague preference of the masses for a particular name'.[2] The radical philosopher Alain likewise swept aside the claim that the Bonapartist, plebiscitary system was really more democratic than the republic: 'What matters,' he said, 'is not the origin of power, but the continuous and efficacious control which the governed exercise over the government.'[3]

---

[1] Cf. A. Thibaudet, *Les Idées politiques de la France* (1932), 167–8; M. Prélot, *Pour comprendre la nouvelle constitution* (1958); E. de Laveleye, *Le Gouvernement dans la démocratie* (1891), ii. 166–70.

[2] *The Works and Life of Walter Bagehot*, ed. Mrs. Russell (1915), x. 241; from an article in *The Economist* of 20 August 1870 entitled 'The Collapse of Caesarism'.

[3] Quoted by C. Nicolet, *Le Radicalisme* (1957), 39. Cf. B. Mirkine-Guetzévitch, 'Some Constitutional Problems facing the French Constituent Assembly', in *Social Research* (1946), xiii. 24–32 for an attack on the notion of 'parliamentary tyranny'.

What kind of government, then, did this constitution establish? It was not quite parliamentary government, nor an ordinary constitutional monarchy, nor yet a Caesarian autocracy. It was a compromise which, if a label is required for it, might be called representative government, as Benjamin Constant also called his constitution of 1815.[1] In conformity with Constant's theories, it gave full power to no one and it was inevitably liable therefore to please no one entirely. It was inspired moreover by two régimes—the Hundred Days and the second republic—and both of these had been unsuccessful. The constitution of the Weimar Republic fifty years later was to incorporate a similar combination of a parliament, an active president, a referendum and likewise ended in disaster. The Vichy régime of Marshal Pétain is said to have planned a constitution which had many points of resemblance with that of 1870 but which came to nothing.[2] Is it possible to argue from this that Ollivier's system had little likelihood of success?

It may have been fair enough thirty years ago to have regarded the second empire as a short-lived autocratic parenthesis in France's gradual development towards parliamentary government, and the liberal empire as a transition between the two; but in the light of recent changes, a new perspective emerges. It is possible now to look on Ollivier's government as part of an entirely different tradition which can be traced through modern French history, from 1815, 1848, 1870 to 1958. The régimes founded in these years have not been essentially parliamentary, but neither have they been right-wing autocracies: they have sought to reduce the power of parliament in order to produce strong government while at the same time reconciling this with liberty and democracy. General de Gaulle's belief in the 'separation of powers, the authority of a Head of State who really is one, recourse to the people by means of referendum

---

[1] Cf. Earl Grey, *Parliamentary Government Considered with Reference to Reform* (new edition 1864); Additional Act of 22 April 1815, preamble.
[2] M. Abeberry, *Le projet de constitution du maréchal Petain* (unpublished typescript thesis, Bordeaux 1951), 202.

whenever its destinies or institutions are involved'; his hostility to government by assembly, his notion of a president 'above party, elected by the people, appointing ministers, with the right to consult the country either by referendum or by parliamentary elections, and with a mandate to ensure the integrity and independence of France in times of crisis',[1] are certainly not inspired by Ollivier, but they belong to the same school of thought. Neither General de Gaulle nor Ollivier established quite the sort of constitution they had hoped for; but they represent a similar effort to find a solution to an old problem.

[1] Charles de Gaulle, *Mémoires de Guerre*, vol. iii, *Le Salut 1944–6* (1959), 103, 240; but cf. Michel Debré, *La République et son pouvoir* (1960); and P. M. Williams and M. Harrison, *De Gaulle's Republic* (1960), 122–30. At the time of the referendum of April 1962 *L'Express* printed a quotation from Emile Ollivier's *Empire libéral* under a large photograph of General de Gaulle on its front page (issue of 5 April); 'One is never weaker than when one appears to be supported by everybody'.

CHAPTER 11

THE PLEBISCITE OF 1870

WHAT was the significance of the plebiscite of 8 May 1870, when the French people approved the new constitution by 7,358,786 votes against only 1,571,939?[1] Ollivier declared it was a triumphant vindication of his own policy, an indisputable proof that the liberal empire was what the people really wanted. 'Had I now died of fever,' he wrote, 'like Cavour, I should have been unanimously celebrated as one of those rare statesmen of the nineteenth century whose aim has been accomplished in its entirety, neither more nor less, and I should also have been cited as evidence of what the will of one person can achieve.'[2] The authoritarian Bonapartists on the other hand asserted that the masses voted simply to show their confidence in the emperor, that no one cared for or even understood the new constitution, and that the plebiscite showed not Ollivier's popularity, but Napoleon's.[3] The republicans on their side denounced the whole episode as a fraud, the product of governmental pressure on ignorant, frightened, and egoistic peasants.[4]

[1] Results in Archives Nationales, F (1c) 130 and *Bulletin des lois* (1870), 11th series, 1st semester, volume 35, bulletin 1813, pp. 675–8.

[2] E.L. xiii. 404.

[3] C. E. de Maupas, *Mémoires sur le second empire* (1884–5), ii. 497.

[4] Taxile Delord, *Histoire du Second Empire* (1869–75), vi. 121; *Discours et Plaidoyers politiques de M. Gambetta* (1881), ii. 17, iii. 77. Cf. the song 'Le Plebiscite':

> Deux grands hommes aux Tuileries,
> Causaient entr'eux un certain soir,
> L'un portrait mille broderies
> Et l'autre le simple habit noir.
> Le premier dit, d'un ton febrile;
> 'Je suis le vrai Napoléon!'
>
> *Refrain:*
>
> 'Majesté, répondit Emile,   } *bis*
> 'Majesté, vous avez raison.'

The plebiscite was indeed confused by numerous paradoxes. Ollivier, who claimed the credit for the result, had not intended to hold it at all. It was principally provoked by the conservative senate—which disliked the new constitution—on the pretext that so radical a change required popular approval, but with obviously hostile motives.[1] In the government its main champion was Daru, anxious for grand measures and delighted with it as a personal success, until his party, the centre-left, protested so strongly at his abetting an infringement of parliamentary government, that he (and Buffet with him), resigned, disassociating himself from his own work.[2] Thus this crowning event of the liberal empire, which was supposed to put the seal on the union of liberals, in fact disrupted it: instead of confirming the trend of progress, it gave the signal for a movement of reaction. 'Thiers', wrote the British ambassador, 'is said to have been the principal mischiefmaker. . . . No one expected that he would long endure that any Government of which he was not a Member should go on smoothly.'[3]

The issues were thus blurred by intrigues and even more so by the wording of the plebiscite. The electorate was allowed either to approve or to reject the liberal empire as a whole, without distinguishing between its approval of the new liberties and its approval of the empire. Ultra-conservative Bonapartists, like Cassagnac, who execrated Ollivier's reforms, were thus

'La cuisine du plébiscite,
Reprit le maître, a du succès,
Faisons donc bouillir la marmite
Avec les bons "oui" des Français.
Il aime, ce peuple imbécile,
Tous les ragouts de ma façon.'

Refrain:

Mon peuple est un mouton docile
Dont je sais tondre la toison. . . .

P. Barbier and F. Vernillat, *Histoire de France par les chansons* (1959), 7.

[1] Drouyn de Lhuys to Ollivier, [early] April 1870, O.P.
[2] D., April 1870.
[3] Lyons to Clarendon, MSS. Clar. Dep. 477, 14 and 29 April 1870. Cf. Thiers to Ollivier, 2 April 1870, O.P.

compelled to vote *yes*.[1] Many supporters of these reforms, on the other hand, disapproved of the plebiscite as anti-parliamentary and therefore voted *no* or abstained (following Thiers' advice), or (like Daru) wrote 'yes, except for Article 44'. The newspapers which had formerly supported Ollivier were now suddenly critical: at best they only hesitatingly and reluctantly advised their readers to vote *yes*. Guizot and Laboulaye alone declared that the plebiscitary method was a minor blemish which should not obscure the importance of Napoleon's concessions.[2]

In many places, moreover, as the campaign grew warmer and the hostile agitation of the republicans became more violent the ground of the debate was changed once again.[3] Terrified by the prospect of a red revolution, the bourgeoisie felt bound to put aside their scruples and to rally in defence of order. The Orleanist newspaper of Toulouse, for example, had on 1 May urged abstention, because of its disapproval of plebiscitary methods, but four days later declared 'liberal conservatives' to be so 'alarmed by the extravagant clamours' of the left opposition, that they ought to vote *yes*.[4] A newspaper of Dijon, suddenly changing its policy in the same way, announced that 'the plebiscite of 8 May is the pacific but relentless struggle of order against revolution'.[5] It was largely for this same reason

[1] Paul de Cassagnac, *Une Politique vraiment nationale* (1905), i. 80–87; H. J. Dugué de la Fauconnerie, *Souvenirs d'un viel homme 1866–1879* (about 1912), 128; cf. A. de Caix de Saint-Amour, *Le Plébiscite et l'hérédité* (1870).

[2] P.R.O., F.O. 27/1802, May 1870; *Journal de Lot-et-Garonne* (Agen), 1 May 1870; *L'Industriel Alsacien* (Mulhouse), 28 April 1870; *L'Indépendant du Lot* (Cahors), 1 May 1870; *Catéchisme élementaire à l'usage des électeurs qui n'ont pas lu le senatus-consulte ou qui, l'ayant lu, n'y ont rien compris* (1870, long poster); Archives Nationales, BB (30) 455; *La Justice et la politique sous le second empire* (n.d., privately printed by the Ministry of Justice), a volume of 856 pages containing the reports of the procureurs-généraux on the plebiscite, the originals of which have since disappeared.

[3] Cf. A. Vermorel, *Le Parti socialiste* (1870); G. Lefrançais, *Souvenirs d'un révolutionnaire* (about 1902), 379–80; S. Maritch, *Histoire du mouvement social sous le second empire à Lyon* (Lyon, 1930), 258–60.

[4] René Amanieu, 'Élections législatives et plébiscites à Toulouse sous le second empire', *Annales du Midi* (1950), lxii. 176.

[5] Josette Michel, *Le Plébiscite du 8 mai en Côte d'Or* (Dijon 1957, unpublished typescript, D.E.S.), 26.

that most of the bishops declared in favour. The constitutional issue counted for very little with the church: the ultramontane *Univers* offered its support to Ollivier in return for a promise that he would never evacuate Rome, and when refused, decided on abstention.[1] The vicars-general of the diocese of Valence issued a circular letter which spoke neither of liberty nor of the emperor but simply declared, '*Yes is Order . . . No is Anarchy*'.[2] Though the parish clergy mostly voted *yes* (with a considerable minority abstaining and even voting *no*) very few showed any enthusiasm at all for the liberal empire.[3] The legitimists, who played hardly any active part in the campaign, usually abstained, but, where there was a strong republican challenge, they some-times emerged to vote conservative.[4]

Apart from the question of the phrasing of the plebiscite, was the vote free? Ollivier in principle intended that it should be so; and instead, therefore, of the government taking the lead in influencing the electorate through the civil service, as had been the practice in the past, he proposed to leave the organi-zation of propaganda to private initiative. He encouraged the formation of an independent committee of leading politicians and journalists, with the duc d'Albufera as president, which soon set up some eighty sub-committees in Paris and a further 350 in the provinces, financed by their own subscriptions (and, it is said, by a gift of one million francs from the Crédit Foncier).[5]

---

[1] Ollivier to Wallon, 1 March 1873, copy, O.P.; *Le Courrier du Bas-Rhin* (Strasbourg), 29 April 1870; Cf. J. W. Pickersgill, 'The French Plebiscite of 1870 and the Catholics', *English Historical Review* (1937), 254–66.

[2] *La Justice et la politique sous le second empire*, 439 n.

[3] Ibid., 18, 100, 101, 123–4, 271, 334, 352, 454, 551, 558, 572, 655–7, 680–3, 709.

[4] Ibid., 40–41, 60, 78–79, 89, 92, 100–1, 311, 532, 572, 585, 648, 667; J. Cornillon, *Le Bourbonnais à la fin de l'empire et sous le gouvernment de la défense nationale* (Moulins, 1924), 23; O. Pichat, *L'Empire devant le peuple* (1870); Vicomte de L'Ecuyer la Papotière, *Le Plébiscite de 1870, son vrai caractère, véritables questions qu'il soulève* (1870); André Armengaud, *Les Populations de l'Est-Aquitain au début de l'époque contemporain* (1961), 439–43.

[5] A. Dumon, *Révélations sur le plébiscite et le comité central* (1870); H. P. O. Lissagaray, *Histoire de la Commune de 1870* (1876, Marcel Rivière edition of 1947), 23.

Admirable though Ollivier's intentions may have been, this procedure in practice meant that he lost control over the direction of the propaganda, which became much more conservative than liberal.[1] Yet at the same time the committees were looked upon as a mere façade. Many civil servants joined them 'in their personal capacity', though the distinction between voluntary and official electoral work was theoretical. 'The committee', the Russian chargé d'affaires observed (with exaggerated cynicism), 'is in close contact with the ministry and receives orders from it'.[2]

The government apparently had intended to found a special newspaper for the occasion, entitled Le Plébiscite, but was stopped by the protests of the journalists, who feared this might reduce the circulation of their own papers: it thus had little control over the way the plebiscite was presented in the press.[3] Again, the civil servants of the old régime who had been largely left in office almost inevitably tended to revive something of the old methods they had perfected to support 'official candidates', despite Ollivier's specific instructions forbidding them to do so. The public prosecutors briefed their subordinates as before, but in private; the judges of the peace toured their cantons, but not in uniform; the firemen were lectured on their political duties; the mayors led their electors to the voting booths—in ways which differed according to the vigour and enthusiasm of the particular individuals.[4] Some officials interpreted the plebiscite liberally,

[1] Quotations from its circulars in Josette Michel, Le Plébiscite du 8 mai 1870 en Côte d'Or (1957), 46.

[2] Okounev to Gorchakov, 16–28 April 1870, letter no. 43, Russian Foreign Policy Archives, Moscow, 1870, file no. 116; see also E. A. Jelubovskaya, The Decline of the Second Empire and the Rise of the Third Republic in France (Moscow, 1956), 205; a few traces of insignificant correspondence between the ministry and the committee in BB (30) 455.

[3] L'Indépendant du Lot (Cahors), 1 May 1870; BB (30) 455.

[4] La Justice. . . . 226–7, 353, 610; Ollivier quotes from p. 318 (E.L. xiii. 339) a report showing abstention by the civil service; but he fails to continue the quotation to the following page, which reveals that there was a great deal of difference between what officials said they were doing, and what they in fact did.

but others so simplified it as to declare that 'authoritarian or parliamentary, the empire remains the empire, and the emperor the emperor and all the emperor's friends must understand that the battle is joined not between two political forms of the empire, but between the empire and the revolution, between ruin and salvation, between social order and its overthrow'.[1]

The opposition nevertheless certainly enjoyed more freedom than ever before under the second empire and it was extremely active within the limits of its inevitably inferior resources. Its propaganda in the press, in pamphlets, and in public meetings probably did not reach every village in the country, as the government's did, but it was very powerful in the strongholds of republicanism, and at times seemed to be on the point of bursting into revolution.[2] In Paris, the extremists of the left were surprised to find that they were able to say with impunity at a public meeting attended by the police that 'after having lived upon France for eighteen years like a veritable louse, the empire is now asking us if we want a change of vermin'. One meeting was indeed stopped when an orator clad in a blouse called the empire a 'government of thieves' but was allowed to continue when he retracted with the explanation that if it was not a government of thieves, it was a government of rascals.[3] On the other hand a hairdresser of Aix-les-Bains was sentenced to fifteen days' imprisonment for calling Ollivier a 'weather-cock, Judas, apostate, turncoat', and for saying 'M. Bonaparte and M. Pius IX founded their thrones on blood: I do not recognize the authority of M. Bonaparte, your emperor; he must be defeated.' A republican barrister of Lyon, Andrieux (later to be a tough prefect himself), was prosecuted likewise for insulting the emperor as 'a decayed old man, worn out by debauchery, ruled by a

---

[1] Procureur Général of Dijon to Ollivier, 19 April 1870, *La Justice* . . . , 343.

[2] BB (30) 455; Procureur Général of Montpellier to Ollivier, 2 May and 'midnight 3 May', 1870, *La Justice* . . . , 520–9.

[3] G. Lefrançais, *Souvenirs d'un Révolutionnaire* (c. 1902), 379, G. de Molinari, *Le Mouvement socialiste et les réunions publiques avant la révolution du 4 septembre 1870* (1872), 112.

Spanish wife and led by a bastard republican deserter'.[1] Newspapers were frequently seized or censured for 'spreading false news': even a cartoon in *Le Charivari* showing a civil servant leading a peasant to the poll, with the legend 'Au printemps tout pousse', was banned.[2] The laws of the authoritarian empire were still in force to allow repression in this wild, erratic way.

Ollivier was not responsible for a great deal of the civil service's activity, but in time he was increasingly provoked by the violence of the attacks against him into urging forceful repression. With the menace of revolution suddenly resurrected, he felt he must show himself to be a strong man, as capable of holding it in check and as resolute in the defence of order as any despotism. (This determination to be strong, as well as liberal, was to be seen again in the foreign policy which led to the outbreak of war.) He telegraphed his subordinates throughout France: 'Do not hesitate to prosecute newspapers . . . containing appeals to civil war or outrages against the emperor. We cannot stand watching the revolutionary excesses with folded arms. Respect liberty; but to provoke assassination and civil war is contrary to liberty. . . . ' 'I am told the public meetings of Marseilles are intolerable in their violence. Do not hesitate to make an example, and above all, strike at the leaders; get the barristers, the *messieurs*, rather than the poor devils of the masses.' 'It is time that the hand of the government was felt.'[3] Finally, just before the poll, Ollivier ordered the arrest of all members of the Workers' International for planning the overthrow of the state; created a further sensation by revealing the details of a gruesome plot to assassinate the emperor; and then prosecuted the newspapers which declared this had been invented by the police. The effect of these measures was to put an end to the relative apathy about the plebiscite, which had prevailed till then, create a nation-wide sense of crisis, and, according to the

---

[1] *La Justice* . . . , 314, 474. Cf. *Le Radical de l'Ouest* (Nantes), 10 April 1870; and *L'Emancipation* (Toulouse), 30 April 1870.

[2] *Le Charivari*, 28 April 1870.

[3] Telegrams in A. Poulet-Malassis, *Papiers Secrets et Correspondence du second empire* (1880), 187, 189, 191.

Russian chargé d'affaires, add one and a half million votes to the government's majority.[1]

This is of course only a guess; and the extant material does not really allow any very precise explanation of why the government's vote was 4·3 million in the elections of 1869 but 7·3 million in the plebiscite of 1870. One can very hesitantly suggest that about half a million men who had abstained in 1869, now voted *for*: this is particularly noticeable in the west, where it indicates not legitimist or clerical pressure, but the strengthening links between the civil service and the masses. Between one and a half and two million votes had formerly been cast for 'opposition candidates' who, on examination, turn out to represent personal, local, or liberal opposition, men who were not hostile to the empire and who were now either supporters to the liberal empire or at least not enemies of it. In addition there was an important section of frightened moderate republicans and others who broke with their extremist allies and came out in favour of 'order'. This can be seen happening in a particularly striking manner among the bourgeoisie of Lyon, where the socialist agitation was exceptionally violent.[2] There are also departments, however, where the alignments of 1869 seem unchanged: the hostile legitimists of Gard and Hérault held firm in opposition and the republican vote in Var, Vaucluse, Pyrénées Orientales, Nièvre, for example, remained as strong as before.

It is important not to simplify the results; and it is incorrect to assert that France was divided on a class basis, the property owners against the proletariat. The peasants did not vote in a solid block for the emperor: there are significant instances of the more prosperous among them voting *no*, while poorer ones voted *yes*.[3] The 'capitalists' were by no means united against the

---

[1] Okounev to Tsar Alexander II, 6–18 May 1870, letter no. 57, Russian Foreign Policy Archives, Moscow, 1870, file no. 116. He adds that the soldiers who voted *no* did so from professional discontent against Niel's army reforms.

[2] M. Moissonnier, *L'Opposition ouvrière à Lyon à la fin du second empire* (unpublished typescript, D.E.S., Lyon about 1957), chap. 7, p. 2.

[3] *La Justice* . . . , 546–7, Procureur-Général of Montpellier to the Minister of Justice, 20 May 1870.

reds: some, as liberals opposed to the plebiscite, others as protectionists opposed to Napoleon's free trade, declared themselves
hostile; there is even a report of manufacturers exerting strong
pressure on their employees to vote *no*.[1] The industrial workers
indeed, except in the largest urban conglomerations, frequently
voted *yes*. 'We vote *yes*,' said the workers of Thann, 'because
the manufacturers vote *no*!'[2] The industrial town of Volvic
approved the plebiscite by 990 votes against only 14; the mining
town of Pontgibaud by 204 against 83.[3] A pamphlet was published to persuade the workers that since the legislature was
the tool of the employers, diminution of its power was a good
thing: they should place their confidence not in it but in
the emperor.[4] The opposition included small artisans, petty
bourgeois, commercial travellers, whose motives were not
always political: some represented the hereditary hostility of
townsmen to peasants,[5] others anticlericalism.[6] These exceptions are very significant in assessing the strength of the liberal
empire.[7]

Despite its complications, the plebiscite was a most remarkable
and indeed perhaps unprecedented victory: after eighteen years
of dictatorship, Napoleon was still able to emerge with the
support of 67·5 per cent. of the electorate—not much less than
the 74·5 per cent. he had obtained in 1851.[8] Ollivier could with
some justice claim that liberty had rejuvenated the empire.

[1] *La Justice . . .* , 288, cf. also 266.
[2] Quoted from *L'Electeur alsacien* by F. L'Huillier, *La Lutte ouvrière à la fin
du second empire* (1957), 62.
[3] A. G. Manry, Le Plébiscite de 1870 et les premières élections législatives
sous le troisième république dans le Puy de Dôme, *Revue d'Auvergne* (1957),
71. 16–22.
[4] Jean Martin, *Les Travailleurs et le plébiscite* (Bordeaux 1870)—in BB (30)
455.
[5] Cf. P. Bois, *Paysans de l'Ouest* (Le Mans, 1960); *La Justice . . .* , 267.
[6] M. Moissonnier, *L'Opposition ouvrière à Lyon à la fin du second empire 1869–70*
(Lyon, about 1957, unpublished typescript, D.E.S.), chap. 2, p. 8; *La
Justice . . .* , 297.
[7] See Jacques Gouault, *Comment la France est devenue républicaine 1870–5*
(1954), for a rather different view.
[8] General de Gaulle won his referendum in 1958 by 66 per cent. (in metro-
politan France).

Punch published a cartoon showing France granting Napoleon and his son a new lease as tenant of the throne. The Comte de Paris abandoned his hopes of an Orleanist restoration and made plans to settle in America.[1] Paradoxically, however, the plebiscite seriously undermined Ollivier's position.

On 18 May 1870, Karl Marx considered it certain that Napoleon, encouraged by his enormous majority, would soon carry out a reactionary *coup d'état*.[2] Haussmann in his memoirs claims he had a conversation with the emperor in June, in which he was positively told that this was indeed intended, for, said Napoleon, 'I had never imagined that there could be anyone so incompetent as the members of the ministry.'[3] Ollivier strenuously denies these allegations and insists that there was no change in Napoleon's attitude towards him. Other observers agree that the large majority really made a coup unnecessary.[4] Napoleon's speech of 19 May supports this latter view: 'The plebiscite', he said, 'had as its aim simply the ratification by the people of a constitutional reform; but in the midst of the conflict of opinions and the enthusiasm of the battle, the debate was raised on to a higher plane. This is not to be regretted. The adversaries of our institutions turned it into a question between the revolution and the empire. The country decided in favour of the system which guarantees order and liberty. Today, the empire is strengthened in its foundations. It will show its strength by its moderation. The government . . . will not depart from the liberal line it has marked out for itself.'[5]

---

[1] Comte d'Haussonville, *Le Comte de Paris: souvenirs personnels* (1895), 17.

[2] Marx to Engels, in Maximilien Rubel, *Karl Marx devant le bonapartisme* (1960), 137.

[3] G. E. Haussmann, *Mémoires* (1890), ii. 564–5.

[4] E.L. xiii. 522–5; P.R.O., F.O. 27/1802, Lyons to Clarendon, 10 May 1870; Bodleian MSS. Clar. Dep. 477, Lyons to Clarendon, 28 May 1870; Arthur Meyer, *Ce que mes yeux ont vu* (1911), 5–6; Marquis de Roux, *Origines et fondation de la troisième république* (1933), 43.

[5] E.L. xiii. 458. Cf. Napoleon's letter to J. David telling him to stop his intrigues against the ministry in Robert Dufourg, Un homme politique girondin au siècle dernier, Jérôme David, *Revue historique de Bordeaux et du département de la Gironde* (1957), N.S., vi. 156.

Yet, though Napoleon probably remained faithful to his liberal ministers, he had other friends beside them. He had contracted obligations of gratitude to the many reactionaries who had served him loyally during his autocratic period and the contacts of these men with the court had not been ended in 1870. The empress particularly was not only kind to them but even emerged as their leader against the liberal empire. On 3 January she had greeted it with the cold remark: 'The ministers who have the confidence of the emperor are certain of my good will'—implying that they did not have her confidence. Her opinion of Ollivier had in fact changed completely since their first meeting in 1865. She had perhaps been drawn to him then largely because his advocacy of the law of combinations fitted in well with her notion of herself as the protector and benefactor of the toiling masses. The charity she favoured was, however, the kind that is dispensed from above and that can go only with paternal despotism. Thus, while the emperor moved increasingly towards liberalism, she on the contrary revealed herself more and more as a thorough conservative. Napoleon, she insisted, ought to remain true to his past (and she had known him only as a dictator). She claimed that 'real strength comes from consistency'—a phrase which shows how widely she differed from her opportunist husband; and she had therefore wished to postpone the inauguration of a liberal régime, at least till her son should ascend the throne. She urged this view all the more strongly because she believed that 'France is losing her rank among the nations' as a consequence of Prussian expansion, that 'she must win it back or die'. The transformation of the European scene after 1866 was probably what finally won her over to right-wing Bonapartism.[1]

This had recently been showing increasing signs of life and of organization. It had extremely powerful leaders in the fallen

[1] G. Lacour-Gayet, *L'Impératrice Eugénie* (1925), 66–67; P. Guiral, *Prévost-Paradol* (1955), 714 and 715 n.; H. Salomon, *L'Ambassade de Richard de Metternich à Paris* (1931), 141, 143, 183; E.L. xii. 347; *The Times*, 10 January 1870, p. 9; M. T. Ollivier, *L'Epouse de L'Empereur; Souvenirs Personnels, Revue de Genève* (January–June 1921), 161–82, 356–74.

but undaunted archangels of the old régime: Rouher (now president of the senate), Pinard, and Forcade la Roquette. These last two men had both been ministers of the interior and so were regarded as the patrons of many official candidates elected under their auspices; significantly, they now obtained seats for themselves in the lower house, the better to lead their clientele. They had at their command zealots of quite outstanding energy: Granier de Cassagnac, the authoritarian empire's 'press-king', Dugué de la Fauconnerie, who had risen very fast after a dynamic career as an iron-fisted sub-prefect, Du Miral, for long vice-president of the legislature, who in June 1869 had hoped for an insurrection as a 'necessary evil',[1] and Baron Jerôme David, the confidant of the empress. They were joined now by one of the least known figures of this reign, a young journalist called Clément Duvernois, whom one repeatedly glimpses flitting backstage in the final act but who remains something of a mystery. He is said to have been a man of great ambition, of much ability and few scruples, who had first written against the emperor and then entered his pay, who had supported Ollivier when he appeared as a rising star, until, disappointed in his hope of obtaining a ministry from him, he became a violent enemy of the liberal empire. He was determined that since he could not serve it he would overthrow and replace it. He saw how the right was dissatisfied with the way Ollivier had deserted it in order to pander to the Burgraves, the Orleanists, and everybody except the old friends of the emperor. He did much to turn their displeasure into active hostility.

On 23 February, the right had already rallied fifty-six votes to protest against the government's abandonment of the system of official candidates. After this first show of strength, however, they played their cards with great skill, tantalizing Ollivier with a half-masked opposition, but refusing to join battle. When, as on 4 June, he insisted on a vote of confidence, they cunningly refused to be drawn, and Duvernois declared with sinister

[1] Archives Nationales, 45 A.P. 3, Du Miral to Rouher, 16 June 1869.

emphasis, 'We are waiting for our hour.'[1] 'To hear [these men] talk . . . ,' wrote Lord Lyons, 'one would suppose them ready to eat Ollivier alive.' On one occasion in parliament they even surrounded the ministers and 'did not scruple to shake their fists in their faces'.[2]

Their intrigues were all the more dangerous now that, with the plebiscite safely won, they felt free to overthrow a ministry which had served its purpose, and which, moreover, was seriously weakened by the defection of the centre left. The resignation from the cabinet of its leaders Daru and Buffet[3] may well have come as a relief to Ollivier. He had little in common with them: they were admirers of the parliamentary government of Louis Philippe, which he execrated; they were interested principally in political liberty, whereas he laid great stress also on civil and and social reforms. He believed in free trade, they were protectionists; he was devoted to the new Italy, they looked askance at it; he was a deist, they were passionate Catholics; he had developed a personal loyalty to the emperor, whom they on the contrary distrusted. Ollivier claimed afterwards that he formed a coalition with them precisely because he despised them: he felt that his personal prestige would render them helpless in the cabinet beside him; their presence was a small price to pay for the considerable number of votes they brought with them. In fact his main motive was probably a desire to show his independence of the emperor's favour: he felt an imperative need to have an absolute majority in parliament.

In order to keep his colleagues in check, Ollivier claimed the position of leading minister, if not of prime minister, unexpectedly emerging as an advocate of the practice of parliamentary government. Buffet and Daru, so as to counter his pretensions, denied that there could be a prime minister while the emperor retained the presidency of the cabinet. They insisted that their

---

[1] *Annales des séances du corps législatif* (1870), iv. 309–12; E. Pinard, *Mon Journal* (1892), vol. ii; H. J. Dugué de la Fauconnerie, *Souvenirs d'un vieil homme 1866–1879* (1912), 100–28.

[2] Bod. MSS. Clar. Dep. 477, 27 February and 1 March 1870.

[3] Talhouet resigned later, in May.

meetings should be held at a different ministry each time; and they eventually agreed to meet at Ollivier's only when this procedure proved too inconvenient.[1] The episode recalls the situation in 1816, when the ultra-royalist believers in divine right had a majority in parliament and therefore became advocates of parliamentary government, while the constitutionalists spoke up for the king's prerogative right to ignore parliamentary majorities.

Government policy was considerably confused by the rivalry of the two groups within it. Thus Buffet, who represented the cotton-manufacturing department of Vosges, issued the decree restoring a measure of protection to industry, which observers found hardly the sort of reform with which the liberal empire should announce itself. Again Buffet and Daru successfully prevented Ollivier from giving a job to Renan, who was too much of an anti-clerical for them, and they quarrelled also about how mayors should be appointed. Above all as foreign secretary Daru pursued a personal policy in direct opposition to that of Ollivier, producing situations as ridiculous as those common under the régime of personal government. No sooner had he taken office than he issued a circular, without cabinet approval, declaring that France would oppose the unification of Germany. Ollivier's policy was that France would not oppose this if it was effected as the result of the freely expressed wishes of the German people, for Napoleon was after all the apostle of the religion of nationalities. So Ollivier was compelled to have recourse to publishing an inspired article in a Cologne newspaper saying that Daru's was not the cabinet's policy. A little later Daru wished to make known his opinions on the ecclesiastical questions which were that time being debated in the Vatican Council (which produced the declaration of papal infallibility). It was the cabinet's policy to respect the church's liberty to decide these matters of dogma for itself, but Daru nevertheless gave it out as his *personal* view that the church should not encroach upon the rights of the state. Once more Ollivier had to contradict his foreign minister, and

[1] See Ollivier's letter to Gréard, 11 October 1891, draft, O.P.

sent private word to the Vatican that France would not intervene. The incoherence of government foreign policy in the Hohenzollern crisis should not therefore come as a surprise.

The plebiscite, which won Ollivier a majority in the country, thus had the effect of destroying his majority in parliament. It lost him the support of the centre left, and encouraged the right to work for his overthrow. Yet he did nothing to strengthen his highly precarious position. He was so elated by the news of the victory of 8 May that he declared, 'The strength given to the government by this vote is such that the emperor can with impunity commit every possible mistake and remain unshaken on his throne. The fate of his dynasty is assured.'[1] He patched up his cabinet by bringing into it Gramont, a career diplomat and two deputies of his own centre right, Mège and Plichon, neither of whom brought any new parliamentary support with them. He could have strengthened himself only by a dissolution; but, arguing that France had had so much electoral agitation and confusion since 1869 that she now needed repose, he refused to take the only step which could have given the liberal empire a firm foundation. At the same time, by announcing his firm determination not to dissolve, he also gave up the weapon he had formerly been able to hold *in terrorem* over the right.[2] So, when the crisis in foreign affairs came soon after and the emperor left for the front, Ollivier had no real majority behind him in parliament, and he soon found himself helpless before the coalition of the empress and the right. The power of his oratory proved evanescent, and ultimately therefore he failed as a parliamentarian.

[1] Amédée Achard, *Souvenirs personnels d'émeutes et de révolutions* (1872), 266.

[2] Jules Pointu, ancien sous-préfet, *Histoire de la chute de l'empire, 6 juillet —4 septembre 1870* (1874), 9–10. According to the *Liberté* of 7 December 1869 the right consisted of about eighty-two members; A. Darimon, *Les Cent Seize* (1889), 198, numbers them as ninety-seven; cf. Pinard's analysis, showing how these figures must be amended, *Annales des séances du corps législatif* (1870), ii. 354. The centre left had about forty members.

CHAPTER 12

THE FRANCO–PRUSSIAN WAR

WHY was it that Emile Ollivier, who came into power with the avowed intention of ending Napoleon III's foreign adventures as well as his despotism, then declared war on Prussia in little more than six months? How was it that he, who had long been an outstanding advocate of non-intervention, disarmament, and friendship with Germany, suddenly resorted to force 'with a light heart', 'unburdened by remorse'? The origins of the Franco-Prussian War have been studied minutely in a great number of books and, though some points of detail and interpretation remain unsettled, there is little likelihood of substantial new discoveries on this subject. Ollivier's own private papers certainly have nothing new to add about *what* he actually did in the decisive days of July. A closer study of his previous opinions can, however, clarify the question of *why* he acted as he did. His conduct is most usually explained as the product of inexperience and confusion, of his losing control of events. Is this in fact all there is to it?

Ollivier's views on foreign affairs may be reduced to four principles. The first was that foreign policy should be simply the application of his motto of 'liberty and democracy' to external problems. His life was dominated by his struggle to achieve these at home; he believed peace was essential if he was to succeed in transforming the despotism and then carrying through his large programme of reforms; and his hope was that all the other peoples would similarly concentrate on their own improvement. He was therefore, secondly, a partisan of the 'principle of nationalities', but by this he understood not that boundaries should be rearranged along 'natural limits', nor that existing countries should necessarily amalgamate into large states, nor that men of the same race should unite politically: he denounced the racial idea as 'barbarous and retrograde'.[1] For him, any group of people, of whatever number or race, had the right to dispose of itself as it pleased in external as in internal matters, to form an independent government if it wished, or to unite itself to more powerful neighbours if that was to its advantage.[2] He thus agreed that the settlement of 1815 was wrong, but he did not think that France should therefore intervene on every side to redraw the map of Europe, to overthrow oppressors and to liberate nationalities. For he maintained, thirdly, that 'the true principle of foreign policy is the principle of non-intervention, precisely because it is the policy of peace'. A country had no right to interfere in the affairs of another unless called upon by a legally constituted government: the first step in revolution must be taken by the people concerned itself.[3]

Finally, he wished to eliminate questions of power from international relations. The rights of nationalities, he said, could not be limited by the supposed necessity of maintaining the balance of power. 'Balance', he wrote, 'is a fine word, just as order is, but a conventional balance established against the will of the people is no more balance than silence produced by despotism is order.'[4] France should not seek to expand territorially, or to advance towards the Rhine. 'I cannot wish for the physical aggrandizement of my country, for was not Athens greater than Macedonia, even though it had only a few leagues of land?' Wars of conquest were always the ruin of civilization and liberty; and the true ideal for France should be intellectual not military leadership. She had 'exercised a veritable kingship over the whole world' in the eighteenth century because, he claimed, 'at that time she menaced nobody', and she had lost her supremacy as soon as she had embarked on war. 'I desire that France should be influential in the world, but I desire that she should be so because she is loved and not because she is feared.' He attacked

---

[1] E. Ollivier, *Démocratie et liberté* (1867), 420.
[2] E. Ollivier, *Le 19 Janvier* (1867), 380.
[3] E. Ollivier, *Démocratie et liberté* (1867), 305.
[4] E.L. i. 178.

therefore her age-old tradition of trying to keep Europe territorially divided and weak, for this degraded her into a jealous obstacle to progress. Her excellence in the civilized arts was such that she had nothing to fear from rivalry: she could be 'great among the great'. He saw no objection to the formation of new large states on her frontiers: in later years he even thought this development should be welcomed as a first step towards the Confederation of Europe 'which will one day be established between its various peoples . . . in the manner of the United States of America'. Meanwhile, he apparently had visions of peace being maintained by an international tribunal with 'sovereign power'.[1]

Ollivier therefore advocated a pacific foreign policy throughout his years of opposition. He welcomed the liberation of his beloved Italy, 'spiritually my second fatherland', whose art and literature had been a major inspiration of his life, but he was not therefore a blind partisan either of the war of independence or of the unification which succeeded it. He looked upon the war of 1859 as the product of a dynastic plan of conquest by the houses of Savoy and Bonaparte. How could he, whose sympathies lay all in Florence, believe in professions of liberty uttered in the 'barbarous language' of despised Piedmont? How could he suppose that any liberty could be introduced into Italy by the autocrat who had passed the law of *sûreté générale* and had exiled his enemies to Cayenne? How could he welcome a war which, if successful, would strengthen the despotism in France? In parliament he neither voted for the war nor against it, but abstained. He looked on the new kingdom of Italy with a critical eye: he considered that under orders from Turin, Tuscany was governed no less despotically than it had been under the grand duke: he insisted that Rome belonged neither to the pope nor to the Italians but to the Romans themselves, who should be left free to decide whether they wished to join the new kingdom or not; and he believed finally that the south of Italy and Sicily

[1] J. i. 215 (13 May 1855), *Démocratie et liberté* (1867), 305–7, 316, 318, E.L. i. 152–182, iii. 98–99, x. 610.

had little in common with the north and would, if freely consulted, prefer to be independent. He placed liberty, that is, above unity.[1]

He opposed any intervention at all on behalf of the Poles, even though republican opinion by long tradition favoured it. He insisted that a war would strengthen Napoleon's despotism and distract Frenchmen from the struggle for liberty: besides, the leaders of the Polish movement of independence were reactionary aristocrats.[2]

On the subject of the unification of Germany, likewise, he took up an independent position. He opposed the policy of both Napoleon and Thiers. Thiers, the leader of the 'realist' school, argued that France should remain loyal to her traditional policy of keeping Germany divided, that Napoleon's championship of nationalism had been disastrous to her position as a great power and that indeed 'there were no further mistakes to be made'. Napoleon on the other hand still believed that to assist unification was to be on the side of progress and of the future but, conscious of mounting criticism and dwindling prestige, he sought to reconcile his idealism with the realities by demanding territorial compensations for France on the Rhine. Ollivier declared that Napoleon was wrong to think that the principle of nationalities necessarily meant the formation of large nations and he denied that French prestige required compensating territorial expansion. He replied to Thiers that if France really was humiliated by the formation of the new Germany, then she should at once declare war and destroy it. Against both he declared that though they might dislike the work of Bismarck, who had indeed acted on the principle of conquest and not on that of nationalities, they had no right to oppose it: it was up to the Germans to do so themselves. He believed that not a few

[1] J. i. 340 (26 August 1858); i. 361–4, 373, 390, 395 (12 January, 10 February, 11 July, and 23 September 1859); 14 October 1864; E.L. iv. 98 and 521, vi. 138; *Démocratie et liberté* (1867), 266; Ollivier to Boggio, 14 October 1864 (J. ii. 157).

[2] E.L. vi. 466–70; cf. Madeleine Amoudruz, *Proudhon et l'Europe: les idées de Proudhon en politique étrangère* (1945), 84.

of the states preferred autonomy to unification with Prussia
and that Germany could find adequate satisfaction for her
nationalist aspirations in a reformed confederation. Nevertheless, now that the new greater Prussia was constituted, France
should accept it as a *fait accompli*. 'The only wise, intelligent,
and decent course,' he said in 1867, 'is to accept without pusil-
lanimity, to accept without anxiety, to accept with confidence
a work which, I am convinced, is not directed against us. Yes,
gentlemen, Germany will join in friendship with France the day
France ceases to threaten it.' Germany ('the land of Mozart
and Beethoven', 'democratic, liberal, cultivated'), far from being
the hereditary enemy of France, had been her ally on countless
occasions, and was now more than ever necessary to be as 'our
rampart, our veritable avant-garde' against autocratic Russia.
When he accepted power in 1870, he made it clear that he could
under no circumstances oppose the unification of north and south
Germany if it were brought about by the will of the people,
and that he could hardly do so even it if were done by Prussian
conquest. 'Have not the treaties of alliance unified Germany
militarily and has not the renewal of the Zollverein united it
economically? German unity against us is accomplished: what
still remains to be done, political unity, is purely Prussia's business, and it will bring it more difficulties than strength. What
interest have we in preventing the democrats of Wurtemberg
and the ultramontanes of Bavaria from going to annoy Bismarck in his parliaments, since in any case when it comes to a
war all Germany will be against us?'[1]

The Prussian ambassador in Paris noted that Ollivier had 'a
very marked sympathy for German culture and German ideas
in general. One day in fact I commented on this to him and he
replied that these sentiments dated from his first marriage, when
he had learnt to know Germany from the distinguished Germans

---

[1] Speech of 15 March 1867, *Démocratie et liberté* (1867), 411–44, 258, 304–6;
Ollivier to Girardin, 12 September 1866 (printed in E.L. ix. 608 ff., xii. 126–7,
xii. 149); Ollivier to Duvernois, 24 October 1869, J. ii. 385; and E.L. viii.
115, 212, 453–4, 554, 593, 622; ix. 181, 288, 608; xii. 135.

whom his first wife, the daughter of Liszt, drew to his house.'[1] Ollivier's attitude to Germany was in fact typical of many of the leaders of 1848 and of the intellectuals of the second empire. The former had seen no danger in German unification. Lamartine declared that he placed 'the interests of civilization and of liberty well above any question of territorial aggrandizement' and that 'a statesman worthy of the name, that is to say, a guide of the people, a co-operator with Providence, must be ruled by two points of view, the human point of view first and the national one second. . . . I am a man before being a Frenchman.'[2] The intellectuals, for their part, saw in Germany a nation of philosophers to whom they felt greatly indebted, leaders in scientific progress whom they admired, a 'people of dreamers' (as Flaubert defined them in his *Dictionary of Received Ideas*) whom they had no cause to fear. A few of them, notably Quinet and Prévost-Paradol, changed their minds after Sadowa, but they were exceptions. In his foreign policy (as in his constitution-making) Ollivier was to repeat the experiments of 1848, despite their failure: the significance of the events in Germany largely escaped him.[3]

In February 1870 Bismarck himself thought that, in view of Ollivier's advent to power, the unification of Germany might be achieved peacefully.[4] The principal act of Ollivier's foreign policy was indeed to inaugurate talks for international disarmament and even to reduce recruitment to the French army unilaterally, as an example and evidence of good faith. All this is well known; but the question which has never been properly investigated is why Ollivier, when it came to the crisis, abandoned this policy to join the party of war. The answer is to be found

---

[1] *Les Origines diplomatiques de la guerre de 1870-1*, vol. xxix (1932), 501-2.

[2] P. Quentin-Bauchart, *Lamartine et la politique étrangère de la révolution de février* (1907), 390, 44-45.

[3] Claude Digeon, *La Crise allemande de la pensée française 1870-1914* (1959), 9-47; L. Reynaud, *L'Influence allemande en France au XVIII et XIX siècle* (1922), 259; A. Bellesort, *Les intellectuels et l'avènement de la troisième république* (1931).

[4] P. Renouvin, *Histoire des relations internationales*, vol. v (1954), 377-8.

partly in his opinions on 'just wars', which were and are far less known. For the Franco-Prussian war was declared not to prevent German unification but to avenge the slighted honour of France. On this latter question Ollivier was far more suscep-tible, and indeed bellicose, long before the crisis. A note in his diary in 1859 suggests that even then he considered the 'outraged honour of France' a legitimate or plausible cause for war, an exception to his general preference for peace. In his speech of 1867 accepting the consequences of Sadowa he explicitly pointed out that he was not asking his country to 'bow her head before a humiliation', and that if she had in fact been humi-liated by these events she should at once declare war. Above all in a conversation with the British ambassador in January 1870 he revealed that even a minor rebuff to French prestige would almost inevitably cause him to declare war. He asked Lord Lyons to put his proposals for disarmament before Prussia as though they came from England, to conceal their real origin, so that if they were rejected, France would not appear insulted. 'He was particularly alive', reported Lyons, 'to the importance of not exposing France to the appearance of being slighted: in fact he would not conceal from me that under present circumstances a public rebuff from Prussia would be fatal—"un échec" (he said) "c'est la guerre". We who have to render an account to Parlia-ment and the Country are less than the former government able to put up with any wound to the national pride. Our main object is peace (he added) but we must show firmness and spirit or we shall not be able to cope with Revolution and Socialism at home.'[1] It was precisely because he advocated a policy ap-parently so detrimental to his country's greatness with regard to German unification that he had to be exceptionally patriotic in everything else. It was in the same way that the philosophers of the eighteenth century had appeared to be cosmopolitan citizens of the world, but on closer examination turned out to possess a 'national pride remaining deep-rooted even among

[1] J. i. 362 (12 January 1859); Speech of 15 March 1867 (*Démocratie et liberté* (1867), 436); Lyons to Clarendon, 30 January 1870, Bod. MSS. Clar. P. C. 474.

those who said and thought they were most freed from it'.[1]

The second cause of his change is hinted at in the last sentence of Lyons' despatch: he was determined to be 'firm'. Just as in domestic affairs he had increasingly tried to show himself 'strong' as well as liberal, so in his foreign policy he was determined to be 'magnanimous', but from a position of strength and not from weakness. He was particularly susceptible to the taunt that he was reproducing Louis Philippe's policy of peace at any price, of doing nothing, a policy which had so notoriously 'bored' the country. He personally looked on France's retreat in 1840 as an intolerable humiliation. 'The fundamental political idea' of his hero Lamartine was, he said, 'the necessity for a strong government'.[2]

Finally, Ollivier allowed a third exception to his policy of peace. 'A war is not legitimate,' he had written in 1863, 'except when it is indispensable, when it is desired by a whole nation.'[3] He believed that what ought to distinguish his ministry from its authoritarian predecessors was that it should reflect public opinion and represent its will; and in July 1870 the principal reason he gave for declaring war was that the people wanted it. 'It is no longer men like Rouher and La Valette who have the direction of the policy of France,' he told the Austrian ambassador. 'It is I, a minister of the people, originating from the people, feeling with the people, I, a minister responsible to the nation, responsible for its dignity. . . . '[4] Thus though Ollivier *said* that peace was essential for the establishment of freedom in France and that the advent of the liberal empire was the best guarantee of peace, by his own admission his régime paradoxically inclined towards war precisely because it was 'popular'. His speeches against war while he was in opposition had been received with much hostility

---

[1] A. Mathiez, Pacifisme et Nationalisme au 18e siècle in *Annales historiques de la revolution française* (1936), xiii. 10.

[2] E.L. xiii. 60; E. Ollivier, *Lamartine* (1874), 150.

[3] Ollivier to Princess Wittgenstein, 10 July 1863, J. ii. 87.

[4] Metternich to Beust, 8 July 1870, H. Oncken, *Die Rheinpolitik Kaiser Napoleons III von 1863 bis 1870 und der Ursprung des Krieges von 1870–71* (1926), iii. 402.

and interrupted to the extent that he was frequently unable to make himself heard; and in July 1870 he was finally faced with the contradiction between his peaceful foreign policy and his role as the representative of the people, who wanted war.

Professor Case's recent book on *French Opinion on War and Diplomacy during the Second Empire* has shown quite conclusively that the Franco-Prussian War was popular, and that therefore what contemporaries really could not forgive Napoleon and Ollivier was not that they declared it, but that they lost it. 'I summarize public opinion in these words,' wrote the prefect of Charente on 9 July, typical of many others: 'no one wants a Prussian prince in Spain; they hail war patriotically; they prefer peace with a moral victory; they would not forgive the government if it showed weakness or even timidity.'[1] The prefects' reports were for long seriously misinterpreted by republicans who claimed that the war was essentially a dynastic adventure; but Professor Case has shown that they strikingly confirm Ollivier's thesis, previously looked on as a piece of special pleading, that French public opinion was a major factor in precipitating the conflict.

In this light it is easier to understand why Ollivier, while protesting his pacific intentions, took actions which contributed in no small degree to the outbreak of war. Thus, first, he strongly urged that the protest against the Hohenzollern candidature should be sent to Prussia and not to Spain. His principle of non-intervention forbade him to interfere in the internal affairs of Spain; national honour required that France should not be trifled with. Yet this was a fatal mistake, for it turned the affair, which a more subtle diplomatic handling might have scotched, into a major international crisis. Secondly, he was personally responsible for the threatening words with which Gramont, the foreign minister, concluded his public statement to the legislature on 6 July: France hoped for the peaceful withdrawal

---

[1] L. M. Case, *French Opinion on War and Diplomacy during the Second Empire* (Philadelphia 1954), 250; cf. J. Stengers, 'Aux origines de la guerre de 1870; Gouvernement et opinion publique', in *Revue belge de philologie et d'histoire* (Brussels, 1956), xxxiv. 701-47.

of the Hohenzollern candidature, but 'if it turns out otherwise, strengthened by your support, gentlemen, and that of the nation, we shall know how to fulfil our duty without hesitation and without weakness'. *The Times* rightly commented: 'It is seldom in these days of diplomatic reserve that such strong language as that of the Duke of Gramont is used in public on an international question.'[1] Ollivier had added the threat because he wished the government to take a 'firm' stand. He believed that it ought to do what Thiers said ought to have been done in 1866: had it then declared, before hostilities began, that it would not allow a war between Prussia and Austria, there would have been no war and no French humiliation. Ollivier thought that by clearly stating that the Hohenzollern prince must withdraw or it would be war, he was using the best method of preventing a conflict. In fact the legislature so obviously took the threat as a virtual declaration of war, that Ollivier got up to supplement Gramont's statement by adding, 'The government wants peace; it passionately wants peace, but with honour.' He clearly did not appreciate how disastrous his firm language was to be, not only by stirring up war sentiment in France, but also because by making the dispute public, he made it almost impossible for Prussia to yield without losing face. Had secret negotiations been undertaken instead, it would have been far easier to obtain satisfaction with an agreed compromise. 'If the further ineptitudes of Gramont's and Napoleon's diplomacy had not a few days later plunged France into war, there would still have been this speech to explain; and as Bismarck more than once remarked in the ensuing week, he was ready to demand an explanation of it so humiliating that France could be relied on to fight instead.'[2]

The third and major criticism to which Ollivier's conduct in this crisis is subject is that after 12 July he lost control of French policy. He was delighted by the announcement by Prince Karl Anton of his son's withdrawal and he publicly stated that this

[1] *The Times*, 7 July 1870.
[2] Michael Foot, 'The Origins of the Franco-Prussian War' in the *New Cambridge Modern History*, vol. x. (1960), 591.

meant peace. However, he then failed to thwart the demand for guarantees against the renewal of the candidature which, without consulting the cabinet, Gramont and Napoleon made, and which produced the rebuff that led to war. In the last decisive cabinet meetings he allowed the initiative to drop out of his hands into those of the empress and General Lebœuf, who destroyed all proposals for a peaceful compromise. Even though he might have been convinced that French national honour required a war, he rushed blindly into it without first making proper preparations. France was not ready militarily and the Prussians were very surprised that she declared war long before she could launch an offensive.[1] She was diplomatically isolated and yet did not pause to make sure of allies first. Gramont had in fact deliberately concealed the inconclusive negotiations with Austria from Ollivier.[2] Ollivier, however, cannot escape blame for Gramont's mistakes, for he had himself appointed Gramont—a notoriously violent enemy of Prussia—to the foreign office; he had vainly believed he could keep Gramont under control, but he thus revealed he had learnt nothing from his experience with Daru.

In this crisis, therefore, the whole structure of the liberal empire appears to have collapsed: cabinet control of policy disappeared into chaos: there might just as well have been an authoritarian government in power for all the difference it made. The declaration of war is generally regarded as an irrefutable condemnation of Ollivier's system. 'It is M. de Gramont,' one historian has written, 'who is responsible for the innumerable faults committed in the negotiations on the Hohenzollern incident, but it is M. Ollivier's political conception which allowed him to commit them.'[3] But this is not entirely fair.

It is not accurate to assert that the absence of cabinet government

[1] Michael Howard, *The Franco-Prussian War* (1961), 78.

[2] H. Oncken, *Die Rheinpolitik Kaiser Napoleons III* (Stuttgart, 1926), iii. 355, 368, 382, 422; W. E. Mosse, *The European Powers and the German Question 1848–1871* (Cambridge, 1958); C. de Grunwald, *Le Duc de Gramont* (1950).

[3] Henry Salomon, 'Une expérience politique en 1870 et ses conséquences', in *Revue de synthèse historique* (1921), xxxii. 90.

(with internal ministerial cohesion, independence of the crown, and a firm parliamentary majority) was a vice peculiar to the liberal empire. Cabinet government had never existed in France, neither during the restoration nor, as Professor Pouthas has recently shown, even under Louis Philippe. Casimir Perier, who came nearest to establishing it, did not choose his own ministers; Guizot, from 1840 to 1846, did not have a permanent parliamentary majority; ministerial unity was never achieved.[1]

Nevertheless, Ollivier must personally bear some of the responsibility for the war; and though in his memoirs he declared his conduct to be beyond reproach, immediately after the event he privately admitted his errors. Little jottings in a tiny notebook he carried about with him contain these questions: 'Did I commit no mistake? Did I bend under pressure? Why did you declare war on Prussia? I did not declare it! It was Prussia which declared it on us. My only two mistakes were to have opposed the country's military reorganization when I was in opposition (but it is true that my exoneration is favoured because I did not excite France against Prussia at the same time) and not to have postponed the declaration of war so as to gain time to be ready. But I did not know that we were not ready.' In another note he says, 'I committed three mistakes. First, I believed in the disinterested grandeur of Germany; secondly, I believed there was an army in France; thirdly, I believed that there was a nation in France, whereas France was as greedy as she was in the middle ages. The army was rotten inside—courageous, but without leaders and without good organization. Instead of a nation there were only violent parties preferring the triumph of the foreigner to that of a Napoleon. . . . Had I seen these three truths, of which I was then ignorant, I should have lowered my head before the insult and tried to give our humiliation a decent façade, in the English manner.' And again, 'I perished at the hands of diplomacy and the army, the two parts of the *ancien régime* into

[1] C. H. Pouthas, 'Les Ministères de Louis Philippe', in *Revue d'histoire moderne et contemporaine* (1954), N.S. vol. i. 102–30; J. Barbey, *Le Conseil des ministres sous la restauration* (1936).

which I did not have time to introduce my ideas of reform.'[1]

Even so, it is important to note that the defeat of the French armies was by no means inevitable, and certainly not in the form in which it occurred. The French did indeed labour under grave disadvantages: they had failed to modernize their military system as the Prussians had done: but their startlingly sudden collapse was due to an extraordinarily large number of individual errors of judgement on the part of their generals. The soldiers fought with brilliant heroism, 'lions led by asses'; the fate of each battle was hardly ever foredoomed when it started; it required mistake after mistake of tactics and strategy before the issue was decided. The one serious mistake that could have been avoided was the appointment of the emperor himself as commander in chief on the field. His health had broken down completely, he was subject to excruciating pain, and what energy he had ever possessed now quite deserted him. It appears that it was the insistence of the empress that was largely responsible for his leading his troops in person.[2]

Again, the collapse of the empire was not a foregone conclusion after the first disasters. The news of these, and the danger of Paris falling into enemy hands, produced a violent agitation in the capital, which was all the more hysterical because most people had been so certain of victory. The republicans made a scarcely disguised bid for revolution by demanding that all the citizens of Paris (who were predominantly their supporters) should be armed in its defence and that its deputies (all republicans) should form a 'committee of defence'. Chevandier, the minister of the interior, replied on 8 August by ordering the arrest of their principal leaders, including twenty-two deputies of the left, but Ollivier secured the postponement of the measure. He said this *coup* involved enormous risk, which might cost them their lives; he was willing to take the risk only in partnership with Napoleon, but not with the empress, who, in the latter's absence at the front, ruled as regent. The empress was being

---

[1] Brown notebook, probably of 1872, 3″ × 4″, O.P.
[2] M. Howard, *The Franco-Prussian War* (1961), 63 and *passim*.

worked on increasingly by the right wing who thought that they could preserve the empire only by turning Ollivier into the scapegoat of defeat and who were urging his dismissal. It was not worth suppressing the left only to be overthrown by the right; Napoleon alone could keep these men in check. In opposition to them, Ollivier argued that the empire would be preserved only if Napoleon handed over the army to competent generals and returned to Paris to lead his threatened people. He would thus cease to prevent victory on the battlefield and he would give his ministry the strength to defeat the enemy at home.

On the morning of 9 August, Ollivier asked the empress to recall Napoleon, planning that he should return that same evening, give his consent at once to the arrests, which would be carried out during the night, and that meanwhile the cabinet would obtain a vote of confidence from the legislature in the afternoon to give it added strength to meet the crisis. The empress at first objected that it would be degrading and cowardly for Napoleon to desert his troops, but, after much sighing and weeping, at length agreed. However, while Ollivier went into another room to draft his declaration to the house, other counsels made themselves heard and she went back on her decision. At this supreme moment in fact the right ultimately won the battle for the ear of the empress, who had till then resisted their efforts to make her dislodge the ministry. They saw how Napoleon's return would strengthen it and they therefore played on her fears that she was asking him to disgrace himself before his troops. They were honest perhaps in believing this, though Napoleon himself was willing to come to Paris if the empress and the ministers thought it best. In any case, the result was that at noon the telegram calling for his return had still not been sent.

And when Ollivier arrived at the legislature, he found that the leaders of the right had got there first. When he rose to speak, he was met with violent jeering and abuse from the left. He turned to the right and to the centre right, to seek their support, but they met his glance with stony silence. Infuriated, he demanded that they should declare themselves openly, and he put the question of confidence. They took up the challenge coolly. It was Clement Duvernois, the diehard Bonapartist of the right, who moved the motion that the house wanted a cabinet 'capable of organizing the defence of the country'. The vote was taken, each side rising to its feet in turn. Only some ten members rose in Ollivier's favour. The cabinet was overthrown.

Ollivier's supporters thus vanished practically overnight. Many of them told him that they did not mean it as a 'personal' vote against him. It was simply that, distraught by the news of defeat, not knowing where to turn, they had been won over by the leaders of the right to the belief that a drastic change was necessary, that only thus could the empire be saved. Jerome David and Clement Duvernois, who now became ministers, had that very day at last found a 'saviour' for the country in General Cousin de Montauban, comte de Palikao, who would be the leader of the new cabinet and minister of war. He was—bitter irony—the grandson of de Launay, the last governor of the Bastille.

From that day the empire was as good as lost. 'The dynasty that still reigns in France,' said *The Times*, 'is commonly thought of almost as a thing of the past.'[1] Napoleon like his uncle lost his throne as much in Paris as on the battlefield, defeated by the politicians quite as much as by the enemy. Just as after Waterloo it was the betrayal of his followers that compelled his uncle's abdication, so now Napoleon III, having given up his command, was condemned to following his army like a piece of baggage—prevented from returning to Paris by the empress' reiterated telegrams that if he did he would have mud thrown at him. This may have been so, but Paris first of all was not France, and how could he rally France except from Paris? 'I do not know what they are doing in Paris,' he said. 'They have lost their heads. They have overthrown the ministry. It is not in the midst of the storm that one changes one's pilot and crew.' And some days later he wrote to Ollivier, 'I have been so preoccupied by military events that I have not yet been able to tell you how much I regretted your

[1] 12 August 1870.

departure from office. You have given me so many proofs of
devotion that I have become used to counting on you to smooth
out difficulties and to imprint a firm and strong course on the
conduct of events. I hope nevertheless that our relations will
remain as intimate as in the past. . . .'[1]

In fact they never saw each other again. Napoleon formally
surrendered to the Prussians within a month, was deposed, and
sought refuge in England. Ollivier had meanwhile gone to Italy
to urge that country to enter the war on France's side. After 4
September his house at St. Tropez was threatened by a republican
mob and his father and son fled to join him in Italy. Rumours
were spread that he had run away with millions made on the
stock exchange, whereas in fact he did not have a single security
to his name at that time. He was compelled to borrow money
to meet his expenses.[2]

It may well be asked why Ollivier did not attempt to eradicate
that special evil of despotism, the back-stairs influence of courtiers
and women. Should he not have done something to convert
the empress from her violent hostility to Prussia, from her belief
in the need for war, and from her preference for autocracy;
or at least ensured that her opinions should be ineffectual?[3] It
seems, in fact, that Ollivier had no illusions on this subject:
in 1866 he had said to the empress, who had claimed that she
was quite willing to give up her power: 'You will never be put
out to grass, Madame. In France a sovereign will always have
more initiative than he can use. He will always remain master of
foreign policy and almost so of internal policy too.'[4] If he really
meant this, ought he not to have remained a republican?

Even more serious was the fact that his relationship to public

---

[1] E.L. xvi. 486, 506.

[2] Cf., however, Ollivier's letter to Maurice Richard, 30 August 1870, draft,
O.P., in which he says, 'I am as unpopular in Paris as, despite everything, I am
popular and respected in the provinces.'

[3] Pierre Muret, 'Emile Ollivier et le duc de Gramont le 12 et 13 juillet 1870',
in *Revue d'histoire moderne et contemporaine* (1909–10), xiii. 305–328, xiv. 178–213.
Cf. A. Sorel, *Histoire diplomatique de la guerre franco-allemande* (1875); H.
Welschinger, *Les Origines de la guerre de 1870* (1910).

[4] J. ii. 262 (1 January 1867) and ii. 236 (3 February 1866).

opinion, on which he based himself more than on anything else, was incoherent. He criticized parliament for being too easily guided by passion, and argued that a strong executive was necessary to keep it in check. But why then did he not resist the clamour for war himself, why did he allow his conduct to be determined by the cries of the mob? Both he and Napoleon finally agreed to declare war because they said that public opinion demanded it. He himself abandoned the idea of a congress because it would cause the people to 'throw mud at our carriages and boo us down'. Napoleon sadly commented, 'You see in what a situation a government can sometimes find itself. Even if we had no admissible reason for war, we should now be compelled to declare it, to obey the will of the country.'[1]

Ollivier admitted that he had reached an impasse. Even resignation could not save him. 'The country', he told the newspaper editor Mitchell, 'has confidence in me. I am the guarantee of the new pact that links the empire to France. If I were to retire, the advent of a Rouher ministry would be considered a sort of *coup d'état* against the liberal reforms. The situation which is already so serious would probably be complicated by internal difficulties. And then the war is inevitable: no human power can avoid it now. Since we cannot prevent it, our duty is to make it popular. Were we to resign, we would discourage the country, we would demoralize the army, we would cast doubt on France's right and on the justice of her cause.'

'What then do you hope?'

'For me, nothing. Whatever happens I shall be sacrificed and the war will carry away the régime to which I have linked my name. If we are conquered, may God protect France. If we are victorious, may God protect our liberties.'[2]

[1] E.L. xiv. 373.

[2] Robert Mitchell, *Un Demi-siècle de mémoires* (1911), i. 266, 14 July. Mitchell (the brother-in-law of Offenbach) was the half-English editor of the newspaper *Le Constitutionnel*, which Ollivier inspired.

CHAPTER 13

OLLIVIER AND THE THIRD REPUBLIC

OLLIVIER was aged forty-five when he fell from power in 1870 and though he lived another forty-three years, the doors of active politics were now permanently closed to him. He was so soundly defeated in the parliamentary election, and even in the local one, for which he was bold enough to stand, that he never tried again. It has been suggested that had he resigned rather than declare war, he would almost certainly have played an influential role in the history of the third republic. But was it in fact simply his unpopularity for bringing on this national catastrophe that exiled him from politics?

Certainly Ollivier was reviled and insulted for it with quite extraordinary violence. 'The English would have shot you like Byng,' wrote one newspaper, 'the Carthaginians would have hanged you like Hanno.' 'You are the most cursed man of a whole historical period. It is to you that the responsibility of all our misfortunes reverts; at the touch of your evil hand, the imperial throne crumbled and France herself collapsed. Wherever you go, indignant cries arise; your voice sounds like a mocking echo of the nation's sobbing.'[1] He was not only execrated by the left as one of 'the assassins of France',[2] who had started the war to save his tottering ministry, but also by the right-wing Bonapartists, who denounced 'the ignorant and treacherous ministers of 2 January, who threw our country into an unjust war so as the better to deliver her to the revolution of which they were but the servants disguised as renegades'.[3] Henri Rochefort called him

---

[1] Paul de Cassagnac, *Le Pays*, 21 and 23 April 1880.

[2] A. Rocher, *Les Assassins de la France* (1872); idem, *MM. les capitulards et les citoyens communards, parallèle entre Judas Ollivier et les hommes de la Commune* n.d.).

[3] E. Dreolle, *La journée du 4 septembre*, quoted by E. Ollivier, *Lettres de l'exil* (1874), 83–84.

an 'ambitious man of seventh-rate capacity', a 'great silly, who
with his natural dirtiness and green spectacles resembled a public
scribe or a shady financial agent',[1] Gambetta said he illustrated
how little one ought to esteem politicians who possessed eloquence alone.[2] Maurice Paléologue declared, 'I consider him a
very honest man in private life. But to me he represents all that
is most disastrous in politics: eloquence, great eloquence, in the
service of ideology and infatuation.'[3] 'I do not say that M. Emile
Ollivier was a wicked man,' wrote Charles Maurras, 'I only say
that in 1870 he acted like a featherbrain and that he ruined his
country.'[4] In cartoons, he now appeared in the guise of a turkey
or a serpent, as though it was uncertain whether he ought to be
criticized more for folly than for treachery.[5]

However, responsibility for the war prevented neither the
rapid return of many other servants of the second empire to
politics nor the formation of a strong Bonapartist movement.
Ollivier's case was different: an extremely important factor in
keeping him powerless was that he could agree with no single
party. During the third republic, as in 1848 and in the years
before 1870, he continued to be an independent and a heretic,
and his activities in this period deserve study because they throw
further light on his opinions and his character.

After 1870 the Bonapartist party became thoroughly and
increasingly conservative, partly as a reaction against the disorders
of the Commune, and partly because Rouher now became master
of its organization and the chief inspirer of its policy. It sought to
win the alliance of the legitimists and the clericals for a campaign

---

[1] Henri Rochefort, *The Adventures of My Life* (1896), i. 236, 244.

[2] *Lettres de Gambetta*, ed. D. Halévy and E. Pillias (1938), Letter 219 to
Juliette Adam, 22 October 1874.

[3] M. Paléologue, *Entretiens de l'Impératrice Eugénie* (1928), 94 (written 1903).

[4] Maurras in *L'Action Française* of 26 August 1913, quoted by A. Mascarel,
Cinquante Ans de souvenirs: quelques portraits (1926), 26; cf. Albert de Broglie,
Mémoires (1938–41), i. 365.

[5] H. Mailly, *Pilori*, *A bas les laches* (n.d.), cartoon no. 2, E. Ollivier, 'Renegat
politique, voleur au cœur léger'; Anon. *La ménagerie impériale* (n.d.), cartoon
no. 9, E. Ollivier as a serpent, species 'Bassesse-Duplicité'; cf. *Le Gaulois*,
5 April 1892.

to overthrow Thiers and the republic, hoping that in the ensuing chaos it would emerge (as it had done in 1851) as the only possible safeguard of order against the menace of social revolution. It offered the country strong government, with a return to the authoritarian constitution of 1852 and it abandoned entirely the idea of the liberal empire. In the opinion of Rouher and his followers the liberal deviation had ruined the dynasty. The empress condemned Ollivier as a 'bungling utopian and a presumptuous rhetorician'.[1] The emperor said he continued to feel great affection for Ollivier; he did not hold him to be the cause of the disaster; he disapproved of the reactionaries' attacks on him; but, in the changed conditions of the country, he no longer considered his policy opportune.[2] In 1874 the prince imperial summoned Ollivier to the meeting of leading Bonapartist personalities from whom he invited advice, but Ollivier found himself in a minority of one in it, and never enjoyed any influence or even friendship with the young man.[3] Prince Victor finally, whom the conservatives acclaimed as the next pretender, had nothing in common with Ollivier: on hearing the latter's talents being highly praised, he dismissed the subject with the words, 'It is true, but he is so badly dressed.'[4]

There was no place for Ollivier in this new Bonapartist party of the third republic. 'They treat me,' he wrote, 'as the church treats the impenitent, they excommunicate me.'[5] His tenure of office had strengthened his authoritarian instincts; he fully agreed that socialism, radicalism, and demagogy were the enemy; but he argued that the answer did not lie in pure reaction, which

---

[1] M. Paléologue, *Les Entretiens de l'Impératrice Eugénie* (1928), 195.

[2] Napoleon to Jerome-Napoleon, 21 July and 21 August 1871, *Napoléon III et le prince Napoléon, correspondance inédite* (1925), 322–3; A. Mels, *Wilhemsloehe, souvenirs de la captivité de Napoléon III* (1880), 162–4; E. Boinvilliers, *La Chute de l'Empire* (*2 Janvier 1870*) (1887), 119 n.

[3] D. 29 June 1874, 12 June, and 15 August 1875; Ollivier to Segris, 31 May 1874, Ollivier to Chevandier, 22 June 1874, O.P. Comte d'Hérisson, *Le Prince Impérial* (1890), 242, claims the prince approved the liberal empire.

[4] Paul Lenglé, *Le Neveu de Bonaparte* (1893), 118–21.

[5] Ollivier to Valerio, 1 February 1873, O.P.

would make Napoleon III indistinguishable from Henri V.[1] The struggle of the poor against the rich could be ended 'only by a Caesar who knows, as the emperor did, how to satisfy them as well as to contain them'.[2] 'The present leaders are convinced', he wrote, 'that the empire can be restored through a clerical reaction. I am persuaded that it will not return except through a popular reaction.'[3] The country 'will accept democratic dictators but never dictators of the *ancien régime*'.[4] 'The Bonapartes must never forget that if Napoleon I saved the revolution from its excesses, he also saved it from its enemies.'[5] He objected to the alliance with the monarchists, except as a 'ruse of war'; he opposed the Bonapartist agitation for a new plebiscite, because he maintained that the empire, which had won the plebiscite of 1870, was still the legitimate government of France; to hold a new plebiscite would be to admit that the people's verdict could legitimately be set aside by a revolution, such as that of 4 September 1870.[6]

It is not surprising therefore that the party refused to sponsor his candidature in Corsica or Charente—which were almost safe seats and where he would very probably have been elected —and that it gave him only very moderate support when he stood in his home department of Var in 1876. He had little chance here, for over 50 per cent. of the electorate had voted against the empire in 1870. The legitimists, moreover, put up a candidate of their own, who then indignantly withdrew when the prefect announced that he would be neutral as between him and Ollivier; and so they too were hostile to Ollivier. He had to do a lot of explaining about his part in the war; he issued a long circular on the subject of his 'light heart'; and many conservatives are said to have abstained or even to have voted radical, rather than

[1] Ollivier to Wallon, 19 July 1872, O.P.
[2] Ollivier to an unknown correspondent, 17 January 1872, O.P.
[3] Ollivier to Cosima Wagner, 8 January 1873, O.P.
[4] Ollivier to Napoleon, 28 December 1873, O.P.
[5] Ollivier to Levert, 29 May 1873, O.P.
[6] Ollivier to Philis, 6 January 1873, O.P.; D. 22 October 1874.

support the author of the national defeat. Nevertheless, standing in both constituencies of the department, he obtained 4,523 votes against the 12,305 given to a republican in one, and 3,116 against 9,737 given to another republican in the second. This was much more than any complete pariah, such as he was supposed to be, would have received; and it was indeed remarkable in view of his having no electoral organization to speak of, and financial resources so inadequate that his propaganda was severely limited. He was apparently given only 5,000 francs (£200) by the central Bonapartist treasury when he estimated that he needed five times as much.[1] The principal lesson of this election was that his association with the liberal empire had damned him not only in the eyes of the republicans but also in those of most Bonapartists.

Ollivier was unable to agree even with that section of the Bonapartists which, under the leadership of Prince (Jerome) Napoleon, sought to be 'progressive'. The two men had been allies against the authoritarian empire and their friendship continued; they corresponded and visited each other frequently. The prince's newspaper Le Napoléon was largely staffed by Ollivier's followers: Philis (secretary-general of Ollivier's ministry in 1870) was its editor, Darimon was in charge of its economic articles, and Mitchell was a frequent contributor.[2] Ollivier himself, however, never played an active or public role in its politics. This was partly because Prince Napoleon would never concede any real authority to him, and said that his unpopularity would ruin the cause: 'Are you mad!' he exclaimed to Paul Lenglé who urged that 'the prodigious orator' should be invited to join them in their public meetings: 'Are we strong enough to

---

[1] A.D. Var, II M 3–30, letters of prefect, sub-prefects, &c.; A.D. Bouches-du-Rhône, Aix depository, 15 U 28, procureur de la république of Draguignan to procureur-général of Aix, 7 and 14 February 1876; Le Var (Draguignan, bi-weekly newspaper), 20 February 1876; Candidature de M. Emile Ollivier dans le Var en 1876 (Draguignan 1876), pamphlet, copy in the Bibliothèque municipale of Draguignan; Gilly La Palud, Elections du Midi, renseignements électoraux (Marseilles, 1876); D. February 1876; Ollivier to Rouher, 9 January 1876 and February 1876, and Ollivier to Laurelli, 15 June 1875, copies; J. M. Pietri to Ollivier, 1876, undated, O.P.

[2] Paul Lenglé, Le Neveu de Bonaparte (1893), 82–83.

swim against such a current?'[1] As important, however, was the
fact that Ollivier disagreed with the prince on two major issues;
in their attitude to the republic and in their opinions on the
church. 'I have as much sympathy', wrote Ollivier, 'towards
an alliance with democratic ideas as I have aversion for a rap-
prochement with the men of the demagogic party, who exploit
democratic ideas much more than they serve them. I still remember very sorely their treason during the war.'[2] He was not willing, that is, to ally indiscriminately with the republican party,
as Prince Napoleon was: he had long distinguished the 'Jacobins'
from the moderates among them and still considered that the
former must be regarded as the enemy. 'I share some of [Prince
Napoleon's] ideas,' he told his brother Ernest, 'but there are
also profound differences between us, notably on religious questions. I like the clergy as much as he hates them, and if I am determined to check their encroachment, I am even more determined
to respect them and to defend them.' 'I do not like clericalism
being brought into politics. It is not the priests who need to be
feared, but les Jacques.'[3]

Thus in 1880, when Ferry attacked the congregations, Ollivier
was on Prince Napoleon's side, as against the conservative Bonapartists, in maintaining that these measures were perfectly legal,
but he objected to the way anti-clericalism was exaggerated into
a wholesale attack on the church.[4] He could agree with neither
side in the dispute: he remained loyal to the forgotten ideals of
1848, in which church and republic (and even Bonapartism) were
all reconciled. 'What have they done to you, these poor priests,'
he said in 1885, 'sons of the people, risen from the soil like us,
that you should persecute them with such refined hatred? You
do not believe what they teach? Who compels you to believe

[1] Ibid., 27; confirmed by E.L. v. 430 and Jules Richard, *Le Bonapartisme
sous la république* (1883), 140.
[2] Ollivier to Prince Napoleon, 4 October 1873, copy, O.P.
[3] Ibid.; Ollivier to Ernest Ollivier, 3 October 1873; Ollivier to Adelon, 4
October 1873, copies, O.P.
[4] Ollivier's articles in *L'Estafette*, 19–23 March, 6 and 8 April 1880; cf. Cassagnac's replies in *Le Pays*, 18, 21 April 1880.

it? Why prevent others from believing it? Do you know how to inculcate some notion of morals into dull brains better than the priest? Have you found something better to say to the wretch dying in destitution, to the mother holding her icy child in her arms, than what the priest tells them when he shows them above the hearse on earth, the resurrection in heaven? . . . For me, in these days when the great aim is to get rich, I venerate those who vow themselves to evangelical poverty; in this world in which everybody thinks only of himself. I admire those who think only of others.'[1]

Ollivier had a passionate interest in theology, and accumulated a vast fund of learning, particularly on the history of Church government. He published two thick tomes on *Church and State at the Vatican Council (1870)* and another two entitled *Manual of Ecclesiastical Law*—both of which remain important works of reference. On his visits to Italy he went to see popes Leo XIII and Pius X, both of whom granted him audiences. Yet he was not quite a believer. His ecclesiastical friends, of whom he had many, sometimes thought they might entice him into the Catholic communion, but in vain. He told them that he believed in a future life and in the divinity of Christ, that he had always criticized Renan for seeing in Him only a man, but that he had no use for the Church himself. When shortly before his death a priest suggested to him that he should make 'an act of religious faith', he assumed a severe mien and refused. 'None of that,' he said. 'I have studied all religions, all philosophies, all systems. I have made up my mind. I have always done my duty. I am not afraid of the future.' He made his wife promise that if by any chance he should lose his lucidity in his last hours and call for a priest, she would not do so.[2]

'Thiers is an Orleanist with a Bonapartist mentality,' said the wits; 'Gambetta is a republican with an Orleanist mentality; Ollivier is a Bonapartist with a republican mentality.' Ollivier

---

[1] *Discours d'Emile Ollivier au banquet de Saint-Tropez* (1885), 12–14.
[2] H. Odelin, Vicaire-Général de Paris, 'Emile Ollivier et le Catholicisme', in *La Revue hebdomadaire*, 12 January 1935.

commented : 'Bonapartist is a bit much.'[1] Rejecting and rejected by both wings of that party, he gradually reverted to being a supporter of the republic, as he had been in his youth; and he was consistent with himself in doing so. He had never been a monarchist on principle: he had always held forms of government to be of little importance in themselves, and systematic opposition to be despicable. Already in October 1870 he had written, 'As soon as any government emerges from the free will of the nation, whether its name is empire, republic, legitimism, or Orleanism, I shall aid it without reservations, as long as it assures order and pursues the amelioration, by the means of liberty and science, of the lot of the humble, the poor, those who suffer and weep. . . . I shall never be the accomplice of a revolution.'[2] With time, the republic had won the support of the majority of Frenchmen and its opponents had degenerated into a cabal of reactionary conspirators.

His break with the Bonapartists came finally in 1883, when they issued a manifesto which, he thought, showed they had quite forgotten their true mission: they said the cause they represented was that of 'the right of the people to choose their chief'. If that was all, replied Ollivier, then they differed from the republic only on the small matter of whether the president should be elected directly by the people or indirectly through parliament. 'It seems to me', he wrote, 'that Napoleon I and Napoleon III gave themselves a mission other than that of resolving correctly a question of political procedure. They made themselves the legislators and the propagators of the cause of the French Revolution, which had been compromised by the impotence of the republic.'[3] The Bonapartists had adopted 'the tradition of the rue de Poitiers', of bourgeois conservatism; and since the Orleanists had now accepted universal suffrage, there was little to choose between the two: they were simply rival pretenders.[4]

[1] D. 17 June 1876.
[2] E. Ollivier, Lettres de l'exil (1921), x. 28.
[3] Ollivier to an unknown person, 1 February 1883, copy, O.P.
[4] Ollivier to Darimon, 12 September 1883, copy, O.P.

'The republic has great strength,' he observed, 'despite its stupidities and meanness. The wisest course would be to compel it to cure itself instead of thinking only of overthrowing it.'[1] 'Instead of living in the Platonic hope of some monarchical restoration whose nature it is impossible to forsee, would it not be better to enter without mental reservations into the republic, not to create a personal role for oneself—former monarchists will remain suspect—but to assist the moderate republicans? . . . Men think not of improving, but only of destroying. The unity of my life will be never to have submitted to such a policy. A republican myself and son of a convict [of the *coup d'état* of 1851], I did not wish to be irreconcilably hostile to the empire. How can I be more severe towards the party from which I sprang than towards that from which I have received nothing but harm? How can I approve that conduct, which I considered it unfair to use against the empire, should be used against the republic, for which I have always had a certain weakness at the bottom of my heart?'[2] In 1885, in a speech which he had printed, he publicly announced his return to the fold. 'The republic is the legal government,' he declared. 'I accept it. . . . How can I speak otherwise? Am I not the child of the republic, and was it not as a republican that I negotiated with the emperor Napoleon III? . . . While the emperor and his son lived, I remained faithful to the pact to establish liberty which I made with him, as Manin and Garibaldi remained faithful to the pact to co-operate for independence [which, though republicans, they had made with the king of Italy]. Now all is finished. God has taken both father and son. They both rest in a foreign land. I am free: my pact is consummated. I am the servant of the interests of no prince, I belong to no party. I belong to no one but to myself, to justice, to truth, to liberty.'[3]

Yet his 'conversion' was, typically, not accepted; and neither

---

[1] Ollivier to Madame de Sourdeval, 11 April 1883, copy, O.P.

[2] Ollivier to Darimon, 20 March 1883, copy, O.P.

[3] *Discours d'Emile Ollivier au banquet de Saint-Tropez, 20 Septembre 1885* (Fréjus, 1885), 22–26.

was it total. When he stood as candidate for the *conseil général* of Var in 1886, the prefect noted: 'He calls himself republican', but then classified him as 'reactionary'.[1] The left-wing press declared that the election of 'the reptile of La Moutte . . . the cursed, funereal spectre of criminal vanity and political madness' would be a national disgrace; and its candidate, though not a local resident, was returned by 658 to 485. Ollivier won in his home commune of Saint-Tropez, but obtained very few votes outside it: Bonapartists and radicals united against him.[2] He was not a man, in fact, who could be contained within any party. Though he accepted the republic, he despised most of the republic's politicians and the way they were running the government. Soon after, he welcomed the successes of Boulanger as 'the republican expression of the people's vigorous dissatisfaction with the intolerable republican government'; and he looked forward optimistically to a new 'consulate' headed by the general.[3] This did not mean that he was going back on his acceptance of the republic, as has been claimed; on the contrary he believed that Boulangisme would replace Bonapartism, not pave the way for its restoration.[4] It was rather that his political ideas placed him on the border-line between republic and empire, and he could never fit satisfactorily into either. Again, when in 1892 Leo XIII urged Catholics to rally to the republic, it was Ollivier who produced one of the most forceful attacks against the pope's encyclical: his articles were 'greatly relished' by the monarchists and 'avidly read in the salons of the Faubourg and in chateaux in the provinces'.[5] His motive, however, was

---

[1] A.D. Var II M (5) 138–144, classification of candidates accompanying prefect's letter to the minister of the interior, 20 July 1886.

[2] *Le Petit Var* of Toulon, 3 and 5 July 1886; A.D. Var II M (5), 138–144, results, letters of the railway police, and Ollivier's circular of 24 July; Ollivier to Kratz, 9 January and 12 August 1886, copy in Chasseloup-Laubat papers.

[3] *Le Gaulois* and *Le Figaro* of 17 April 1888; both have reports of interviews with Ollivier.

[4] Ibid.

[5] Cardinal Dominique Ferrata, *Mémoires: ma nonciature en France* (c. 1921), 246–8.

not hostility to the republic, but a conviction that just as the state should not interfere in religion (a policy he had implemented in 1870), so likewise the pope should not interfere in politics. He was really arguing a point of political theory and yet the inevitable consequence was that he appeared to be an enemy of the régime itself.[1]

The perpetual ambiguity of his position, now as before 1870, is explained in a letter he himself wrote in 1872. 'You say,' he told his correspondent, 'that I was the left-wing of the empire, of which Rouher was the right wing. No. My aim was to be better and more than just the left wing of the empire. I tried to be above the left as well as above the right, and to form a new mean in which both could meet and draw closer without humiliation, so as at last to ensure in France the regular working of liberty. . . . To speak the language of Proudhon, I was no more on the side of the *thesis* than on that of the *antithesis*, I tried to construct a *synthesis*. If I had to choose between the right and the left, I should hesitate, because there is as much truth in the one as in the other and drawn by my instincts of a man of government, it is probable that I should decide for the right. And do not think that this results in the centre left. The centre left is not a synthesis, it is a medium position: for clever men it is a position for intrigue, for honest men it represents weakness or indecision of the will or of the intelligence; it is that *mezzo* system cursed by Machiavelli as the cause of all defeats. The truth in politics as in all else is at the centre, provided this is not turned into immobility between two contrary movements but is the conciliation by synthesis of two practical truths. . . . The synthesis [should be] conservative and democratic, liberal and not revolutionary, offering order to the conservatives and social progress to the people. . . . Louis Philippe was on the right,

---

[1] A. Dansette, *Histoire religieuse de la France contemporaine* (1951 edition), ii. 151; R. P. Lecaneut, *L'Eglise de France sous la troisième république* (1910), ii. 517–18, E. Ollivier, *Solutions politiques et Sociales* (1894), 284–95; H. Martin, 'L'Eglise et l'Etat d'après M. Emile Ollivier', *Etudes réligieuses philosophiques, historiques et littéraires par des Pères de la Companie de Jésus* (1879), iv. 247–68, 423–44, 563–85.

although his ministers ceaselessly talked of the *juste milieu*, a wretched and misleading phrase. M. Thiers, when he is angry, is on the left; when he is in control of himself, is on the centre left, that is nowhere. The emperor was veritably the man of the centre; that is why he attracted me.'[1]

Ollivier's methods as well as his aims made it impossible for him to come out clearly on any one side. He had never been an obedient member of any party and he now said: 'If I re-enter political life, I want to remain master of myself, independent and not at the mercy of some party.'[2] He repeated his objections to all systematic opposition, his wish to reform, convert, moderate, but never to overthrow governments by violence or revolution: this of course meant that he supported governments of which he did not approve—deserting the opposition but not quite rallying to the other side. He persisted in this course systematically. 'In this century, there is in my opinion but one form of glory to be won in politics: to be a man of progress, a democrat, to love and serve the people, despite its injustices and its crimes, but never to become a revolutionary, even for a cause that one considers good and just. For a time, I thought that there had been such a man in this century, M. Guizot, because of the fine maxims in his writings. A more thorough study has, alas, undeceived me and has shown me that he was one of the most ardent of revolutionaries, under the restoration at the time of the address of the 221,[3] and under Louis Philippe during the immoral coalition of 1838;[4] I am now no longer astonished by his scandalous approval of the *coup de main* of 4 September after having given his support to the plebiscite of 1870. As for M. Thiers, he has carried the revolutionary method to its ultimate

---

[1] Ollivier to Wallon, 16 March 1872, copy, O.P. All but the first two sentences of this quotation are omitted (without any indication of an omission) in the text printed in *Lettres de l'exil* (1921), 115–16.

[2] Ollivier to his brother Ernest, 9 May 1873, copy, O.P.

[3] The address to the throne by the Chamber of Deputies in March 1830, which led to the overthrow of Charles X.

[4] The coalition of Guizot, Thiers, and Odilon Barrot to overthrow Molé, 'immoral' because they had nothing in common except a desire for power.

degree of perfection and deserves that it should be designated by
his name. From him in fact the art of overthrowing governments without danger, and on the contrary, with profit to oneself, really dates. I shall be very surprised if, after so much
destruction carried out by his hand, he succeeds in constructing
anything at all. The least revolutionary man of this century
was Lamartine. He sinned only on one day, at the banquet of
Paris, and he made honourable amends. On 24 February, when
he rejected the chimerical regency of the duchess of Orleans,
he was being perspicacious and not revolutionary. I should like
to make it my honour to have never been revolutionary at all.
So far I have succeeded. Contemporaries have not realized that
this is my sole originality.'[1]

Ollivier's political writings after 1870 bear out this interpretation.[2] They are loaded with learned historical references, foot-
notes, and appendices, designed to prove that the constitution
and policy he had advocated in the past and which he continued
to advocate (with embellishments but without any profound
change of principle) were the distillation of the wisdom of the
world's best minds, from Plato downwards. He continued to
demand a responsible president, plebiscites, 'mixed government',
and the limitation of parliamentary powers. He now produced
detailed plans for turning the lower house into an academy of
legislation, which would meet only to decide the general principle of each law, but would do most of its work divided into
groups of specialists (agriculturalists, physicians, &c.), each dealing only with matters in which they were competent. This
would save much time and 'restore to our country the legislative
superiority she had under the first empire'. He proposed plural
voting, women's suffrage, and the transformation of the Senate
into a Supreme Court of Justice. He quoted in support of these
reforms the experience of Florence, Belgium, Switzerland, and
the U.S.A., and the works not only of his favourite Benjamin

---

[1] Ollivier to an unknown person, 8 March 1872, copy, O.P.
[2] See especially *Principes et conduite* (1875); *1789 et 1889* (1889); *Solutions
politiques et sociales* (1894).

Constant[1] but also of those specialists in reconciliation, Jean
Reynaud and Pierre Leroux.[2] He was much encouraged by a
trend he thought he saw developing in the home of parliamentary government itself, England: Bulwer Lytton told him, 'Our
parliamentary system is finished: we must rejuvenate it and
adapt it to the new times', and he was delighted when the conservative party in 1908 made the holding of referenda part of its
political programme.[3]

In the social sphere likewise Ollivier advocated compulsory
arbitration, participation in profits, and a national pensions and
unemployment scheme; he continued to declare that 'the improvement of the lot of the poor ought to be the principal preoccupation of the statesman'[4]; but on the other hand he opposed
legislation for the control of wages and factory conditions, he
denounced compulsory education, and he did not wish to abolish
economic inequality or to give workers any control over management. The contradiction between his simultaneous championship
of social legislation and his anathemizing against state intervention, might appear to be another of the inevitable contradictions of the liberal empire. Certainly Ollivier continued to be
attached to the optimistic doctrine of economic harmony
preached by Adam Smith's leading French pupil, Bastiat: his
ideal remained the *laissez-faire* system of early nineteenth-century
England, before she 'adopted the follies of state socialism'.[5]
Social legislation thus meant for him only the removal of the
obstacles which prevented the working class from bargaining
freely with their employers, the destruction of the legal privileges
of the bourgeoisie. That is why his law of combinations seemed
to him to be such a tremendous step forward. He insisted that

---

[1] Cf. The Additional Act of 1815, Article 33, providing for the representation of industry, commerce &c.

[2] Robert Talmy, *Le Vote familial en France 1870–1939* (unpublished typescript, D.E.S., Lille, 1959), pp. 3–6, gives Lamartine as a principal originator.

[3] Article by Ollivier in *Le Figaro* of 15 December 1910; Cf. Lord Newton,
Lord Lansdowne (1929), 403–7.

[4] *Discours d'Emile Ollivier au banquet de Saint-Tropez* (1885), 16.

[5] E. Ollivier, *Solutions politiques et sociales* (1894), 23, 59, 65, 86, 87 n.

'the state ought to be the liberty-state and sometimes the police-man-state, if necessary, but not the welfare-state'. He wanted the reduction of government expenditure, he opposed income-tax as 'demoralizing',[1] and objected to the government seeking to 'make working men . . . happy against their will'.[2] 'A man's work', he wrote, 'is proportionate to his ability to bear the responsibility of life: he from whom you remove responsibility for himself is like the slave in Homer, he has lost half his soul.' He enveighed against Marx and Lassalle as enemies of liberty: 'To compulsory military service and compulsory education there will be added compulsory jobs, compulsory thought, compul-sory health, and—who knows?—compulsory food and cloth-ing. We shall have compulsory trade unions, compulsory charity, compulsory atheism or religion. One does not stop on such an easy road. Those who are distressed at still not being sufficiently governed will have their wishes granted. More and more the state—and God knows what absurdities will be included under this word—will think, act, will, and foresee for us; and we, besotted flock, will have nothing to do but to bend our heads and pay our taxes. Happy those who do not see such days!'[3]

It might seem therefore that Ollivier differed very substanti-ally from Napoleon III on these matters. The latter had written that the state should be the 'beneficient motor' of society, 'lead-ing' the people 'towards a better future', and 'putting itself at the head of true ideas', 'satisfying the masses' by 'grand measures'.[4] But one also finds him saying later the exact opposite, and the difference between the two men was perhaps only on the question of timing. Napoleon declared in 1863 that in England social and political conditions 'freed the government from the need to be the sole promoter of the vital forces of the nation, so that, instead of regulating everything, it leaves to each the

---

[1] E. Ollivier, *1789 et 1889* (1889), 495.
[2] E.L. xiii. 241–7.
[3] E. Ollivier, *Solutions politiques et sociales* (1894), 93–94.
[4] Napoleon III, *Œuvres* (1856), i. 4, ii. 122, iii. 22; *Napoleon III et le prince Napoléon* (1925), 58–59.

responsibility of his own acts'. 'France will also achieve ... this marvellous activity, this absolute independence ... when we shall have consolidated the foundations indispensable to the establishment of complete liberty.'[1] Napoleon certainly had no desire to reduce all Frenchmen to a level uniformity, as Tocqueville feared; he was on the contrary a strong believer in the hierarchic structure of society. He would have approved Ollivier's statement that the French were 'envious rather than egalitarian', anxious above all for their own prosperity and for decorations.

In his social ideas generally Ollivier in fact had much in common with Napoleon III. Both men wished to be simultaneously left wing and right wing.

[1] *Moniteur universel*, 26 January 1863, p.115.

CHAPTER 14

CONCLUSION

WHAT then is Ollivier's legacy and what is his significance in French history? He consoled himself in his old age with the thought that a 'really great man' was not one who 'won political or oratorical success in the eyes of contemporaries more or less blinded by ephemeral passions', but one who had the 'merit of having bequeathed to the future one of those truths of theory or of conduct which thenceforth shine like torches before men's footsteps'.[1] He maintained that his liberal empire had represented 'the highest summit of liberty France has ever reached',[2] and that the method by which he had achieved it, which men denounced as treachery and tergiversation, was in fact, in its consistent preference for evolution as opposed to revolution, the most commendable of the century.[3] Immediately after the war he had suffered the most agonizing doubts about this foreign policy: he had hallucinations of the cries of dying soldiers and the curse of two nations pursuing him; but he came to the conclusion that 'I fulfilled my duty, that I was guided neither by the desire to keep power nor by that of winning glory, but solely by the preoccupation of preserving our poor country strong and intact in her honour'.[4]

Contemporaries, however, regarded his claims as the product of a ridiculous vanity. 'M. Ollivier', one said, 'has much talent; nature has endowed him richly; but unfortunately the wicked fairy of the fable who comes to spoil everything with her malevolence was not absent from his cradle, that fairy who brings the

[1] E.L. xiii. 223-4.
[2] E. Ollivier, *Principes et Conduite* (1875).
[3] E. Ollivier, 'De la methode politique', in *Le Correspondant* (1893), vol. 171, pp. 985-1011; idem, *Thiers à l'académie et dans l'histoire* (1879), 67; idem, *Lettres de l'exil* (1921), 114.
[4] E. Ollivier, *Lettres de l'exil* (1921), 134.

finest promise to nothing and who transforms advantages into
weaknesses. For him, this fairy was self-infatuation. . . . M.
Ollivier is in fact infallible, he has never been wrong. . . . He
knows only one form of plea, that which Cicero called *pro
domo sua*. . . . [He] does not know how to applaud himself enough
. . . [though] he has an excuse that disarms the severities of criticism—his excess of naïveté, which makes him forget his own
past.'[1]

Ollivier believed that with time the country would at length
see him in his true light. 'I shall have my revenge, as France will,
but on condition that I wait, wait, wait.'[2] He signed the articles
he wrote for newspapers with the pseudonym 'Patiens' and over
his front door he placed the motto 'Certa viriliter, sustine patien-
ter'.[3] He looked upon the literary activities of his forced retirement as a preparation for an ultimate return to politics, a useful
interlude in which he could 'increase his physical and intellectual
strength, so as to bear valiantly the struggles that might still
be reserved for me'. 'I am firmly convinced', he told the newspaper reporters who came to ask him his plans, 'that this generous
and intelligent nation will one day regret having kept me out
of its assemblies for so long, and that it will restore me to the
tribune. That is my entire ambition.'[4] He was wrong: his unpopularity lost its bitterness, but instead it became legendary, almost
sacred. 'Because he was the emblem of defeat, he was not par-
doned, to show that France did not accept her defeat.'[5]

When Ollivier realized this, he decided to justify his conduct
and his claims to posterity instead of to his contemporaries. At
the age of sixty-five he began writing his memoirs, entitled *The
Liberal Empire*, to which he devoted the rest of his life. They
took the form of an enormous and nominally impartial history

---

[1] E. de Pressensé, 'Les évolutions de M. Emile Ollivier', in *La Revue politique
et littéraire*, 3rd series (1882), iv. 204–6.

[2] E. Ollivier, *Letters de l'exil* (1921), 196.

[3] 'Fight with virility, bear with patience.'

[4] *Le Gaulois*, 4 September 1879.

[5] André Beaunier, 'L'historien de l'Empire Libéral', *Revue des deux mondes*
(1915), xxix. 338.

of the reign of Napoleon III, though their ultimate purpose was
to serve as an apology of his own role in it. He himself admitted
that he wrote them not only for 'the delicious pleasure of render-
ing disinterested witness to truth' but also because 'in the depths
of my despair there remains alive an indestructible hope' that
men would one day do justice to him, when political circumstances changed. France, he wrote, 'is waiting for the time when,
roused by the great man of whom she dreams, she will emerge
from her bed of pettiness, once more astonish the world and
again give it the joy of which it has been deprived since she
has ceased to lead it. Then some curious historian will perhaps
discover in the depths of a library the last copy of this work [*The
Liberal Empire*] which has escaped being eaten by worms or whose
leaves do not crumble into dust. He will say: Really! Is this then
what really happened? And he will recount it to readers who
will listen to him. It is to you, O unknown justiciary of the
future, that I dedicate this history.'[1]

His book has largely failed in its purpose perhaps, first of all,
because of its sheer bulk. It consists of no less than seventeen
volumes, of over 600 pages each—three million words. There
can be very few people who have read this straight through;
he would probably have been wise had he separated the history
from the memoirs and given a more consecutive account of his
own life and a clearer exposition of his aims. Secondly, though it
claimed to be impartial history, it gave a very individual interpretation, in which the protagonists were painted in the brightest
colours and sometimes in uncompromising black and white.
Ollivier maintained that impartiality does not 'condemn [the
historian] to having no opinion, to expressing neither admiration
nor blame' but only 'not to travesty opinions or acts, to report
opinions he does not share and acts he criticizes with such scrupu-
lous exactness that their very authors would have nothing to
object to or add'.[2] However, he did not quite succeed in doing
this: an English reviewer considered it a polemical work in

[1] E.L. xiv. 6–7.
[2] E.L. ix. 268–9, cf. ii. 3–24.

which special pleading was not avoided, even though by 'con-
scientious reaction' it sought to be fair: it 'pour[s] out vials of
unmitigated wrath' against Bismarck, though at the same time
admiring him as Milton admired Satan.[1]

The book defends Napoleon III with vigorous partisanship.
The emperor had, Ollivier says, generosity, good sense, 'the
royal quality of justice', moderation, but also audacity. The
only defect he admits is the undeniable one that he was unable
to supervise the details of administration. Napoleon was no
despot; he agreed to the *coup d'état* 'with tears in his eyes'; he
even gave far more liberty than existed under the third republic.
His aim at home was 'order' simply as a means to social progress.
Abroad he planned disinterestedly to help oppressed nationalities.
He never sought aggrandizement for himself; his Mexican adventure was the product of 'misinformation'; his policy of compensations was pushed on to him by his minister Drouyn; and as
for his war of 1870, had not Bismarck himself 'confessed' to
having craftily engineered it all?[2] All this is so overdone that the
plausibility of Ollivier's own defence is much diminished. His
habit of devoting several pages to answering one line of criticism
and of quoting fulsome praise of himself whenever he found a
record of it, inevitably stimulated resistance in his readers; nor
did his bitterly severe judgements on his contemporaries encourage compassion for their author.[3] Thus Haussmann 'had the
impudent air of a lacquey in a good household'; Fould, minister
of finance, was a 'man of wit, a man of clubs and salons, a patron
of the arts, who even knew a little about finance, which he had
learnt from his brother Benoit, an eminent banker' (that is,
Ollivier's friend); Thiers' whole philosophy was that 'he had
been predestined by a special decree of Providence to govern
in chief the society born of the [French] Revolution, that every
political régime which did not give him this position was afflicted

---

[1] *Fortnightly Review* (January 1910), 122.

[2] E.L. ii. 437; iii. 18, 77–81, 83, 97; iv. 368, 516; v. 74, 241–2; viii. 477;
xii. 536.

[3] P. de Quirielle, 'Le Cas de M. Ollivier', in *Le Correspondant* (25 September
1913), vol. 252, pp. 1094–1116.

with an incurable imperfection'; Grévy was 'cold, with little good will, egoistic, sarcastic, incapable of being moved by a generous inspiration'; Garnier-Pagès was 'a clown'.[1]

However, Ollivier's book has been successful in a different way. As history, *The Liberal Empire* will always remain a work of essential value for its period and the most important single work on it by a contemporary. It is a product of formidable industry and contains a great deal of original material. It incorporates information obtained from conversations with many leading figures of the second empire as well as drawing on Ollivier's own remarkable memory. It uses manuscript sources not generally available and some of which have since disappeared.[2] It is true that he sometimes makes slight changes in the documents he transcribes, usually for reasons of style, and that on occasion he omits inconvenient passages without warning.[3] Sometimes, even in matters with which he was most closely associated, his account is not altogether reliable. Nevertheless, modern specialists are unanimous in attesting its enormous and enduring value.

It is also worth reading for its literary qualities. It has rightly been called a 'monument of French literature, an unrecognized monument or rather an unknown one'.[4] 'I place [it]', André Bellesort has said, 'in the first rank of memoirs. I know none that

---

[1] E.L. iii. 86, ii. 259, vi. 376, xii. 381, ii. 492. Contrast this judgement of Garnier-Pagès with the latter's generous reference to Ollivier in his *Histoire de la révolution de 1848* (1861–72), vii. 267, as 'a young man of promise and talent'.

[2] His manuscript sources include notably the diary and correspondence of Marshal Vaillant, the correspondence of Niel with the emperor, documents lent by Gramont, Chevreau, Chasseloup, Segris, Buffet, and other colleagues, in addition to his own papers. He does not always name his sources, and his book is thus more solidly founded than sometimes appears. For example ii. 510 is based on a letter from Buffet and ii. 274–9, the account of a meeting of the Burgraves with a report of Thiers' speech, on a manuscript lent by Buffet. He also quotes from Chasseloup-Laubat's diary, which has been lost.

[3] E.g. cf. the difference between E.L. vi. 534–5 and *Annales du corps législatif* (1864), vi. 171; and the difference between E.L. vii. 404–7 and J. ii. 197–9. There are important passages omitted from E.L. xii. 612–14, as revealed by comparing it with the letter preserved among his papers.

[4] A. Dansette in *Revue de Paris* (July 1961), 146–51.

is as full of verve and of fire.'[1] Even a hostile critic has written, 'M. Ollivier's politics have been and will remain debatable: his literary talent is above all dispute.'[2] There are passages in his work, wrote *The Times*, which 'are as graphic and sombre as anything in Tacitus, and there is no modern historian, unless it be Kinglake, who so vividly depicts scenes of which he was an eye-witness.'[3]

His style is a dazzling combination of mellifluence and vigour. He is perhaps at his most brilliant in the character studies with which this work is studded: 'he carries to a rare degree of perfection the peculiarly French art of the portrait'.[4] Both the form and the content of his work have a remarkable richness resulting from his political experience on both the left wing and the right and from his exceptionally wide reading: 'There

[1] A. Bellesort, *La Société sous Napoléon III* (1932), X.
[2] L. de Lanzac de Laborie in *Bulletin critique* (1901), 22. 698.
[3] *The Times*, 21 August 1913.
[4] L. de Lanzac de Laborie reviewing volume x. in *Bulletin Critique* (1905), 26. Here, for example, is part of his portrait of Jules Favre. 'Of great height and broad body, with a large and powerful head lit up by charming, delicate, and soft eyes, crowned by an Olympian head of hair, with a protruding chin hiding in the depths of its curve a grimacing lip which seemed to have been twisted by the invective that had so often crossed it, such was Jules Favre's appearance at the tribune or the bar. He did not know vanity, but he did not guard himself against envy. He was not a good man. Was he a bad one? He was sensitive—that is to say he was as capable of goodness as of wickedness. One had no security in one's relations with him; there was no friendship he would not sacrifice for the pleasure of intoning a well-constructed period: one was always exposed to having his speech changing catlike from caress to an attack with open claws. Though of unclouded integrity and of unlimited disinterestedness no man has gratuitously torn more decent people to pieces. . . . Although his youth had been austere and devoted unremittingly to work, he had no deep knowledge of politics, finance, history, or even law, nor of anything at all, except rhetoric, whose resources he knew as no one has done since Cicero, his model. . . . Doubts about truth did not torment him and every argument seemed true to him as soon as it lent itself to being turned into a speech. Then he felt himself to be really superior, not that this speech was solid in the manner of Guizot or Dufaure, but because it was copious, flexible, of long and gracious undulation, with vivid traits heightened by the brilliance of his imagery, the ingenious juxtaposition of his observations, well suited to a correct, equal, pure, indefatigable, cadenced voice, which neither rose nor fell too much and whose mere sound charmed his audience with the pleasures of artistic enjoyment.' E.L. iv. 78–79.

was never yet a grand history written', as Clarendon has said, 'but by men conversant in business and of the best and most liberal education.'[1] *The Liberal Empire* was considered by Bergson to be reminiscent of the Duc de Saint-Simon's Memoirs: but it is perhaps most comparable to Clarendon's *History of the Great Rebellion*. On the strength of it, Toynbee has classified Ollivier as one of the pleiad of historians whose expulsion from active life has revealed their true talents and who 'has made a greater mark and achieved greater distinction in the last chapter of his career . . . than he would ever have achieved if the first chapter had not been cut short by his withdrawal as . . . a fallen minister of state'.[2]

Others have considered that Ollivier's chief claim to fame is that he was one of the greatest orators of his century.[3] His opponents, while granting him this, have replied that he was nothing more. 'M. Emile Ollivier', said Camille Pelletan, 'was an admirable instrument of rhetorical music; no one could sing—with accents more melodiously unctuous—rich, rolling Lamartinian periods. He really deserved his high reputation at the tribune [but] everybody knows how he lacked political sense.'[4] A colleague of his in the French Academy recorded how that body was frequently 'charmed by a warmth of accent, a profusion of imagery, an amplitude of periods, an oratorical torrent which carried us away on its potent wave and sent through us the thrill of great eloquence'.[5] Another wrote: 'We were subjected to the charm which he himself felt in the way a singer is moved by his own voice. When one heard him, one forgot his face of an unfrocked priest, his scowling eyes, his black nails, his shabby

---

[1] Edward, Earl of Clarendon, *An Essay on an Active and Contemplative Life, and why the one should be preferred before the other* (Glasgow, 1765), 40.

[2] A. J. Toynbee, *A Study of History* (1951 edition), iii. 287–8. The pleiad consists of Thucydides, Xenophon, Polybius, Josephus, Ibn Khaldun, Machiavelli, Clarendon, and Ollivier.

[3] E.g. Jules Delafosse, *Etudes et portraits* (1894), 261.

[4] C. Pelletan, 'L'Opposition républicaine sous l'empire', *Revue politique et parlementaire* (May 1910), 220.

[5] Speech of René Doumic, Séance de l'Académie Française, 24 January 1918.

clothes, his unkempt hair, one only saw his rhetorical gestures, whose amplitude was admirable and which seemed to beat time to his marvellous eloquence. The grandeur of the imagery, the sonority of the voice, the incomparable harmony of the phrases moved even the most unfeeling: everything in it, even his slightly southern accent, gave additional grace to his diction. As to Martignac, one could cry out to him: Silence, siren. He had the strange ability to speak impromptu on everything and anything, without even having doubts on the subject he was treating. It seemed as though there suddenly grew in him a power for which he was not responsible and to which he yielded, as though obeying an irresistible impulse. I often saw him coming to the French Academy after the proceedings had begun and a debate had unexpectedly been started: he would ask his neighbour, who was usually Mezières, 'What are they talking about?' He would scarcely have heard the answer before he asked to speak and enraptured us. His audience, however, was not sympathetic to him: he was not liked here and was kept at a distance. Men bore him a grudge for so many misfortunes, which he continued, at least outwardly, to bear "with a light heart", but they could not prevent themselves from admiring him and no one could resist the pleasure of listening to him. That was all: his influence was negative and it was enough for him to move a motion for it to be defeated.'[1]

His reputation indeed was such that the young Paul Deschanel, the future president of the republic, came all the way down to the south coast specially to submit to him for his criticism the draft of his maiden speech.[2] But to possess oratorical skill is a dangerous distinction: 'rhetoric is very good, or stark nought: there is no medium in rhetoric. If I am not persuaded, I laugh at the orator.'[3]

Maurice Barrès picked on Ollivier as epitomizing a species of

---

[1] M. Du Camp, *Souvenirs d'un demi-siècle* (1949), i. 238-9.
[2] H. Odelin, 'Emile Ollivier et le Catholicisme', in *La Revue hebdomadaire* 12 January 1935; and cf. also Gen. du Barail, *Mes Souvenirs* (1894-6), iii. 121.
[3] John Selden, *Table Talk* (1689), s.v. Preaching.

unsuccessful politician. 'All these men—the Emile Olliviers—
are men of letters at bottom. Their essential need is to express
themselves in speech or in writing. They are not statesmen.'[1]
Ollivier himself claimed that he was on the contrary 'above all
a man of action', though the fact was obscured by his belonging
to an unusual type, 'to the school of the phlegmatics, of William
III and Napoleon III' who worked by gradual and not by revolutionary methods.[2] He believed that his hero Lamartine was
likewise 'above all a man of action'[3]—a judgement which seems
to echo Lamartine's frustrated cry in 1838: 'My destiny was in
the field of action: events deny it to me and I am withering.'[4]
Ollivier's failure was in one sense a purely personal one: he
was inadequate for the role to which he aspired. He was too full
of enthusiasm to distinguish illusion from reality, to such an
extent that he has been called the second empire's Madame
Bovary of politics.[5] He was blinded by an unbounded optimism:
he was 'a victim of his very gifts' Adrien Dansette has said, 'and
particularly of his eloquence. . . . He thought that men and things
would be as easy to manage as words and he saw facts as his
imagination created them.'[6] Alphonse Daudet likewise summed
him up as 'an idealist poet who went astray into politics'. He had
'the look of an interrogating and undecided dreamer behind the
crystal of his spectacles, the face of a talker in which all is in the
fold of the lips, the outline of the mouth, full of audacity and
without will'.[7]

---

[1] M. Barrès, Mes Cahiers, vol. vii. (1933), 63.

[2] Ollivier to his brother Ernest, 3 October 1873, copy, O.P. Presumably
1688 and 1851 were revolutions to prevent revolutions.

[3] E. Ollivier, Lamartine (Conférence faite à l'Université des Annales, 1 May
1907), 3.

[4] P. Thureau-Dangin, Histoire de la monarchie de juillet (1906), v. 144.

[5] G. Duveau, De 1848 à nos jours (1953), 229. See the criticism of his L'Eglise
et l'Etat au Concile du Vatican in E. Beau de Lomenie, Maurras et son système
(Bourg 1953), 35, and of his plebiscite in A. Thibaudet, Les Idées politiques de
la France (1932), 167–8.

[6] Revue de Paris (July 1961), 146–51.

[7] Alphonse Daudet, Quarante Ans de Paris 1857–1897 (Geneva, 1945), 75–81.

Yet Ollivier was far from being a misfit in the reign of Napoleon III. Renan (who had followed him into the liberal empire) confessed of himself that 'I was predestined to be what I am, a romantic protesting against romanticism, a utopian preaching down-to-earth politics, an idealist vainly giving himself much trouble to appear bourgeois, a tissue of contradictions'.[1] Ollivier was all the more typical of his times, all the more interesting historically, because he saw no conflict in being simultaneously idealist and bourgeois. His career is important because it illuminates a whole generation and perhaps even a permanent section of French society. A few of his opponents at least did him the credit of admitting that he really did represent the deep-felt aspirations of his contemporaries. 'La France bourgeoise', wrote Allain-Targé, 'est tiers parti. It always has been and always will be for the middle party. It dreams of the reconciliation of contradictions. Under Louis Philippe, it wanted peace and a martial attitude, liberty without excess, a monarchy surrounded with republican institutions, electoral reform, the rule of civil servants. This was mad, but this was its idea. Today it has a similar idea which is just as stupid. It wants the gradual progress of moderate liberties and the conservatism of a strong government, militarism, repression of the masses, and universal suffrage.'[2] The 'crime of Ollivier' in Allain-Targé's eyes was that he had abandoned the republican party, which popular opinion rejected at that time, which 'was impossible today but would be necessary tomorrow', and which aimed at effecting 'the transition from the domination of the bourgeoisie of 1789 to the democracy of the twentieth century'. In fact Ollivier's conduct was more complicated. He did indeed wish to 'reassure' the middle classes, but he was hostile to the idea of a government exclusively dominated by them: he went over to the empire

[1] E. Renan, Souvenirs de'enfance (1883), 73.

[2] Allain-Targé to his mother, April 1866, in Revue historique (1937), vol. 179, p. 140. Jules Delafosse, Etudes et portraits (1894), 254, likewise says, 'The liberal and parliamentary empire was without doubt a chimera. . . . But it must be agreed that this transfiguration, of which M. Emile Ollivier was the principal artisan, corresponded with the universal wish of the time.'

partly because he preferred it to the rue de Poitiers. However, he also wished to give a greater say to the masses: his solution to the problem of the conflict of bourgeoisie and proletariat was to turn the proletariat into bourgeoisie. This again was a widespread ideal among his generation.

'The special characteristic of radical policy,' wrote Jules Simon in his important book *La Politique Radicale*, 'is that it rejects compromise, half-measures, and that it goes . . . to the limit of its principles. . . . [It seeks] all or nothing.'[1] Ollivier held the very contrary view and he got the better of his critics, for, once in power the radicals abandoned most of their demands. He rightly claimed that the policy of 'opportunism' which flourished under the third republic was his very own.[2] The once fiery Gambetta accepted the monarchical institutions with which the royalists endowed his republic, after having vehemently denounced them; the new radicals who arose on his left in 1875 accused him in turn of going over to the bourgeoisie and one of his bitterest critics exclaimed, 'Gambetta has become Marshal Macmahon's Emile Ollivier!'[3] Jules Simon performed a complete *volte face*, condemned the policy of 'all or nothing' and declared that Ollivier was a man to whom they had been 'very unjust'.[4] The opportunist republican Freycinet wrote in his memoirs that 'but for the woeful war with Prussia, the transformed empire had a good chance of lasting'.[5]

Ollivier, however, lacked a vital quality which explains to a considerable extent why Gambetta, though he died almost as frustrated as Ollivier and though he held power almost as briefly, has universally been regarded as far superior. Gambetta knew how to work with men and how to win their affection:

---

[1] Jules Simon, *La Politique radicale* (1869), 4–5.

[2] *Discours d'Emile Ollivier au banquet de Saint-Tropez* (1885), 6.

[3] *Letters from Paris 1870–1875, written by C. de B., a political informant to the head of the London House of Rothschild*, translated and edited by Robert Henrey (1942), 209.

[4] J. Simon, 'Notice historique sur . . . Carnot', in *Mémoires de l'académie des sciences morales et politiques* (1896), xxix. 3–55; E.L. vi. 564.

[5] C. de Freycinet, *Souvenirs 1848–1878* (1914), 92.

his modest and open nature enabled him to make an enormous number of friends, and these created a legend around him, after his death, so powerful that no republican has ever dared to challenge it since. Ollivier on the other hand was too full of his own self to win real trust from others; his wizardry with words, for all its emotional power, lacked the complement of an attractive personality to make its effect more than evanescent. 'The tinted spectacles prevent one catching his eye. One is not quite sure with whom one is dealing. One does not feel confidence in him.' So he was for ever after stamped as 'a man who has committed a mistake'.[1]

In 1857 Proudhon had given this piece of advice to Darimon: 'Never depart from this rule: a deputy must always take the point of view of his party: say what he thinks, give his advice, and if this advice does not prevail, follow the general opinion. By making this sacrifice of your personal judgement, you will be recognized as a trustworthy and loyal man.'[2] Ollivier lacked the patience and the humility to accept this maxim. The result was that though he may have had the 'passion of Fox', no colleague ever spoke of him with tears in his eyes, as many did of Fox and Gambetta.

Opinion on Ollivier is not likely to change until the idea that the second empire was capable of being made liberal finds wide acceptance. This cannot happen until opinion on Napoleon III has itself altered and until the view gains ground that he was more than a farcical parody of his uncle, that he has an independent claim to statesmanship, particularly in domestic affairs. H. A. L. Fisher hailed Ollivier as 'a true liberal', but condemned

---

[1] Henry Michel, Le Quarantième Fauteil (1898), 57–61.

[2] Proudhon to Darimon, 29 June 1857, P. J. Proudhon, Correspondance (1875), vii. 259. Cf. the opposite view, expressed by Peel (and criticized by Disraeli); 'However painful it may prove to me to sever party connections . . . still . . . I cannot purchase their support by promising to adhere at all times, and at all hazards, as minister of the Crown, to arguments and opinions which I may have heretofore propounded in this House. I reserve to myself, distinctly and unequivocally, the right of adapting my conduct to the exigency of the moment and to the wants of the country.'—Speeches of Sir R. Peel (1853), i. 767–8.

him because he was deceived into allying himself with Napoleon III, who was not.[1] Modern scholars are, however, revising the old estimate of the emperor and one has recently said, 'For me Napoleon *le petit* is not only morally better than Napoleon *le grand*, but is historically superior to him.'[2] Only when, and if ever, this view prevails, will Ollivier stand a chance of a more favourable hearing. Yet inevitably nothing will outweigh the fact that when the test of his statesmanship came in the crisis of July 1870, he was unable to meet it. In the late 1930's it was claimed that the Provençal word for *olivier* was *daladié*.[3]

Ollivier's comparison of himself with a large number of famous men reflects an almost pathological obsession by visions of grandeur; but historically the comparisons are important. Mirabeau, Constant, Lamartine, and Ollivier do indeed belong to a single tradition and their political aims, despite the many years that separated them, were basically similar. Mirabeau wanted to do for the *ancien régime* what Ollivier almost succeeded in doing for the second empire—to combine monarchy with democracy—but like him he was overbearingly conceited, failed to inspire confidence, and was accused of treason for his compact with the court.[4] Constant tried again with Napoleon's I's empire. Several republicans urged the same theory under Louis Philippe too: not only Carnot but even Gustave Chaudey (who in 1870 declared a liberal monarchy to be impossible) had argued that the reform of the July monarchy would be preferable to its violent overthrow.[5] Proudhon himself flirted with Louis Napoleon, and

---

[1] H. A. L. Fisher, *Studies in History and Politics* (Oxford, 1920), 52.

[2] Luigi Salvatorelli, 'L'Europe de Napoléon III et l'Europe de Mazzini', in *Revue historique* (April–June 1960), vol. 223, p. 283.

[3] *La Table ronde* (January 1962), 92.

[4] O. J. G. Welch, *Mirabeau* (1951), 329–32, 124. Cf. Mirabeau's view that politics 'is concerned with what is possible' (188), and that the king's veto was 'nothing but a right of the people entrusted to the prince'; 'I can conceive nothing more terrible than the soveriegn autocracy of 600 persons' (189).

[5] G. Chaudey, *De la formation d'une véritable opposition constitutionelle* (January 1848).

in 1848 wrote that 'the progress of France . . . could have been achieved as well with the fallen government just as it was, and would have cost much less'.[1] Lamartine and Cormenin represent the same idea in the second republic. France in fact finally but accidentally adopted the solution for which Ollivier and these men had worked in vain, when in 1875 she established a republic with monarchical instutions. It was precisely because the third republic neither pleased nor offended anyone too much that it lasted so long; and now the fifth republic derives its strength in part from the same cause: it is a régime, like the liberal empire, which is somehow both of the left and of the right, stimulating much controversy but based nevertheless on wide popular support or acquiescence.

'In problems of state,' wrote the seventeenth-century Trimmer Halifax, 'where men may or may not be in the right, do not deserve the good opinion of one side so entirely as to forfeit your credit with the other.'[2] Ollivier was a trimmer who did not quite succeed in establishing this delicate balance. His importance must lie in his aims much more than in his achievements. Yet he has few equals for perseverance. 'I am getting old,' he said when he was eighty-six, 'it is annoying, for I have never been more intelligent.' He worked indefatigably on his apology, The Liberal Empire, to the very end, surviving as though from sheer determination to finish it. It was only when he was within a few hundred pages of completing the seventeenth and final volume that, at the age of eighty-eight, he was struck down by an illness which he recognized would be his last. On 20 August 1913 he was visibly ebbing fast away when suddenly raising himself up with extraordinary energy he cried out, 'The soldiers, the soldiers!' Then he fell back and lost consciousness. Half an hour later he was dead.[3] None can say what he saw in this

[1] P. J. Proudhon to Maurice, 25 February 1848, Correspondance (1875), ii. 280.

[2] The Earl of Halifax to Henry Savile, 5-15 February 1680-1, quoted by H. C. Foxcroft, A Character of the Trimmer (1946), 131-2.

[3] Marie-Louise Pailleron, 'Emile Ollivier', in Revue hebdomaire (January 1918), i. 451-62.

last moment. Was it a vision of the revenge of France, or a return of the awful, tortured moments of 1870?

He was buried without pomp at the cape of La Moutte, on a rock that stands out into the Mediterranean sea, at a short distance from his house. A simple monument of granite was placed on the spot with this one inscription engraved on it, which he had himself chosen: *Magna quies in magna spe.* It is a deserted beach and there is no sound there but that of the waves. One recalls his statement that he had known the waves caressing and that he had known them in storm, but that he had greeted both alike, in the certainty that each would fall in turn. The motto on his tomb expresses his last feelings well; and it is curiously confirmed by some verses of Byron which are heavily marked in his copies of *Childe Harold*, both in the English original and in a French translation:

> Have I not had to wrestle with my lot?
> Have I not suffer'd things to be forgiven?
> Have I not had my brain sear'd, my heart riven,
> Hopes sapp'd, name blighted, Life's life lied away?
> And only not to desperation driven,
> Because not altogether of such clay
> As rots into the souls of those whom I survey.
>
> From mighty wrongs to petty perfidy
> Have I not seen what human things could do?
> From the loud roar of foaming calumny
> To the small whisper of the as paltry few
> And subtler venom of the reptile crew,
> The Janus glance of whose significant eye,
> Learning to lie with silence, would *seem* true,
> And without utterance, save the shrug or sigh,
> Deal round to happy fools its speechless obloquy.
>
> But I have lived, and have not lived in vain:
> My mind may lose its force, my blood its fire,
> And my frame perish even in conquering pain;

But there is that within me which shall tire
Torture and Time, and breathe when I expire:
Something unearthly, which they deem not of,
Like the remember'd tone of a mute lyre,
Shall on their soften'd spirits sink, and move
In hearts all rocky now the late remorse of love.

BIBLIOGRAPHY

I. Manuscript Sources

The Ollivier Papers, at La Moutte and in Paris, are here used in their entirety for the first time. They were widely dispersed over the three family houses, but may be divided into three rough categories. 1. *Correspondence.* Copies of many letters sent by Ollivier are to be found in his diary for the period before 1870; and for the period after in a series of bound volumes of carbon copies; there are also bundles of drafts of letters. The originals of his letters to Mme de Sourdeval were returned by her; those to Guiter were borrowed from the latter's descendants; those to his father likewise survive in part. Copies of his letters to his second wife are extant in her manuscript account of their marriage. Letters received were arranged, probably by his widow, in annual files and envelopes. 2. *Diary.* A series of seven bound volumes, 1846–8, 1851–3, 1853–7, 1857–63, 1863–5, 1866–9 and 1870, and in addition loose sheets for 1853 and 1874–6 and small pocket notebooks of about 1870–3. I have published extracts from these under the title *Journal 1846–1869* (Paris, 1961, 2 volumes): this is inevitably a limited selection, but I included the passages which I considered most important and which I can therefore refer to instead of quoting at length in this book. 3. *Documents.* For 1848, bound and unbound collections of speeches, newspaper cuttings, and official documents regarding his prefecture. For 1870, envelopes containing letters received during his ministry, miscellaneous notes, drafts, &c. Also newspaper cuttings for the period after 1870. Ollivier's papers are not in their natural order, because he used them to write his memoirs. Documents on 1870 are thus sometimes to be found embedded in proofs of his *Liberal Empire*. Only after 1870 are they in a condition the historian finds really satisfactory, that is to say not artificially re-grouped and edited. On the other hand there is the compensation that a good number of letters and documents are printed in the text or appendices of the *Liberal Empire*.

Other Private Papers. I give a list of some twenty other collections of private papers of the second empire which I have been able to consult in my *Political System of Napoleon III* (1958), 177–82. Those of Buffet, Chasseloup-Laubat, Montalembert, Segris, Thiers, Rouher, and Baroche, are particularly important for the study of Ollivier. I may add that I have also consulted the Morny papers, which were offered for sale to me, but they were only a small remnant of what he left and were disappointing: they are now in the National Archives. Another collection of thirty-eight letters from Morny, mainly to Magne, is in the possession of M. Maillard, who kindly allowed me to examine it.

NATIONAL ARCHIVES, PARIS

The records of Ollivier's ministry have largely disappeared. Useful information was, however, found in the following boxes:

F (1c) I 130: Plebiscite of 1870, results.

F (90) 408 and 591: Telegrams on Ollivier's election, 1869.

BB (18) 1786: Var file, Ollivier in 1869.

BB (30) 358: Marseilles in 1848. BB (3) 455: Plebiscite of 1870: part of this box disappeared, but this is because the documents abstracted were printed privately under the title *La Justice et la politique sous le second empire* (n.d.). This very rare book contains the reports of the senior officials of the ministry of justice during the period of the plebiscite.

C 1340–1378: Election results 1857–69.

43 A.P.: A letter from Jules Favre to Ollivier, 17 March 1848.

AB xix 178, file 69: projected ministries, 1869.

DEPARTMENTAL ARCHIVES

BOUCHES-DU-RHÔNE. (a) *At Marseilles:*

M (6) 24: Correspondence to Ollivier from mayors, &c., 1848.

M (6) 25–27 and 270: Miscellaneous correspondence and also decrees and proclamations.

M (6) 5309: Telegrams between Ollivier and the ministry.

M II (3) 22: Formalities of 1848 election.

vii 0 10 2: Public works.

R (4) 1: Mayor of Marseilles to the prefect, 1850, about Ollivier.

22 V 1: Circulars of the bishop of Marseilles.

33 V 1: Complaints of the clergy.

Y (2) 139: Letters about the men accused in the rising of June 1848.

(b) *At Aix-en-Provence*:

12 U 1: Political reports addressed to the procureur-général in 1848.

14 U 9: Correspondence and documents on the rising of June 1848.

14 U 10: 'Affaire des montagnards'.

15 U 3 and 5: Election of 1848.

15 U 4: Reports from the procureur de la republique on the June days.

15 U 28: Ollivier's election in 1876.

VAR. *At Draguignan.*

II M 3–30: Election of 1876.

II M (5) 78–81: Conseil général election of 1865.
    138–144: Conseil général election of 1886.

IV M 16: 'Ésprit publique, événements politiques', 1848–50.

IV M 36: The same for 1854–70.

7 U 29–2: Political trials 1850–65.

HAUTE–MARNE. *At Chaumont.*

2 M i: Ollivier's personal dossier as prefect: virtually nothing; and other files investigated yielded nothing.

MUNICIPAL ARCHIVES

Marseilles:

1 D 73: Municipal council's deliberations for 1848.

2 D 133–4: Documents 'annexes aux deliberations'—formal.

5 D 9: Copies of letters from mayor to prefect.

BIBLIOTHÈQUE NATIONALE, DEPT OF MSS., PARIS

Nouvelles acquisitions françaises 9587: brief biography of Ollivier by Auguste Blanqui, scathing.

BRITISH MUSEUM, LONDON

Add. MSS. 40124: Letter from Louis Blanc to Karl Blind about Ollivier.

BODLEIAN LIBRARY, OXFORD

MSS. Clarendon Deposit C. 477: Private letters from the British Ambassador in Paris to the Foreign Secretary, January–June 1870. C. 474 (3): Letters from Clarendon to Lyons.

PUBLIC RECORD OFFICE, LONDON

F.O. 27 1789–92 and 1797–1810: Despatches from Lyons, 1870. The Consular reports from Marseilles in 1848 contain no political information, but requests from the consuls for the payment of their salaries and little else.

ARCHIVES OF THE DIOCESE OF MARSEILLES

File 142: Letters from Ollivier.
Register of Correspondence for 1844–51: Copies of letters from the Archbishop to Ollivier.

BIBLIOTHÈQUE DE LA VILLE, MARSEILLES

MSS. 47794, vol. 12. no. 58 f. 304: Letter from Ollivier, 4 April 1848.

RUSSIAN FOREIGN POLICY ARCHIVES, MOSCOW

Minister's Chancery, 1870, files nos. 116 and 117. Letters (written in French) from the Russian Embassy in Paris, including reports of interviews with Ollivier, January–September 1870.

UNPUBLISHED BOOKS AND THESES

QUATRELLES L'EPINE: Biography of Morny, using papers which have since been lost.

F. CHALAMON DE BERNARDY: Le Comte Walewski. Doctoral thesis 1951, at the Sorbonne.

M. ABEBERRY: Le projet de constitution du maréchal Pétain, Bordeaux D.E.S. 1951, contains comparisons with that of 1870.

JOSETTE MICHEL: *Le plebiscite du 8 mai 1870 en Côte d'Or*, Dijon
D.E.S. 1957.

M. MOISSONNIER: *L'opposition ouvrière à Lyon à la fin du second
empire*, Lyon D.E.S. 1957.

ROBERT TALMY: *Le Vote familial en France 1870-1939*, Lille
D.E.S. 1959.

II. Parliamentary Debates

Compte-rendu des séances du corps législatif and also
Procès-verbeaux des séances du corps législatif for 1852-60.
Annales du sénat et du corps législatif for 1861-70.
Débats parlementaires for the third republic.

III. Newspapers

PARIS: *Moniteur universel*, later *Journal officiel*.

For the period up to 1870: *La Liberté*, *Le Constitutionnel*, *Le
Charivari*, *L'Illustration*, *Le Père Duchêne*, *La Mère Duchêne*,
Le Journal des débats, *Le Journal des economistes*.

For the third republic: *L'Estafette*, *Le Figaro*, *Le Gaulois*, *Le Pays*.
Also *La Revue des deux mondes*.

MARSEILLES: collection of newspapers in the municipal library:
Le Semaphore de Marseille, *Le Gazette du Midi*, *Le Progrès
Social*, *L'Indépendant de Marseille*, all for 1848. Also cuttings
from *Le Courrier Bouches des du Rhône*.

VAR: *Le Démocrate du Var*, 1850; *Le Petit Var* of Toulon and
Le Var of Draguignan for 1876 and 1885-6.

Extracts from other provincial newspapers: *Le Bien Public* of
Chaumont, for 1849, *Le Suffrage universel* of Montpelier
for 1851, and for 1870: *Le Journal de Lot et Garonne* of
Agen, *L'Industriel alsacien* of Mulhouse, *L'Indépendant du
Lot* of Cahors, *Le Courrier du Bas-Rhin* of Strasbourg, *Le
Radical de l'Ouest* of Nantes and *L'Emancipation* of Toulouse.

English newspapers: *The Times*, using its valuable index; *The
Saturday Review*; and for his period in office the *Daily
Telegraph*, *Vanity Fair*, and *Punch*.

IV. Published Works of Emile Ollivier

Du mariage consideré dans ses effets à l'égard des époux, des enfants et des parents, thesis, 1846.

Commentaire de la loi portant modification des articles du code de procédure civile sur les saisies immobilières (part-author, 1858).

Commentaire de la loi du 25 mai 1864 sur les coalitions, 1864.

Démocratie et liberté (speeches 1861–7), 1867.

Le 19 Janvier, compte rendu aux électeurs de la troisième circonscription de la Seine, 1869.

Une Visite à la chapelle des Medicis, 1872.

Lamartine, 1874.

Le Ministère du 2 janvier: mes discours, 1875.

Principes et conduite, 1875.

L'Eglise et l'état au concile du Vatican, 2 vols., 1879.

Thiers à l'Académie et dans l'histoire, 1879.

De la Liberté de la presse, 1880.

Le Pape est-il libre à Rome? 1882.

Le Concordat est-il respecté? 1883.

Le Concordat et le gallicanisme, speech, 1885.

Le Concordat et la séparation de l'église et de l'état, speech, 1885.

Discours au banquet de St. Tropez, 1885.

Nouveau Manuel de droit ecclésiastique français, 1885 and 1907.

Commentaire de l'encyclique de Léon XIII (Immortale Dei), 1886.

1789 et 1889, 1889.

Le Jugement dernier de Michelange, 1891.

Michelange, 1892.

Du régime de la presse, 1892.

Discours sur les prix de vertu, 24 November 1892.

Solutions politiques et sociales, 1894.

L'Empire libéral: études, récits, souvenirs, 18 volumes, 1895–1918:
  1. *Du principe des nationalités*, 1895; 2. *Louis Napoléon et le coup d'état*, 1897; 3. *Napoléon III*, 1898; 4. *Napoléon III et Cavour*, 1899; 5. *L'Inauguration de l'empire libéral, le roi Guillaume*, 1900; 6. *La Pologne, les élections de 1863, la loi des coalitions*, 1902; 7. *Le Démembrement du Danemark, le syllabus, la mort de Morny, l'entrevue de Biarritz*, 1903;

8. *L'Année fatale, Sadowa*, 1904; 9. *Le Désarroi, le Luxembourg, le 19 janvier, Queretaro*, 1904; 10. *L'Agonie de l'empire autoritaire, Mentana, la loi militaire, loi sur la presse et les réunions publiques*, 1905; 11. *Le Veillée des armes, l'affaire Baudin, préparation militaire prussienne, réorganisation de l'armée française par l'empereur et le maréchal Niel, les elections de 1869, l'origine du complot Hohenzollern*, 1907; 12. *Le Ministère du 2 janvier, formation du ministère, l'affaire Victor Noir, suite du complot Hohenzollern*, 1908; 13. *Le Guet-apens Hohenzollern, le conseil œcuménique, le plébiscite*, 1908; 14. *La Guerre, explosion du complot Hohenzollern, déclaration du 6 juillet, retrait de la candidature de Hohenzollern, demande de garantie, soufflet de Bismarck, notre réponse au soufflet de Bismarck, la déclaration de guerre*, 1909; 15. *Etions-nous prêts? préparation, mobilisation, Sarrebruck, alliances*, 1911; 16. *Le suicide, premier acte, Woerth-Forbach, renversement du ministère*, 1912; 17. *Bazaine, général en chef, Rezonville-Metz, le second acte de suicide, déposition de l'empereur, suicide de l'armée, la révolution à Paris, les dernières convulsions, la fin, le 4 septembre*, 1915; 18. *Table générale et analytique*, 1918.

Marie-Magdeleine, récit de jeunesse, 1897.

Le Féminisme, speech, 1902.

Lettres de l'éxil 1870–4, published by his widow, M. T. Ollivier, 1921.

Le XIX Siècle, published by his son, 1924.

Journal, 1846–1869, published by Theodore Zeldin and Anne Troisier de Diaz, 2 volumes, 1961.

A considerable portion of these books appeared first as articles in periodicals. Most of what he wrote for periodicals found its way into his books, and for reasons of space, therefore, his articles are not listed here.

V. Selected Books and Articles on Ollivier

P. SAINT-MARC, *Emile Ollivier 1825–1913* (Paris, 1950) is the only full-length biography. It is based almost entirely on published material.

ANON., *Saint Ollivier, ministre et martyr*, 1869.

MAURICE AGULHON, 'Emile Ollivier, son voyage en Provence et sa pensée politique en 1850', *Les Conférences de l'Institut historique de Provence*, October–December 1957, 55–57.

LÉON BARRACAND, Review of Marie-Magdeleine, *Revue bleue*, 1896, 663–6.

MADELEINE BARRÉ, 'Emile Ollivier et Michelange', *Le Correspondant*, 10 October 1927, vol. 309, pp. 124–8.

ANDRÉ BEAUNIER, 'L'historien de l'Empire libéral', *Revue des deux mondes*, 1915, 29. 330–56.

HENRI BERGSON, *Discours de Réception*, Séance de l'Académie Française du 24 Janvier 1918.

HENRI BERTEYLE, 'Emile Ollivier et l'Allemagne', *Revue politique et parlementaire*, 10 March 1927, vol. 130, pp. 412–21.

H. BONDILH, *Les Parvenus de la république: réponse à M. Emile Ollivier et ses courtisans*, Marseille, 1868.

EDOUARD CHAPUISAT, 'Souvenirs sur Emile Ollivier', *Revue bleue*, 1922, vol. 60, pp. 515–17.

FRANCIS CHARMES, 'Chronique', *Revue des deux mondes*, 1913, 17. 239–40.

ALPHONSE DAUDET, *La Trahison d'Emile Ollivier*, 1864, published anonymously.

JULES DELAFOSSE, *Etudes et portraits*, 1894.

RENÉ DOUMIC, Speech at the reception of Henri Bergson at the Académie Française, 24 January 1918.

NOEL FELICI, *Emile Ollivier*, 1934.

L. U. FERRAGUS, *Emile Ollivier*, 1870.

MGR. FÈVRE, *La Vie, action politique et œuvres de M. Emile Ollivier*, c. 1905.

H. A. L. FISHER, *Studies in History and Politics*, Oxford, 1920.

PAUL GAULOT, Review, *Revue hebdomadaire*, February 1910, 95–96.

G. P. GOOCH, *The Second Empire*, 1960.

E. D'HAUTERIVE, 'Correspondance du Prince Napoléon et d'Emile

Ollivier', *Revue des deux mondes*, October–December 1930, 159. 787–818, 160. 345–71, 591–615.

H. DE LACOMBE, Review, *Le Correspondant*, 1894, vol. 177, pp. 969–98.

L. DE LANZAC DE LABORIE, *De la royauté absolue à l'empire libéral: portraits historiques*, 1923.

FREDERICK LAWTON, 'Emile Ollivier and the War of 1870', *Fortnightly Review*, January 1910, 113–22.

SIR A. C. LYALL, *Studies in Literature and History*, 1915.

Z. MARCAS [Pseudonym of G. Biard d'Aunet], *Emile Ollivier*, 1865.

HIPPOLYTE MARTIN, 'L'Eglise et l'Etat d'après M. Emile Ollivier', *Etudes réligieuses, philosophiques, historiques et littéraires*, 1879, 4. 247–68, 423–44, and 563–85.

ARNOLD MASCAREL, *Cinquante ans de souvenirs: quelques portraits*, 1926.

SALVO MASTELLONE, 'Emile Ollivier et la guerre de 1859', *Revue d'histoire diplomatique*, July–September 1959, 243–56.

E. MERSON, *La Politique de M. Emile Ollivier*, 1875.

HENRY MICHEL, *Le Quarantième Fauteuil*, 1898.

H. MONTROUZIER, 'Le Gallicanisme de M. Emile Ollivier', *Revue du monde catholique*, 10 August 1868, 321–52.

PIERRE MURET, 'Emile Ollivier et le duc de Gramont', *Revue d'histoire moderne et contemporaine*, 1909–10, 13. 305–28, 14. 178–213.

H. ODELIN, 'Emile Ollivier et le Catholicisme', *Revue hebdomadaire*, 12 January 1935.

MARIE-THÉRÈSE OLLIVIER, *Emile Ollivier, sa jeunesse*, 1919.

MARIE-LOUISE PAILLERON, 'Emile Ollivier', *Revue hebdomadaire*, January 1918, 1. 451–62.

ARMAND DE PONTMARTIN, Review, *Le Correspondant*, 10 March 1890, vol. 158, pp. 909–25.

E. DE PRESSENSÉ, 'Les Evolutions de M. Emile Ollivier', *La Revue politique et littéraire*, 1882, 3rd series, 4. 204–6.

P. DE QUIRIELLE, 'Le Cas de M. Ollivier', *Le Correspondant*, 25 September 1913, vol. 252, pp. 1094–1116.

PAUL RAPHAEL, 'Emile Ollivier et la suppression du recteur d'Aix en 1848', *La Revolution de 1848*, 1928, vol. 25, 6–15.

PAUL REYNAUD, *Emile Ollivier*, lecture delivered 20 February 1933, printed in *Conferencia*, 15 July 1933, 107–24.

M. DE ROUX, 'Emile Ollivier', *Revue critique des idées et des livres*, 10 September 1913, vol. 22, pp. 513–24.

H. SALOMON, 'Une expérience politique en 1870 et ses conséquences', *Revue de synthèse historique*, January–July, 1921, vol. 32, 1–30, 62–90.

J. VIER, 'La Comtesse d'Agoult, Emile Ollivier et le ministère du 2 janvier', *L'Information historique* (November–December, 1961), 190–5.

R. L. WILLIAMS, *Gaslight and Shadow*, New York, 1959.

VI. Other Books and Articles to which Reference is made in the Footnotes.

(This list is in no way intended to be a comprehensive bibliography of the period.)

ANON., *Catechisme élementaire à l'usage des électeurs qui n'ont pas lu le senatus-consulte, ou, qui, l'ayant lu, n'y ont rien compris*, 1870.

ANON., *La Ménagerie impériale*, n.d.

ANON., *Une Famille républicaine: Les Carnot, 1753–1887, par un Député*, 1888.

AMÉDÉE ACHARD, *Souvenirs personnels d'émeutes et de révolutions*, 1872.

JULIETTE ADAM, *Mes premières armes littéraires et politiques*, 1904.
Mes sentiments et mos idées avant 1870, 1905.

DUC D'ALBA, *Lettres familières de l'impératrice Eugénie*, 2 vols., 1935.

F. H. R. ALLAIN-TARGÉ, *La République sous l'empire, lettres 1864–70*, 1939.
Souvenirs d'avant 1870, *Revue de Paris*, September 1903, 5. 1–16.

COMTE D'ALTON-SHÉE, *Souvenirs de 1847 et de 1848*, 1879.

RENÉ AMANIEU, 'Elections législatives et plebiscites à Toulouse sous le second empire', *Annales du Midi*, 1950, vol. 62, 151–80.

MADELEINE AMOUDRUZ, *Proudhon et l'Europe: les idées de Proudhon en politique étrangère*, 1945.

P. M. ACARI, *Il pensiero politico di Cavour*, Milan, 1944.

A. ARMENGAUD, *Les Populations de l'Est-Aquitain au début de l'époque contemporain*, 1961.

C. DE B., *Letters from Paris, 1870–1875*, ed. R. Henrey, 1942.

W. BAGEHOT, *Works*, vol. 10, 1915.

EUGÈNE BALLEYGUIER, alias Loudun, alias Fidus, *Souvenirs d'un impérialiste: journal de dix ans*, 1886.

Journal de Fidus sous la république opportuniste, n.d.

GEN. DU BARAIL, *Mes Souvenirs*, 1894–6.

J. BARBERET, *Les Grèves et la loi des coalitions*, 1873.

JEAN BARBEY, *Le Conseil des ministres sous la restauration*, 1936.

PIERRE BARBIER AND FRANCE VERNILLAT, *Histoire de France par les Chansons: La république de 1848 et le second empire*, (vol. 7), 1959.

ODYSSE BAROT, *Histoire des idées au 19e siècle: Emile de Girardin, sa vie, ses idées, son œuvre, son influence*, 1866.

M. BARRÈS, *Mes Cahiers*, vols. 3 and 7, 1933.

J. BARTHÉLEMY, 'Un Grand Industriel de la presse, Emile de Girardin', *Revue politique et parlementaire*, June 1934, vol. 159, 514–20.

LOUIS BARTHOU, 'Des Attentes à la liberté de travail', *Nouvelle Revue*, 1 February 1901, 321–34.

FRÉDÉRIC BASTIAT, *Œuvres complètes*, 1854–5.

PAUL BASTID, *Doctrines et institutions politiques de la seconde république*, 1945.

Un Juriste pamphletaire: Cormenin, 1948.

CHARLES BAUDELAIRE, *Correspondance générale*, ed. J. Crépet, vol. 5, 1949.

EVARISTE BAVOUX, *Du Principe d'autorité et du parlementarisme*, 1869.

E. BEAU DE LOMENIE, *Maurras et son système*, Bourg, 1953.

A. BELLESORT, *La Société sous Napoléon III*, 1932.

Les Intellectuels et l'avènement de la troisième république, 1931.

V. BENEDETTI, *Ma Mission en Prusse*, 1871.

A. BERTAULD, *La Liberté civile: nouvelle étude critique sur les publicistes contemporains*, 1864.

H. BERTIN, *Evolution constitutionnelle du second empire*, 1900.

CHARLES BIGOT, *Les Classes dirigeantes*, 1875.

J. BILLIOUD et al., *Centenaire de la deuxième république, l'époque 1848 à Marseille et dans les Bouches du Rhône*, Marseilles, 1948.

E. BOINVILLIERS, *La Chute de l'Empire (2 janvier 1870)*, 1887.

P. BOIS, *Paysans de l'Ouest*, Le Mans, 1960.

A. BONNARD, *Les Moderés*, 1936.

T. B[OSQ], *Notice . . . suivie d'un précis des evénéments du 22 et 23 juin 1848*, Marseilles, 1850.

BOUTROUX, 'Notice sur la vie et les œuvres de M. Etienne Vacherot', *Mémoires de l'Académie des sciences morales et politiques*, 21 May 1904, 25 83–114.

J. BOUVIER, 'Banquiers devant l'actualité politique en 1870–1871', *Revue d'histoire moderne et contemporaine*, 1958, N.S., 5. 137–51.

ALBERT DE BROGLIE, *Mémoires*, 1938–41.

Bulletin des lois, 1870.

AMEDÉE DE CAIX DE SAINT-AMOUR, *Le Plébiscite et l'héredité*, 1870.

ALVIN R. CALMAN, *Ledru-Rollin après 1848 et les proscrits français en Angleterre*, 1921.

RENÉ CAPITANT, 'Le Conflit de la souveraineté parlementaire et de la souveraineté populaire en France depuis la liberation', *Revue international d'histoire politique et constitutionnelle*, 1954, N.S., 4. 153–69.

MME CARETTE, née BOUVET, *Troisième série des souvenirs intimes de la cour des Tuileries*, 1891.

H. CARNOT, *Les Radicaux et la charte*, 1847.

ARMAND CARREL, *Œuvres politiques et littéraires*, ed. Littré and Paulin, 1857.

L. M. CASE, *Public Opinion on War and Diplomacy during the Second Empire*, Philadelphia, 1954.

JEAN CASEVITZ, *La Loi Niel 1866–68, l'armée française à la veille de la guerre de 1870*, privately printed, c. 1960.

PAUL DE CASSAGNAC, *Une politique vraiment nationale* (articles), 1905.

E. CASTRE, *Le Conseil général des Bouches du Rhône*, Marseilles, 1912.

G. CAVAIGNAC, *La Force révolutionnaire*, 1838.

J. M. and B. CHAPMAN, *The Life and Times of Baron Haussmann*, 1957.

D. G. CHARLTON, *Positivist Thought in France during the Second Empire*, Oxford, 1959.

ANTONIN CHATEL, *Napoléon III et l'opposition*, 1870.

GUSTAVE CHAUDEY, *De la formation d'une véritable opposition constitutionnelle*, 1848.

L'Empire libéral est-il possible?, 1870.

C. CHESNELONG, *Les Derniers Jours de l'empire et le gouvernement de M. Thiers. Mémoires publiées par son petit-fils*, 1932.

AIMÉ CHÉREST, *La Vie et les œuvres de A.-T. Marie*, 1873.

J. J. CHEVALLIER, *Histoire des institutions politiques de la France de 1789 à nos jours*, 1952.

J. J. CLAMAGERAN, *Correspondance 1849–1902*, 1906.

JACQUES COHEN, *La Préparation de la constitution de 1848*, 1935.

IRENE COLLINS, *The Government and the Newspaper Press in France 1814–1881*, Oxford, 1959.

Liberalism in Nineteenth Century Europe, 1957.

BENJAMIN CONSTANT, *De la Force du gouvernement actuel de la France et de la nécessité de s'y rallier*, 1796.

De la responsabilité des ministres, 1815.

De la doctrine politique qui peut réunir les partis en France, 1816.

Principes de Politiques, 1815.

EMILE CONSTANT, 'Notes sur la presse dans le département du Var sous le second empire', *Provence historique*, July–September 1960, 10. 239–59.

LOUIS VICOMTE DE CORMENIN, *Reliquiae*, 1868.

Œuvres, vol. 3, *Pamphlets anciens et nouveaux*, 1870.

J. CORNILLON, *Le Bourbonnais à la fin l'empire et sous le gouvernement de la défense nationale*, Moulins, 1924.

COURS D'ASSISES DE LA DRÔME, *Procès des accusés de juin de Marseille, sous la présidence de M. Bertrand*, Marseilles, 1849.

GUSTAVE CUNEO D'ORNANO, *La République de Napoléon*, 1894.

ARMAND CUVILLIER, *Hommes et idéologies de 1840*, 1956.

L. and W. D[AGUSAN], *Récit historique des événements des 22 et 23 juin à Marseille*, Marseilles, 1848.

A. DANSETTE, *Histoire religieuse de la France contemporaine*, 1951 ed.

A. DARIMON, *Histoire d'un parti: Les Cinq sous l'empire*, 1885; *L'Opposition libérale sous l'empire*, 1886; *Le Tiers parti sous l'empire*, 1887; *Les Irreconciliables sous l'empire*, 1888; *Le Ministère du 2 janvier*, 1889.

A travers une révolution, 1847–55, 1884.

Histoire de douze ans, 1857–69, 1883.

L'Agonie de l'empire, 1891.

De la réforme des banques, 1856.

ALPHONSE DAUDET, *Souvenirs d'un homme de lettres*, 1889.

ERNEST DAUDET, *Souvenirs de mon temps*, 1921.

TAXILE DELORD, *Histoire du second empire*, 1869–75.

ALFRED DELVAU, *Histoire de la révolution de février*, 1850.

Les Murailles révolutionnaires, 1851.

DELUNS-MONTAUD, 'La Philosophie de Gambetta', *Revue politique et parlementaire*, 10 February 1897.

M. DESLANDRES, *Histoire constitutionnelle de la France*, 1932–7.

JEAN DIETZ, 'Les Débuts de Jules Ferry', *Revue de France*, 1 October 1932, 501–21.

CLAUDE DIGEON, *La Crise allemande de la pensée française, 1870–1914*, 1959.

E. DOLLÉANS, *Histoire du mouvement ouvrier*, 1948.

M. DOMMANGET, *Blanqui et l'opposition révolutionnaire à la fin du second empire*, 1960.

G. DOUTREPONT, *Les Proscrits du coup d'état en Belgique*, 1938.

P. DUBOSC, *Quatre Mois de république à Marseille*, Marseilles, 1848.

A. DUBUC, 'Frédéric Deschamps, commissaire de la republique en Seine Inférieure', *Actes du Congrès historique du centenaire de la révolution de 1848*, 1949, 381–95.

M. DU CAMP, *Souvenirs d'un demi-siècle*, 1949.

ROBERT DUFOURG, 'Un Homme politique girondin au siècle dernier: Jérôme David', *Revue historique de Bordeaux et du département de la Gironde*, 1957, N.S. 6. 153–66.

H. J. DUGUÉ DE LA FAUCONNERIE, *Souvenirs d'un vieil homme*, *1866–79*, c. 1912.

A. DUMON, *Révélations sur le plébiscite et le comité central*, 1870.

V. DURUY, *Notes et souvenirs 1811–1894*, 1901.

M. DUVERGER, *Droit constitutionnelle et institutions politiques*, 3rd ed., 1958.

La Cinquième République, 1959.

P. DUVERGER DE HAURANNE, *Histoire du gouvernement parlementaire en France*, 1857–72.

J. B. and J. DUVERGIER, *Collection complète des lois, décrets, etc.*, vol. 70, 1870.

G. DUVEAU, *La Vie ouvrière en France sous le second empire*, 1946.

HENRI DURIF, *M. Félix Esquirou de Parieu, essai sur sa vie et ses ouvrages*, Aurillac, 1868.

A. ESMEIN, *Eléments de droit constitutionnel français et comparé*, 5th ed., 1909.

D. O. EVANS, *Le Socialisme romantique*, 1948.

Social Romanticism in France 1830–48, Oxford, 1951.

JULES FAVRE, *Discours parlementaires*, 1881.

Henri Belval, 1880.

Mélanges politiques, judiciaires et littéraires, 1882.

CARDINAL DOMINIQUE FERRATA, *Mémoires, ma nonciature en France*, c.1921.

H. FERRETTE, *Manuel de législation industrielle*, 1909.

MAURICE FLORY, 'L'Appel au peuple napoléonien', *Revue internationale d'histoire politique et constitutionnelle*, 1952, N.S. 2. 215–22.

CLAUDE FOHLEN, 'Crise textile et troubles sociaux: Le Nord à la fin du second empire', *Revue du Nord*, 1953, 35. 107–23.

HENRI FONFRÈDE, *Œuvres*, ed. C. A. Campan, Bordeaux, 1844–7.

P. L. FOURNIER, *Le Second Empire et la législation ouvrière*, 1911.

MICHAEL FOOT, 'The Origins of the Franco-Prussian War', *New Cambridge Modern History*, vol. 10, 1960, 577–602.

MARCEL FOURNIOL, 'Epilogue des journées marseillaise de juin', *La Révolution de 1848*, 1929, 26. 356–77.

C. DE FREYCINET, *Souvenirs, 1848–78*, 1914.

E. E. FRIBOURG, *L'Association internationale des travailleurs*, 1871.

M. FRIDIEFF, *Les Origines du réferendum dans la constitution de 1793*, 1931.

L. GAMBETTA, *Discours et plaidoyers politiques*, 1881.

Notes et Impressions, *La Grande Revue*, July–September 1900, 3. 29–55, 379–400.

Lettres 1868–82, ed. D. Halévy and E. Pillias, 1938.

L. A. GARNIER-PAGÈS, *Histoire de la révolution de 1848*, 1861–72. *L'Opposition et l'empire*, 1870, 1872.

A. G. GARRONE, *Il Figlio di Mazzini*, Florence, 1951.

S. GENTON, *Une Année au corps législatif, 1869–70*, Lyon, 1871.

L. GIRARD, *Les Elections de 1869*, 1960. *La Politique des travaux publiques du second empire*, 1952.

RAOUL GIRARDET, 'Introduction à l'histoire du nationalisme français', *Revue française de science politique*, September 1958, 505–28.

EMILE DE GIRARDIN, *L'Empire avec la liberté*, 1859. *La Politique universelle*, 1852.

FERNAND GIRAUDEAU, *Napoléon III Intime*, 1895.

E. and J. GONCOURT, *Journal*, édition définitive, 1935.

JACQUES GOUAULT, *Comment la France est devenue républicaine, 1870–5*, 1954.

HENRI GOUGELOT, *L'Idée de liberté dans la pensée de Benjamin Constant*, Melun, 1942.

GEORGES GOYAU, *L'Idée de patrie et l'humanitarisme: essai d'histoire française 1866–1901*, 1913.

DUC DE GRAMONT, *La France et la Prusse avant la guerre*, 1872.

[E. G. GRENVILLE-MURRAY], *Men of the Second Empire*, 1872.

MARQUIS DE GRICOURT, *France and Germany, or Imperial Rule under Napoleon III*, 1871.

CONSTANTIN DE GRUNWALD, *Le Duc de Gramont*, 1950.

HENRI GUILLEMIN, *Cette curieuse guerre de 1870*, 1956.

PIERRE GUIRAL, *Prévost-Paradol*, 1955.

' Les Evénements de 1860 et les libéraux français', *Annales de la Faculté des Lettres d'Aix*, 1961, 35. 69–91.

'Marseille', in *Aspects de la crise et de la dépression de l'économie française au milieu du xix e siècle*, ed. E. Labrousse, 1956.

Marseille et l'Algérie, 1957.

LUDOVIC HALÉVY, *Carnets*, 1935.

S. W. HALPERIN, 'Visconti-Venosta and the Diplomatic Crisis of July 1870', *Journal of Modern History*, 1959, 31. 295–309.

ETHEL HARRIS, *Lamartine et le Peuple*, 1932.

P. HAURY, 'Les Commissaires de Ledru-Rollin en 1848', *La Révolution Française*, 1909, 57 (ii). 438–74.

G. E. HAUSSMANN, *Mémoires*, 1890–3.

COMTE D'HAUSSONVILLE, *Le Comte de Paris, souvenirs personnels*, 1895.

J. L. HENON, *Notice sur, d'après les documents conservés par sa famille*, Lyon, 1874.

COMTE D'HÉRISSON, *Le Prince Impérial*, 1890.

EMILE HERVET, *Le Plébiscite de 1870: Oui ou Non*, 1870.

MICHAEL HOWARD, *The Franco-Prussian War*, 1961.

R. JACQUELIN, 'Les Cent Jours et le régime parlementaire', *Revue du droit public et de la science politique*, March–April 1897, 193–220.

LÉON JACQUES, *Les Partis politiques sous la troisième république*, 1913.

E. A. JELUBOVSKAYA, [*The Fall of the Second Empire and the Founding of the Third Republic in France*], Moscow, 1956.

HANS KOHN, 'France between Britain and Germany', *Journal of the History of Ideas*, 1956, 283–99.

ARPAD F. KOVACS, 'French Military Institutions before the Franco-Prussian War', *American Historical Review*, 1946, 51. 217–35.

EDOUARD DE LABOULAYE, *Le Parti libéral: son programme et son avenir*, 4th ed., 1864.

ERNEST LABROUSSE, *Le Mouvement ouvrier et les idées sociales en France 1815–1900. Aspects de la crise économique et sociale de la France et du Royaume Uni, 1815–1880*. Cours de la Sorbonne, 1949.

G. LACOUR-GAYET, *L'Impératrice Eugénie*, 1925.

F. LAGRANGE, *Vie de Mgr. Dupanloup*, 1884.

VICOMTE DE LA GUERONNIERE, *Aux Electeurs de France: Le Vote du 8 mai*, 1870.

A. DE LAMARTINE, *La France Parlementaire*, 1865.
La Politique rationale, 1832.

GILLY LA PALLUD, *Elections du Midi: renseignements électoraux*, Marseilles, 1876.

SUZANNE DE LA PORTE, 'Autour du 19 Janvier: tiers parti et opposition républicaine: Fragments inédits de la correspondance d'Allain-Targé', *Revue historique*, 1937, 179. 135–45.

C. LATOUR DU MOULIN, *Autorité et liberté*, 1874.
Lettres à un membre du parlement d'Angleterre sur la constitution de 1852, 1861.

C. LATREILLE, *Les Dernières Années de Lamartine 1852–69*, 1925.

R. P. LECANUET, *L'Eglise de France sous la troisième république*, 1910.

VICOMTE DE L'ECUYER LA PAPOTIÈRE, *Le Plébiscite de 1870*, 1870.

A. A. LEDRU-ROLLIN, *Discours politiques et écrits divers*, 1879.
De la décadence de l'Angleterre, 1850.

GEORGES LEFRANC, *Histoire du mouvement syndical français*, 1937.

G. LEFRANÇAIS, *Souvenirs d'un révolutionnaire*, c. 1902.

G. LEIBHOLZ, 'Démocratie representative et état des partis modernes', *Revue internationale d'histoire politique et constitutionnelle*, 1952, N.S. 2. 51–67.

PAUL LENGLÉ, *Le Neveu de Bonaparte, souvenirs de mes campagnes politiques avec le prince Napoléon Bonaparte 1879–1891*, 1893.

P. LÉON, 'Les Grèves de 1867–70 dans le département de l'Isère', *Revue d'histoire moderne et contemporaine*, 1954, N.S. 1. 272–300.

G. LEPOINTE, *Histoire des institutions du droit publique français au dixneuvième siècle 1789–1914*, 1953.

PIERRE LEROUX, *Projet d'une constitution democratique et sociale*, 1848.
La Grève de Samarez, 1863.
De l'humanité, 1840.
D'une réligion nationale, 1846.

EMILE LE SENNE, *Frédéric Bastiat et l'extension du rôle de l'Etat*, 1906.

EMILE LEVASSEUR, *Questions ouvrières et industrielles en France sous la troisième république*, 1907.

Histoire des classes ouvrières et de l'industrie en France de 1789 à 1870, 2nd ed. 1903–4.

L. LIARD, 'Notice sur la vie et les œuvres de M. Jules Simon', *Mémoires de l'Académie des sciences morales et politiques*, 1898, 21. 621–52.

CHARLES LIMET, *Quatre-vingts ans de souvenirs 1827–1907*, 1908.

H. P. O. LISSAGARAY, *Histoire de la Commune de 1870*, 1876, new ed. 1947.

F. LISZT, *Correspondance de Liszt de de Mme Emile Ollivier*, 1936.

F. L'HUILLIER, *La Lutte ouvrière à la fin du second empire*, 1957.

F. D. LONGE, 'The Law of Trade Combinations in France', *Fortnightly Review*, 1867, 220–5, 296–309.

A. LAWRENCE LOWELL, *Public Opinion and Popular Government*, New York, 1913.

COMTE DE MAC-CARTHY, *Les Assemblées départementales devant la France parlementaire*, 1870.

H. MAILLY, *Pilori, à bas les laches*, cartoons, n.d.

H. MALO, *Thiers*, 1932.

A. G. MANRY, 'Le Plébiscite de 1870 et les premières élections législatives sous la troisième république dans le Puy-de-Dôme', *Revue d'Auvergne*, 1957, 71. 10–22.

M. MARION, *Histoire Financière de la France depuis 1715*, vol. 5, 1928.

S. MARITCH, *Histoire du mouvement social sous le second empire à Lyon*, 1930.

JEAN MARTIN, *Les Travailleurs et le plébiscite*, Bordeaux 1870.

A. MATHIEZ, 'Pacifisme et nationalisme au 18e siècle', *Annales historiques de la révolution française*, 1936, 13. 1–17.

C. E. DE MAUPAS, *Mémoires sur le second empire*, 1884–5.

P. MASSON, *Les Bouches-du-Rhône, encyclopédie départementale*, 1924–35.

J. MAURAIN, *La Politique ecclésiastique du second empire*, 1930.

Baroche, 1936.

A. MELS, *Wilhemshoehe, souvenirs de la captivité de Napoléon III*, 1880.

ERNEST MERSON, *Confessions d'un journaliste*, 1890.

ARTHUR MEYER, *Ce que mes yeux ont vu*, 1911.

ROBERT MITCHELL, *Un Demi-siècle de mémoires*, 1911.

G. DE MOLINARI, *Le Mouvement socialiste et les réunions publiques avant la révolution du 4 septembre 1870*, 1872.

A. DE MORNY, 'La Genèse du coup d'état, mémoires du duc de Morny publiées par son petit-fils', *Revue des deux mondes*, 1 December 1925, 512–34.

Fragments of Memoirs in *L'Intermédiaire des chercheurs et curieux*, 30 April 1904, 49. 659–64.

'Quelques reflexions sur la politique actuelle', *Revue des deux mondes*, January 1848, 151–63.

W. E. MOSSE, *The European Powers and the German Question, 1848–71*, Cambridge, 1958.

HENRI MOUGIN, *Pierre Leroux*, 1938.

NAPOLEON III, *Œuvres*, 1856.

Discours, messages et proclamations de l'empereur, 1860.

Œuvres posthumes, ed. Comte de La Chapelle, 1873.

ERNEST NEWMAN, *The Life of Richard Wagner*, 1933–47.

HAROLD NICOLSON, *Benjamin Constant*, 1949.

R. G. NOBÉCOURT, *Vie d'Armand Carrel*, 1930.

G. DE NOUVION, *Frédéric Bastiat*, 1905.

M. T. OLLIVIER, 'L'Epouse de l'Empereur, souvenirs personnels', *Revue de Genève*, January–June 1921, 161–82, 356–74.

H. ONCKEN, *Die Rheinpolitik Kaiser Napoleons III von 1863 bis 1870*, Stuttgart, 1926.

E. ORDINAIRE, *Du Perfectionnement de la race préfectorale*, 1870.

COMTE D'ORNANO, *La Vie passionnante du Comte Walewski*, 1953.

Origines de la guerre de 1870–1, 1910–30.

M. PALÉOLOGUE, *Entretiens de l'impératrice Eugénie*, 1928.

ERNEST PASCAL, *Discours politiques 1878–87*, 1889.

CAMILLE PELLETAN, 'L'Opposition républicaine sous l'empire', Lecture to the Ligue Française de l'Enseignement, 26 January 1910, published in *Revue politique et parlementaire*, May 1910, 211–35.

R. PELLOUX, 'Remarques sur le mot et l'idée de revolution',
  Revue française de science politique, 1952, 42–55.

GABRIEL PERREUX, *La Propagande républicaine au début de la
  monarchie de juillet*, 1930.

HECTOR PESSARD, *Mes Petits Papiers 1860–70*, 1887.

ERNEST PICARD, *Discours parlementaires*, 1882–90.

OLIVIER PICHAT, *L'Empire devant le peuple*, 1870.

J. W. PICKERSGILL, 'The French Plebiscite of 1870 and the Catholics', *English Historical Review*, 1937, 254–66.

E. PINARD, *Mon Journal*, 1892.

JULES POINTU, *Histoire de la chute de l'empire, 6 juillet–4 Septembre
  1870*, 1874.

P. POIRSON, *Walewski*, 1943.

PIERRE PONSOT, *Les Grèves de 1870 et la commune de 1871 au
  Creusot*, 1957.

A. POULET-MALASSIS, *Papiers secrets et correspondance du second
  empire*, 1880.

C. H. POUTHAS, 'Les Ministères de Louis Philippe', *Revue d'histoire moderne et contemporaine*, 1954, I. 102–30.

M. PRÉLOT, *Pour Comprendre la nouvelle constitution*, 1958.
  'La Signification constitutionnelle du second empire', *Revue
  française de science politique*, 1953, 31–56.

L. A. PRÉVOST-PARADOL, *La France nouvelle*, 1868.

P. J. PROUDHON, *Correspondance*, 1875.
  De la capacité politique des classes ouvrières, 1924 ed.

P. QUENTIN-BAUCHART, *Lamartine et la politique étrangère de la
  révolution de février*, 1907.

LÉON RADIGUET, *L'Acte additionnel aux constitutions de l'empire
  du 22 avril 1815*, Caen, 1911.

M. RECLUS, *Emile de Girardin*, 1934.
  Jules Favre, 1912.
  Ernest Picard, 1912.

HENRY REEVE, *Royalist and Republican France*, 1872.

ELIAS REGNAULT, *Histoire du gouvernement provisoire*, 1850.

ERNEST RENAN, *Souvenirs d'enfance*, 1883.
  Œuvres complètes, ed. H. Psichari, 1947–60.

P. RENOUVIN, *Histoire des rélations internationales*, vol. 5, 1954.

ACHILLE REY, *Histoire de Mgr. C. J. E. de Mazenod*, Marseilles, 1928.

L. REYNAUD, *L'Influence allemande en France au 18 et 19 siècles*, 1922.

JULES RICHARD, *Le Bonapartisme sous la république*, 1883.

HENRI ROCHEFORT, *The Adventures of My Life*, 1896.

A. ROCHER, *Les Assassins de la France*, 1872.

  MM. les capitulards . . . , n.d.

L. DE RONCHAUD, *La Politique de Lamartine*, 1878.

PROSPER ROSSI, *Mes Souvenirs, 1848*, Toulon 1888.

MAXIMILIEN RUBEL, *Karl Marx devant le bonapartisme*, 1960.

G. RUDLER, 'Benjamin Constant, son ralliement à l'empire', *Revue de Paris*, 15 December 1930, 832–47.

J. SABBATIER, *La Tribune judiciaire*, 1885–61.

C. H. DE ST.-SIMON, *Œuvres choisies*, 1859.

H. SALOMON, *L'Ambassade de Richard de Metternich à Paris*, 1931.

JOSEPH SALVARELLI, *Les Administrateurs du département du Var 1790–1897*, Draguignan, 1897.

LUIGI SALVATORELLI, 'L'Europe de Napoléon III et l'Europe de Mazzini', *Revue historique*, April–June 1960, 275–86.

ALBERT SARRAUT, *Le Gouvernement direct en France*, 1899.

A. SCHEURER-KESTNER, *Souvenirs de Jeunesse*, 1905.

GUSTAVE SCHLUMBERGER, *Mes Souvenirs*, 1934.

JAMMY SCHMIDT, *Les Grandes Thèses radicales*, c. 1931.

R. SCHNERB, *Rouher*, 1949.

  Ledru-Rollin et le suffrage universel, 1948.

J. A. SCOTT, *Republican Ideas amd the Liberal Tradition in France 1870–1914*, New York, 1951.

COMTE L. DE SÉGUR, *L'Agriculture et la liberté*, 1869.

C. SEIGNOBOS, *Histoire de la France contemporaine* ed. E. Lavisse, vols. 6–8, 1921.

J. SIGNOREL, *Le Referendum législatif*, 1896.

JULES SIMON, *La Politique radicale*, 1869.

  La Liberté, 1859.

  'Notice sur la vie et les travaux de M. L. H. Carnot', *Mémoires de l'Académie des sciences morales et politiques*, 1896, 29. 3–55.

Premières Années, [1901].

D. MACK SMITH, 'Cavour and Parliament', *Cambridge Historical Journal,* 1957, 13. 37–57.

E. SPULLER, *Petite histoire du second empire utile à lire avant le vote du plébiscite,* 1870.

J. STENGERS, 'Aux origines de la guerre de 1870: Gouvernement et opinion publique', *Revue belge de philologie et d'histoire,* Brussels, 1956, 34. 701–47.

DANIEL STERN, *Essai sur la liberté considerée comme principe et fin de l'activité humaine,* 1847.

Histoire de la révolution de 1848, 1851.

A. J. P. TAYLOR, *The Struggle for Mastery in Europe,* Oxford, 1954.

I. TCHERNOFF, *Le Parti républicain sous la monarchie de juillet,* 1905.

Le Parti républicain au coup d'état et sous le second empire, 1906.

EUGÈNE TENOT, *Etude historique sur le coup d'état,* new ed., 1877–80.

A. THIBAUDET, *Les Idées politiques de la France,* 1932.

THIBAULT-LEFEBVRE, *Adhésion a l'empire libéral,* 1870.

ALBERT THOMAS, 'The Liberal Empire 1859–70', *Cambridge Modern History,* 1908, 11. 467–506.

P. FÉLIX THOMAS, *Pierre Leroux, sa vie, son œuvre, sa doctrine,* 1904.

'Pierre Leroux en exil', *Revue de Paris,* 1903, 623–48.

GUY THUILLIER, *Les Idées politiques d'Emile de Girardin, La Revue Administrative,* 1959, 134–6.

D. B. TODOROVITCH, *Le Droit syndical et les doctrines syndicalistes,* 1934.

G. TRIDON, *Gironde et Girondins: la Gironde en 1869 et en 1793,* 1869.

E. VACHEROT, *La Démocratie,* 1860.

A. VERMOREL, *Le Parti socialiste,* 1870.

LOUIS VIÉ, *Renan: la guerre de 1870 et la 'reforme' de la France,* 1949.

J. VIER, *Daniel Stern: lettres républicaines du second empire,* 1951.

Emile de Girardin inconnu, 1949.

AUGUSTE VITU, *Les Réunions électorales à Paris, mai 1869,* 1869.

R. WALDECK-ROUSSEAU, *Questions sociales,* 1900.

R. Warlemont, 'La Representation économique suivant l'acte additionnel aux constitutions de l'empire', *Revue internationale d'histoire politique et constitutionnelle*, 1954, N.S. 4. 244–56.

G. Weill, *Histoire du parti républicain*, 1928.

F. A. Wellesley, *The Paris Embassy during the Second Empire*, 1928.

H. Welschinger, *La Guerre de 1870*, 1910.

G. Woodcock, *P. J. Proudhon*, 1956.

Gordon Wright, 'French Public Opinion and Conscription in France 1866–70', *Journal of Modern History*, 1942, 14. 26–45.

INDEX